Where to Watch Birds

With *Where to Watch Birds*, his first book, John Gooders scored an immediate success. He left a career as a teacher and lecturer at a college of education to become editor of the nine-volume encyclopedia, *Birds of the World*. In 1970 he took two months off on a Churchill Fellowship to study migration through North Africa. Subsequently he launched his own magazine *World of Birds*, but left after a year to write television scripts for Anglia Television's *Survival* series and to edit the company's house magazine, *The World of Survival*. He now devotes his time to full-time writing about birds and natural history. He lives in London, where his wife runs the wildlife photographic agency, Ardea. They have two children and a cottage in Sussex, where bird-watching and the family come first.

John Gooders

Where to Watch Birds

illustrated by David Thelwell
introduction by Roger Tory Peterson

Pan Books London and Sydney

First edition published 1967 by André Deutsch Limited
Second revised edition published 1974
This edition published 1977 by Pan Books Ltd,
Cavaye Place, London SW10 9PG
© John Gooders 1967, 1974
ISBN 0 330 25030 2
Printed and bound in Great Britain by
Richard Clay (The Chaucer Press) Ltd, Bungay, Suffolk

To all who have contributed
this book is gratefully dedicated

Introduction

Bird-watching, bird-finding, bird-spotting, tick-hunting, or birding – call it what you will – has come of age. It is moving beyond the stage of identification guides into the era of Baedekers. North America has had such Baedekers since 1951 when Dr Olin Sewall Pettingill, Jr, published his *Guide to Bird Finding East of the Mississippi* (Oxford University Press), and 1953 when he supplemented it with his *Guide to Bird Finding West of the Mississippi*.

Normally Great Britain, the mother country of the modern bird-watcher, is the first to launch a useful device or new tool, but perhaps the reason that this inevitable book has not appeared earlier is that the number of choice spots of ornithological interest in England, Wales and Scotland runs into the hundreds. Where does a compiler start? It took the encyclopaedic James Fisher to break the ice with his *Shell Nature Lover's Atlas* (1966) which gives capsule summaries of sites and areas of interest to the field naturalist (including those of every stripe and hue from paleontologists to beetle-watchers).

This new book by John Gooders, which has long been awaited by the field-glass fraternity, goes into depth on the birds, giving explicit directions for reaching more than five hundred bird-rich areas and a breakdown by season of some of the species that might be seen. There is also a useful listing of local natural history societies, bird clubs and conservation organisations, their current secretaries and publications.

How I wish I had owned such a guidebook when I was trying to fill in my own British list (I went years before I saw my first cirl bunting, finally shown me by Richard Fitter). Had I owned such a book I would not have waited until 1966 before 'discovering' Noss in the Shetlands (while on the Scottish cruise of the International Ornithological Congress). I intend to return to Noss for a week or two of photography some June, and in this guide Mr Gooders informs me that the way to do it is to cross from Lerwick to Bressay, then taxi (or walk) 2½ miles to Noss Sound and summon the shepherd to row me across.

This valuable book will not only enhance the thoroughness of coverage of bird-spotting in Britain (few transient rarities or waifs will escape scrutiny!) but it will also aid the conservationist in his perennial fight to preserve key wildlife areas against deterioration or outright destruction. The more people travel about to see birds the more they become a recreational resource to be reckoned with and to be preserved. As an example, I might point to a world-famous vantage point across the Atlantic – Hawk Mountain in Pennsylvania, where the hundreds of watchers on any October weekend may far outnumber the migrating birds of prey. The important by-products of this visitation have been the conversion of the local populace from hawk-shooters to hawk-watchers and the passing of protective legislation.

Birds with their high rate of metabolism and furious pace of living, demonstrate life forces perhaps better than any other animals. Like the canaries once used by miners to detect gas leakage, they may act as sensitive indicators of subtle (or drastic) environmental changes. Therefore the growing army of bird-watchers, which ranges all the way from enthusiastic *aficionados* to scientific ornithologists, has become an important watchdog over our environment.

ROGER TORY PETERSON

Contents

List of Maps

Addresses of
National Organisations

BRITISH ORNITHOLOGISTS' UNION,
c/o Zoological Society of London, Regent's Park, London NW1

BRITISH ORNITHOLOGISTS' CLUB
As for the Union

BRITISH TRUST FOR ORNITHOLOGY,
Beech Grove, Tring, Herts.

COUNCIL FOR NATURE,
41 Queen's Gate, London, SW7

FIELD STUDIES COUNCIL,
9 Devereux Court, Strand, London, WC2

NATURE CONSERVANCY,
England: 19 Belgrave Square, London SW1
Scotland: 12 Hope Terrace, Edinburgh 9
Wales: Penrhôs Road, Bangor, Carm.

ROYAL SOCIETY FOR THE PROTECTION OF BIRDS,
The Lodge, Sandy, Beds.

SCOTTISH ORNITHOLOGISTS' CLUB,
21 Regent Terrace, Edinburgh 7

WILDFOWL TRUST,
Slimbridge, Glos.

Acknowledgements

Thanks are due to all helpers, friends, and acquaintances who have endured my persistent brain-picking for so long. In particular to Jeremy Brock and Pat Sellar who have provided a sounding board for my ideas and read large parts of the book in draft, to Bruce Coleman who stimulated the germination of an idea that I had long toyed with, to my wife, who read the entire book in draft and offered many useful ideas, and to the typists, Ann Livingstone and Judith Innes for their patience and interest.

The Royal Society for the Protection of Birds, through their Director Peter Conder, read the book in draft and offered much valuable advice and criticism and checked the security side of my comments on certain species.

Among many other helpers too numerous to mention the following have provided information, read sections in draft, or offered valuable advice on anything from one to thirty localities.

E. J. Abrahams, E. K. Allin, R. H. Appleby, R. H. Baillie, D. K. Ballance, T. H. Bell, A. Belshaw, P. F. Bonham, J. A. Black, F. Brady, A. D. Brewer, Miss H. J. Brotherton OBE, G. H. Clegg, Major P. F. S. Clifford, E. Cohen, R. K. Cornwallis, G. D. Craine, H. H. Davis, R. F. Dickens (late), H. Dollman, J. Donovan, Major Hon. H. Douglas-Home, R. Felton, J. K. Fenton, Miss L. S. Garrad, G. Gibbs, D. Griffin, J. Griffiths, A. W. Guppy, R. J. Howells, D. C. Hulme, P. N. Humphreys, W. E. Jones, E. D. Kerruish, R. Kettle, Lt.-Col. Logan-Home, S. G. Madge, J. D. Magee, J. R. Mather, D. A. McQueen, B. S. Milne, C. K. Mylne, J. Niles, R. C. Parkinson, A. G. Parsons, M. J. Penistan, Mrs M. Price, A. Pringle, N. Pullen, Mrs P. Rendell, J. S. Roberts, Col. H. Morrey Salmon CBE, D. R. Saunders, J. W. Scott, P. Schofield, Mrs M. M. Seabroke, M. J. Seago, D. Shepherd, E. Skinner, F. R. Smith, R. W. J. Smith, Brigadier C. E. H. Sparrow OBE MC, M. A. Stewart, R. Stokoe, Dr C. Suffern, C. M. Swaine, W. H. Truckle, A. J. Vickery, A. E. Vine, D. Watson, J. P. Widgery, D. T. Wilks, R. Wilson, B. Zonfrillo.

Bedfordshire Natural History Society, Brecknock County Naturalists' Trust, Burgh of Hamilton, Buxton Field Club, Cambrian Ornithological Society, Cardiff Naturalists' Society, Christchurch Harbour Ornithological Group, Cornwall Bird Watching and Preservation Society, Derbyshire Ornithological Society, Devonshire Bird Watching and Preservation

Society, Forestry Commission, Gower Ornithological Society, Kyle and Glen Mini-coaches, Lancaster and District Bird Watching Society, Lundy Field Society, David MacBrayne Ltd, Manx Museum, Monmouth Ornithological Society, Nature Conservancy, Northamptonshire Natural History Society and Field Club, North Gloucestershire Naturalists' Society, North of Scotland, Orkney and Shetland Shipping Co. Ltd, Orkney Islands Shipping Co Ltd, Royal Society for the Protection of Birds, Salop County Council, Scottish Tourist Board, Teesmouth Bird Club, Tyneside Bird Club, West Wales Naturalists' Trust, and the Wildfowl Trust.

Preface

The recent expansion of the number of bird-watchers is merely the visible tip of a national interest in birds, nature and the countryside as a whole. A movement that is reflected in the rapid expansion of the membership of the Royal Society for the Protection of Birds and the popularity of television nature programmes. At the same time there has been a growth in the demands of other seekers after fresh air and field sports, notably sailing, fishing, shooting and water-skiing. Unfortunately, these activities sometimes serve to destroy what are ideal spots for the naturalist, or important scientific sites. More unfortunate still, naturalists are unable to compete with sports whose participants are willing to pay large sums of money for facilities.

Industry and government frequently threaten, and sometimes destroy, good sites. An area as important to naturalists as Dungeness has not been spared. The Cairngorms skiing hotels will want to attract visitors in summer as well as winter and the chair lift takes the public to the tops and dotterel territory for a few shillings. The beach at Minsmere is no longer safe for little terns. Only by fully embracing the huge numbers of people that form the television audience of *Look* can naturalists hope to compete with other demands on the countryside.

Peterson, Mountford and Hollom's *Field Guide* has made a key to identification readily available. I hope that this book too will encourage people to go out and see birds, join local societies and become active supporters of the conservation movement. It will doubtless be argued that everything is being put on the plate for the beginner and that the pressure of watchers on certain well-known localities will increase. Though I hope for more watchers I also hope to tempt them, and the established expert, by accounts of places unknown. Even if this ideal fails and more and more watchers swarm to Cley I doubt whether it will create over-watching. More watchers go there than almost anywhere, yet there are still plenty of birds, including rare breeding species. I suppose Cley marshes are safe – or would someone like to build a fully fledged marina in Blakeney Harbour? Or would it be a good site for a nuclear power station? Or what about a storage depot for North Sea gas?

The pressure is on. If the choice is more watchers or more marinas and commercial development most will surely prefer to share their pleasures rather than be denied them altogether.

One of the best things about bird-watching is that it can be enjoyed anywhere. The Carmargue, a Surbiton back garden, Timbuktu, Buckingham Palace all provide bird-watching in different forms. Even rare or unusual birds can occur in the apparently most unlikely places – a greenish warbler at Dollis Hill, London NW; a rufous warbler at Billy Butlin's Holiday Camp, Skegness; or a Wilson's phalarope near Shrewsbury. It seems something of a contradiction, therefore, to produce a guide to where to watch birds when they can be watched at almost any spot on earth. Yet ask a bird-watcher, 'Where should I go for a day's bird-watching?' and you will get an answer. Different watchers will give different answers but a surprising degree of agreement will be found – from Cley and Dungeness, through Minsmere, Rothiemurchus, Dornoch Firth, Chew Valley, Eye Brook, to Clo Mor and Marazion Marsh. Some areas, it is agreed, are good for birds.

Such areas will have birds either in quantity as on Hilbre Island in the Dee Estuary, or in quality as at Loch Garten, or most likely a mixture of both. The blackbird, swallow, chaffinch and a host of other birds that are generally distributed are hardly mentioned in this book. As the beginner improves the number of species that he can easily find grows larger. But a number of species remain worth looking for either because they are migrants and are present in the country for only short periods of the year, or because they are exceedingly rare. Montagu's harrier, kite, wryneck and Savi's warbler all breed but are persecuted by egg-collectors and over-zealous bird-watchers to such an extent that their whereabouts are not usually published. As a general rule breeding birds should be disturbed as little as possible, and those who have purchased this book to find rare breeders have wasted their money.

On the other hand there seems to be no reason why a passage rarity, even the most extreme vagrant, should not be seen by all interested. Luckily the days of 'the bird was collected . . .' are now past and a houbara bustard can tramp up and down a Suffolk mustard field being watched by chara' loads of tick-hunters without fear. The disturbance to the bird is generally slight and cases of harm through pestering are very few. The experts usually sit in the right place and wait for the bird to show itself, it is certainly impossible to get a field description while beating around the bushes. Passage migrants like curlew sandpiper, little stint, spotted redshank, black tern, shore lark and Lapland bunting are unusual enough for bird-watchers to be prepared to travel to see them and, together with the true rarities and unusual or localised winter visitors, form the backbone of this book. Though even here, there is a danger when a declining species is faithful to a particular wintering area. A resort of bean geese in southern England has been omitted on this score at the request of a local watcher.

Birds in quantity are another draw, though commonplace species like starling, rook and some species of gull do not hold the same attraction as the less widespread waders and wildfowl. Vast flocks of knot, dunlin, wigeon and teal exist all round our coasts and watchers travel miles to see them. Doubtless they also hope for a hen harrier or some other unusual winter bird, but they will have a good day if they see nothing more than ten thousand dunlin. If more space has been devoted to these species than any others it is because of their dependability. Their habitats, water and mud flats, are restricted and even a single visit can be relied upon to produce birds.

HOW TO USE THE GUIDE

Over five hundred places in England, Wales and Scotland are described and grouped alphabetically in counties or county groups in line with current ornithological practice. Counties are arranged alphabetically, and brief details of local societies are given together with the titles of any particularly relevant books. If societies can arrange a permanent for-warding address for publication, perhaps through a museum or library, they will be doing the nature movement a great service, with obvious benefits to themselves. I would be pleased to receive any such addresses for future revisions of this guide. The addresses of most societies can be obtained from the Council for Nature, address on page 14.

After each place name the Ordnance Survey (OS) one inch map number is given, and this is followed where appropriate by the high tide (HT) constant prefixed by a + or — and the base point. This enables high tide on any occasion to be calculated by reference to a current almanac like Whitakers or a local paper.

The most interesting regular species are listed under seasonal headings roughly in order of interest but with concessions to family ties. Thus all waders are generally grouped together. The entries show what is found at the different seasons; though seasons are bird seasons and not human. A calendar giving a brief outline of the main ornithological events each month follows this Preface.

Detailed instructions on routes from the nearest large town or trunk road should be read in conjunction with the appropriate Ordnance Survey one inch map, an indispensable aid to the British bird-watcher. Access details including details of how to obtain permits, plus help with local accommodation, where relevant, follows. Access and permit details are always changing, paths are being closed and new reserves created. Though every effort has been made to check material there will be mistakes. This is inevitable in a work of this kind where information is supplied by so many people, and observers should check locally all details of access to private property *before* entering. Where permits are available they generally have to be obtained well in advance of any visit.

In some areas the vast majority of watchers will be on holiday and more general accounts, including a county or county group introduction, are given. This applies to the Scottish islands where the choice has deliberately been selective. Many wonderful places like Shiants, the Bulgachs and North Rona have been omitted.

To improve future editions of this guide it is hoped that users will take advantage of the invitation on page 335 and send in suggestions or corrections to the publishers. Corrections and changes of access details and accounts of new localities would be welcomed and acknowledged if used.

Very few abbreviations are used and are then readily understandable:

BTO	=	British Trust for Ornithology
HT	=	High Tide
NT	=	Naturalists' Trust
OS	=	Ordnance Survey
RSPB	=	Royal Society for the Protection of Birds
WAGBI	=	Wildfowlers' Association of Great Britain and Ireland

Apart from these abbreviations one or two pieces of ornithological shorthand (i.e. 'commic terns' for common and Arctic terns) have been used.

Preface to the Second Edition

Though British ornithology has changed remarkably over the seven years since *Where to Watch Birds* was first published, the reasons for producing this guide are as valid now as they were then. The 'car to people' ratio has predictably increased and a lot more of this highly mobile population is evidently getting out into the countryside and enjoying birds. The Royal Society for the Protection of Birds is increasing in size at the most gratifying rate and the British Trust for Ornithology is enjoying a membership boom. Perhaps it isn't then so surprising that the RSPB is opening more and more reserves, for longer hours and providing better facilities for viewing birds. Already their reserves booklet looks like a *Where to Watch* in miniature.

Even more gratifying is the inquiry by the BTO into bird habitats – a sort of blue book of bird spots that are worth saving and *ipso facto* worth visiting to see birds. Six years ago I asked about the safety (for birds) of Cley Marshes – that was before Maplin and plans to barrage The Wash, the Solway and Morecambe Bay. Perhaps we shall be spared these areas, though I doubt it. If the first edition of this book helped to pick out some of these valuable but vulnerable areas and encourage people to enjoy them then it served its purpose. Only by continuing to increase the number of devotees to our cause will we stand any chance of saving anything. Unfortunately, it is might not right that counts today.

This edition is the result of a complete and thorough revision together with the addition of many new areas and the deletion of others whose bird appeal has declined. Some changes are the direct result of experience, such as the abandonment of the addresses of local societies. They *do* change too quickly for this sort of publication.

With this, as with the first edition, information is everything and I thank all those friends (and new friends) who have written to me and parted with their best kept secrets. Perhaps when they see a young bird-watcher clutching a copy of the book they will feel as satisfied as I do.

John Gooders, Sussex, March 1974

Calendar

JANUARY

Most species are settled in their winter quarters with wildfowl and waders particularly numerous on estuaries, lakes and reservoirs. Periods of snow and sub-freezing temperatures can initiate heavy movements of birds seeking milder conditions, and these are frequently followed by movements back again when the weather improves.

FEBRUARY

There are heavy influxes of wildfowl from the frozen coasts of the southern North Sea and most of the swans, geese and duck reach their peak numbers during this month. For crossbills the breeding season has already started.

MARCH

There is a great increase in the number of birds singing, and the numbers of the commoner winter visitors drop considerably. There are movements of the commoner finches, skylarks and lapwings overhead and many species try a first brood. The first summer visitors, the chiffchaffs and wheatears, are present in southern England – but it is still winter in Scotland.

APRIL

The remainder of the winter visitors depart and there is a heavy migration of birds entering Britain to breed – particularly willow warblers, wheatears and swallows – and of passage migrants. The variety of waders on the coast increases as the number of the winter knot and dunlin decline. Bird-watchers rush around ticking off new species for the year as they arrive, and people write letters to *The Times* about first cuckoos. For the commonest birds the breeding season is in full swing.

MAY

A major proportion of our summer visitors arrive including swifts and most of the warblers and flycatchers. As most species are singing and easy to locate it is an ideal month for bird-watching holidays.

JUNE

This is the breeding season for almost all birds. There are numbers of non-breeding birds around and post-breeding movements of lapwings begin.

JULY

Though generally thought of as the quietest and most uneventful month the return passage of waders and warblers begins, and sea-watching in the south-west can be very good.

AUGUST

An excellent month for passage of waders with the greatest variety of species present. Warblers and other night migrants are sometimes numerous and 'falls' occur in suitable places. Towards the end of the month most migrants are moving.

SEPTEMBER

Migration continues to be very heavy with perhaps a greater chance of an unusual bird than in August though the numbers of the commoner chats and warblers are smaller.

OCTOBER

Most summer visitors have left and the first of the winter visitors begin to arrive. There are heavy movements of finches, larks, thrushes and ring ouzels, and goldcrests are seen in unusual places. Snow buntings and shore larks are frequently seen, and several species begin to sing again.

NOVEMBER

Winter visitors are present in large numbers and there can be dramatic movements of these birds early in the month. Finch flocks in the fields are often very large and occasionally winter predators are seen.

DECEMBER

Though present earlier, wildfowl numbers really begin to build up now and the less usual species are more often seen inland. Coastal wader numbers are dramatic and collared doves come to the end of their breeding season.

Part 1
England

Bedfordshire

FELMERSHAM GRAVEL PITS   OS 134

The pits lie 6½ miles north-west of Bedford on the north side of the River
Ouse opposite Felmersham village. The 52 acres of flooded gravel workings
are a nature reserve of the Bedfordshire and Huntingdonshire NT. There
is a variety of breeding waterfowl and a good collection of warblers on
autumn passage.

   WINTER: waterfowl.
   SUMMER: great crested grebe, shoveler.
   AUTUMN: sedge, reed and other warblers.

Leave the A6 6 miles north of Bedford westwards to Sharnbrook. Turn
left in the village towards Odell and in threequarters of a mile turn left
towards Felmersham. The entrance is on the left 200 yards before the
bridge. Access is only open to members of the Bedfordshire and Huntingdonshire Trust.

THE LODGE, SANDY   OS 147

Situated 2 miles south-east of Sandy alongside the A603. It is the headquarters of the RSPB and visitors are welcome. The 102 acres provide an
attractive area of woodland and heath supporting a wide range of common
breeding birds. The Society has constructed a polythene lined lake that
has attracted a number of aquatic species.

   SUMMER: nightjar, redstart, tree pipit, lesser spotted woodpecker,
   woodcock.

The reserve is open from 9 am to 5 pm April-September: every day,
but members only on Sunday. October-March: week-days only. Leave
Sandy on the A603 and the entrance is on the right after 1¾ miles.

STEWARTBY LAKE

OS 147

The lake lies 5 miles south-west of Bedford and immediately south-west of Stewartby village. Originally a clay pit the area has now been worked out and is fully flooded. Though possibly less interesting than during the partially flooded period it still holds a variety of interesting species including wildfowl and is a gull roost in winter.

WINTER: teal, wigeon, pochard, tufted duck, great crested grebe, gulls.
SPRING: shoveler, black tern.

Leave Bedford southwards on the A418. After 5 miles turn right to Stewartby, and at the T-junction turn left past the station. The water can be seen from the road over the level crossing.

WYBOSTON GRAVEL PIT

OS 134

The pit is 5 miles north of Sandy on the eastern side of the A1. A large area of gravel excavation has created some quite extensive areas of open water that are frequented by a variety of duck in winter. Bewick's swans are often noted and great crested grebes breed. Passage brings small numbers of the commoner waders as well as little ringed plovers.

WINTER: teal, pochard, goosander, Bewick's swan.
SPRING: garganey, little ringed plover.
SUMMER: great crested grebe.
AUTUMN: little ringed plover, terns.

A sign on the eastern side of the A1 1 mile south of Eaton Socon directs the visitor to Wyboston Quarry. A straight lane between two houses leads past cooling towers to the workings and good views by casual visitors can be obtained from this. Regulars should contact the Site Manager.

Berkshire, Buckinghamshire, and Oxfordshire

ABINGDON NATURALISTS' SOCIETY.

MIDDLE-THAMES NATURAL HISTORY SOCIETY.
The Society covers half of Buckinghamshire and Berkshire and holds a full programme of indoor and field meetings. It has a strong bird section, and has published a check-list of the birds of the area. There is a thrice yearly Bulletin.

BANBURY ORNITHOLOGICAL SOCIETY.

OXFORD ORNITHOLOGICAL SOCIETY.
The Society covers Oxfordshire and Berkshire, produces a very good report, and is actively pursuing a policy of co-operation with other societies covering the same area. It holds an interesting range of indoor and field meetings, including expeditions to the coast.

BERKSHIRE, BUCKINGHAMSHIRE AND OXFORDSHIRE NATURALISTS' TRUST.

READING ORNITHOLOGICAL CLUB.
An active group that organises a first-rate series of winter lectures and adventurous field trips.

READ: *Birds of the Middle Thames*, A. C. Fraser; available from Middle-Thames NHS. *The Birds of Berkshire and Oxfordshire*, M. C. Radford.

CHURCH WOOD, HEDGERLEY (Bucks) OS 159

The wood lies 5 miles north of Slough, covers 40 acres and is owned by the RSPB and administered by the Middle-Thames Natural History Society. There are no rarities here but a large range of common woodland species breed and winter.
WINTER: woodpeckers, woodcock.
SUMMER: willow warbler, blackcap, nuthatch, tree creeper, ringed-necked, golden and common pheasants.
Leave Slough northwards on the B473 and turn right to Hedgerley at

Egypt after 3½ miles. Visitors are asked to sign the Visitor's Book and borrow a key against a returnable deposit from Mrs Hatson, 2 Deans Cottages (opposite the pond), Hedgerley, Nr. Slough.

FARMOOR RESERVOIR (Berks)   OS 158

This is a comparatively recent reservoir about which virtually nothing is known, though it will probably attract wildfowl in some numbers. It is completely embanked and is used by a sailing club.

WINTER: wildfowl.
PASSAGE: waders.

Leave Oxford westwards on the A420 and fork right in Botley on to the A4141. Turn left at Farmoor on to the B4017 and the reservoir is on the right. Access by permit obtained from the City Water Engineer, Oxford Corporation, The Town Hall, Oxford.

FOXCOTE RESERVOIR (Bucks)   OS 146

The reservoir lies 2 miles north-east of Buckingham, immediately south of Foxcote Wood. It was flooded in 1956, covers 50 acres, and is a wildfowl refuge of the Berkshire, Buckinghamshire and Oxfordshire NT. Duck are undoubtedly the main attraction, though watching for passage waders and terns would probably be rewarding.

WINTER: wigeon, pintail, shoveler, pochard, tufted duck, goosander.
SPRING: waders, terns.
SUMMER: great crested grebe.
AUTUMN: waders, terns.
See Map.

HAM ISLAND BIRD SANCTUARY (Berks)   OS 159

This is a marshy part of an old sewage farm lying 2 miles south-east of Windsor on an island between two arms of the Thames and covers 100 acres. The island and the surrounding water are used by numbers of wildfowl, especially in hard weather. Waders on passage are more reliable.

WINTER: Canada goose.
SPRING: green and common sandpipers.
SUMMER: yellow wagtail.
AUTUMN: ringed plover, green and wood sandpipers, dunlin.

The Sanctuary is managed by the Middle-Thames Natural History Society, from whom permits are obtainable. Leave the A308 eastwards on the northern edge of Old Windsor and follow OS.

LAMBOURN DOWNS (Berks)   OS 158

These hills are the eastern extension of the Marlborough Downs. They are ploughed chalklands rising to almost 800 feet, lying on either side of the B4001 north of Lambourn village near Hungerford. Typical chalkland birds include stone curlew and cirl bunting. There are always heavy passages of wheatears and, out of the breeding season, a variety of raptors are noted. Though not regular, the latter include the occasional harrier.

WINTER: golden plover, stonechat, corn bunting.

SPRING: wheatear.

SUMMER: stone curlew, wheatear, whinchat, corn and cirl buntings.

AUTUMN: turtle dove, wheatear.

Leave the A4 at Newbury and follow the B4000 to Lambourn. The B4001 leads northwards over the downs and there are numerous tracks and paths to the north that are rights of way.

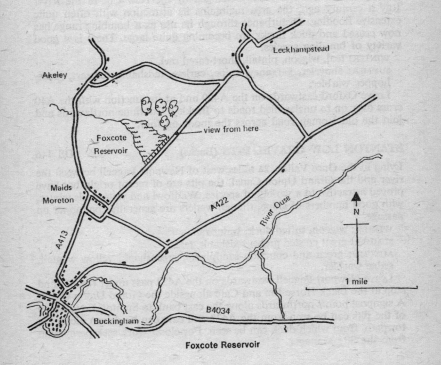

Foxcote Reservoir

MARLOW GRAVEL PITS (Bucks)   OS 159

The pits lie immediately east of Marlow on the north bank of the Thames, and will eventually extend to 200 acres. They hold numbers of the commoner duck and occasionally turn up surprises.

WINTER: tufted duck, pochard, goosander.

SUMMER: great crested grebe, yellow wagtail, sedge and reed warblers.

AUTUMN: common sandpiper, little ringed plover, redshank.

Enter Marlow across the bridge and turn right on the north side to the old station. Turn right just before the station and left at the end. Follow the road to a gate across the railway. Park and cross to main gate of pits. Ask at site office for access.

OTMOOR (Oxon)   OS 145 and 146

Otmoor lies 5 miles north-east of Oxford and is a lonely stretch of inland grazing marsh. Though greatly changed by the New Cut of the River Ray a century ago, the area maintains its attraction with often quite extensive flooding. Disturbance through its use as a bombing range has now ceased and duck flocks are becoming quite large. There is a good variety of breeding species.

WINTER: teal, wigeon, pintail, short-eared owl.

SUMMER: shoveler, garganey, snipe, curlew, redshank, redstart, grass-hopper warbler.

Leave Oxford eastwards on the A429 and at its junction with the A40 cross over on to unclassified roads to Beckley. Continue northwards and join the old Roman road across the moor on foot.

STANTON LOW GRAVEL PITS (Bucks)   OS 146

Lying in the Ouse Valley, 2½ miles west of Newport Pagnell between the river and the Grand Union Canal, the pits are of recent origin but have proved attractive to a variety of species. Wildfowl and water rails winter, with good numbers of snipe, though waders are generally commoner on passage.

WINTER: wigeon, tufted duck, water rail.

SUMMER: great crested grebe, redshank, teal.

AUTUMN: green and common sandpipers, greenshank, yellow wagtail, sedge warbler.

Leave Newport Pagnell westwards on the A422 pass under the M1 and stop at the Black Horse Inn and Café alongside the Grand Union Canal. A signpost points northwards along the east bank to Stanton Low. Many of the pits can be seen from the A422 and cars can be driven along the towpath, from which duck can be seen. For closer work seek permission from the Site Manager.

THEALE GRAVEL PITS (Berks) OS 158

The pits lie 1 mile south of Theale alongside the Kennet and Avon Canal, with another pit immediately west of the village. The wildfowl include the common diving ducks.

WINTER: tufted duck, pochard, shoveler, Canada goose, great crested grebe.
SPRING: waders.
SUMMER: yellow wagtail.
AUTUMN: greenshank, green and common sandpipers, commic terns.

Leaving Reading westwards on the A4 to Theale, turn left in the village and at the second bridge walk along the south bank of the canal to east and west. Leaving Theale westwards view to the south from the A4 after threequarters of a mile.

VIRGINIA WATER (Berks) OS 169

The lake lies north of the A30, 2½ miles south-west of Egham. The lake covers 130 acres with several long arms stretching to north and west. Its wildfowl population includes quite large numbers of mandarin ducks and garganey are regular on passage. The surrounding mixed woodland holds interesting breeding species.

WINTER: mandarin duck, wigeon, shoveler, pochard, tufted duck, goosander, smew, siskin, goldcrest.
SPRING: garganey.
SUMMER: great crested grebe, mandarin duck, warblers, woodpeckers, hawfinch, woodcock.

Stop on the A30, 3 miles west of the Thames at Egham before the Wheatsheaf Hotel. The lake can be seen on the right from the road. Access unrestricted.

WESTON TURVILLE RESERVOIR (Bucks) OS 159

This is an old canal reservoir, lying 4 miles west of Tring and the same distance south-west of the Tring Reservoirs. Though less than half a mile long and subject to considerable casual disturbance, it is one of the most notable wetland habitats in Buckinghamshire. Its natural banks have quite extensive reed beds and the area is well covered by a ringing group. Passage often brings a few black terns, some fresh waders and large numbers of hirundines.

WINTER: wigeon, pochard, shoveler.
SPRING: black tern, waders.
SUMMER: great crested grebe, sedge and reed warblers.
AUTUMN: common sandpiper, redshank, greenshank, swallow, sand martin.

Leave Tring westwards on the A41 and turn left after 3½ miles, just past Aston Clinton. Turn left at the far end of Weston Turville and watch for fishing sign on the left. Though not a right of way, access is generally unrestricted. It is a reserve of the Berkshire, Buckinghamshire and Oxfordshire NT.

WINDSOR GREAT PARK (Berks)   OS 159 and 169

The Park is immediately south of Windsor and the A332 runs through its north-western corner. It covers a huge area of predominantly open parkland with plantations and coverts of coniferous and deciduous trees. To the north-west, outside the park proper, lies Windsor Forest. The Great Meadow Pond is an excellent centre for wildfowl, including mandarin and passage garganey, and there are frequent hobbys in summer.

WINTER: wigeon, shoveler, pochard, mandarin duck.
SPRING: garganey.
SUMMER: hobby, nightjar, woodpeckers, grasshopper, reed and wood warblers, tree pipit.

Leave Windsor southwards on the A332 for direct access to the Park. Turn right on to the B383 alongside Windsor Forest.

WYCHWOOD FOREST (Oxon)   OS 145

Wychwood is a large deciduous forest lying south-west of Charlbury, 12 miles north-west of Oxford, and was a royal forest in the medieval period. Among a wide range of woodland birds, buzzards are frequent visitors.

SUMMER: buzzard, barn owl, woodlark, redstart, wood warbler.

Leave Oxford westwards on the A40 and turn right on to the B4022 at Witney. Turn left after 4 miles. Part of the area is a National Nature Reserve and a permit is required to visit any part.

Cambridgeshire

CAMBRIDGE BIRD CLUB.

The Club enjoys a constantly changing undergraduate as well as a more fixed town membership. Its Report covers the area worked by its members and overlaps neighbouring counties, notably Lincolnshire and Norfolk around the Wash, and the Brecks in Suffolk. It holds a programme of indoor and field meetings and is generally strong and active.

CAMBRIDGESHIRE AND ISLE OF ELY NATURALISTS' TRUST.

BRECKLAND   OS 135 and 136

Breckland lies roughly in the rectangle between Mildenhall, Bury St Edmunds, Watton and Methwold and covers parts of three counties. As it lies within 20 miles of Cambridge, it receives full cover from the University and is most fully reported in the Cambridge Bird Club Report. The last hundred years have seen the former sandy wastes turned into areas of productive farming and forestry. Over half is now coniferous forest of varying age and comparatively few large areas of open heath remain.

Nevertheless, the Brecks are good for birds and the traditional species are still found, though often in changed habitats. Stone curlew now breed on agricultural land while the other speciality, the crossbill, has benefited from the planting of conifers. Amongst the best remaining heaths, East Wretham belongs to the Norfolk NT and includes the two important meres of Langmere and Ringmere. The Trust also owns Thetford and Weeting Heaths, which are National Nature Reserves and there is a further National Nature Reserve at Cavenham Heath, access to which is partly restricted. The RSPB's Reserves at Horn and Weather Heaths are totally restricted.

The mere at Livermere Park holds an interesting variety of wildfowl and the heathland meres often hold Bewick's swans and goosander.

WINTER: Bewick's swan, goosander, shoveler, brambling, siskin.

SUMMER: gadwall, shoveller, Canada goose, ringed plover, snipe, redshank, curlew, stone curlew, long-eared and short-eared owls, nightjar, woodlark, willow tit, wheatear, whinchat, redstart, nightingale, grasshopper warbler, goldcrest, red-backed shrike, siskin, redpoll, crossbill.

The whereabouts of unusual breeding species is unlikely to be disclosed but interesting birds can be found with searching. The following are among the better spots:

1. LIVERMERE: leave the A143 3 miles north of Bury and half a mile north of Great Barton northwards to Great Livermere. Take the lane to the Church. There is generally no objection to bird-watchers walking along the main track to the mere, provided one keeps to the footpath.

2. RIVER LARK AND CAVENHAM HEATH: leave Bury northwards on the A1101 to Icklingham. Past the village and a quarter of a mile past the junction with the B1112 turn left on a track to Temple Bridge. General access along river and over heath.

3. BRANDON SAWMILL: leave Brandon northwards on the A1065. Between the fork on the northern side of the level crossing is an old pine wood which is worth a look.

4. EAST WRETHAM: leave Thetford northwards on the A11 and fork left after 1¾ miles. Stop near Ringmere and explore, especially the old pines to the west.

CAMBRIDGE SEWAGE FARM   OS 135

Lies immediately east of the A10 north of Cambridge, and is one of the frequent resorts of the Cambridge Bird Club. The sludge drying beds attract waders, especially in autumn, and the gravel pits on the northern boundary hold diving duck in winter and black terns in autumn.

WINTER: ruff, pochard, tufted duck.

AUTUMN: green and wood sandpipers, spotted redshank, little ringed plover, black tern.

Leave Cambridge northwards on the A10. Less than 2 miles from city centre, cross a level crossing and turn right after a quarter of a mile, through an iron gate. If travelling by car, park on convenient space on the left side of road opposite the gate. Access is granted to members of the Cambridge Bird Club.

ELY BEET FACTORY   OS 135

The factory lies immediately east of the River Ouse some 1½ miles east of Ely. In spite of the high chemical content of the water, the waste beet

RIGHT

The Ouse Washes provide 20 miles of outstanding ornithological interest. In exceptionally hard winters, when the whole of this area is deserted, the river north of Denver is sometimes very exciting

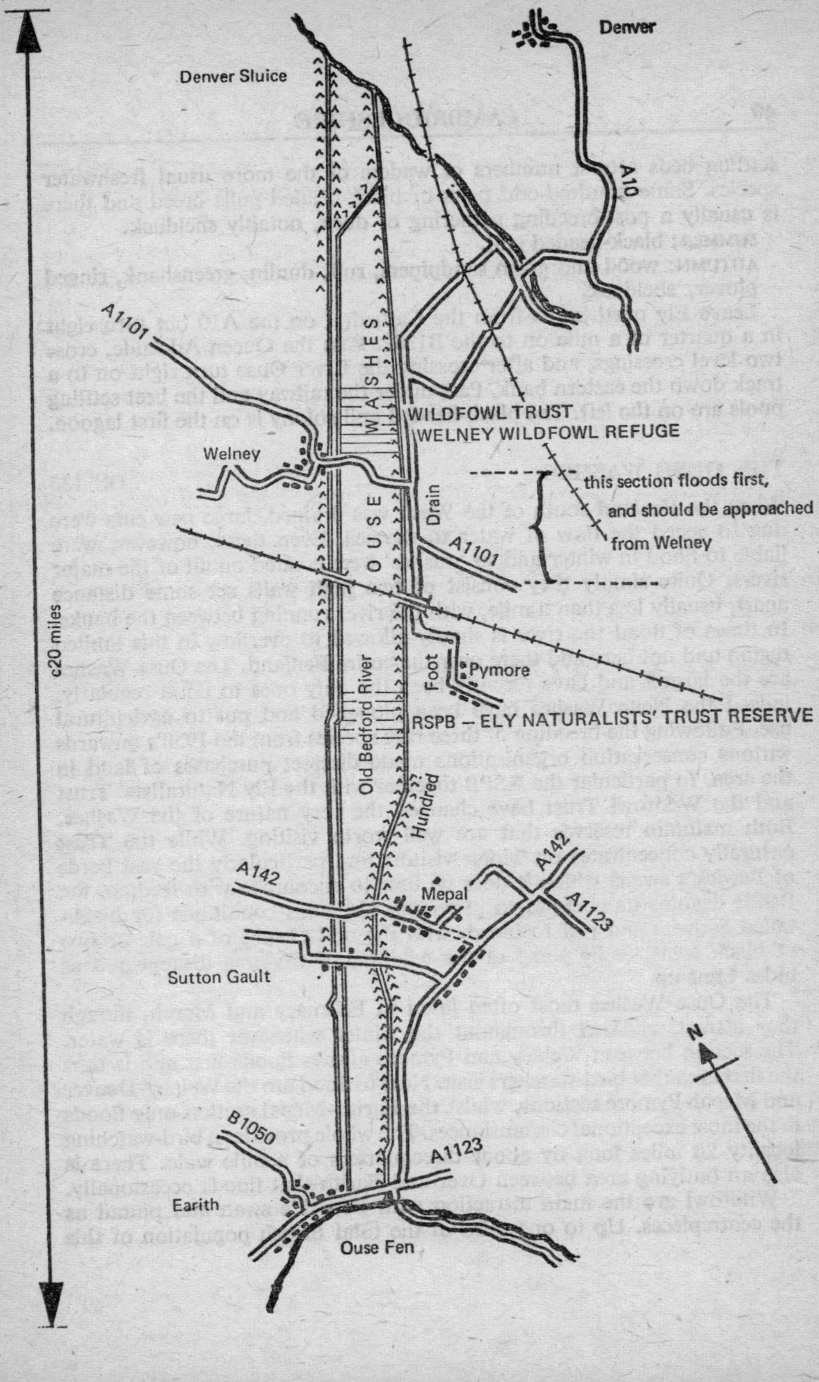

Denver

Denver Sluice

A10

A1101

WILDFOWL TRUST
WELNEY WILDFOWL REFUGE

Welney

OUSE WASHES

Drain

A1101

this section floods first,
and should be approached
from Welney

Pymore

Foot

Old Bedford River

Hundred

RSPB – ELY NATURALISTS' TRUST RESERVE

A142

A142

A1123

Mepal

Sutton Gault

B1050

A1123

Earith

Ouse Fen

c20 miles

N

settling beds attract numbers of waders of the more usual freshwater species. Some hundred-odd pairs of black-headed gulls breed and there is usually a post-breeding gathering of duck, notably shelduck.

SUMMER: black-headed gull.

AUTUMN: wood and green sandpipers, ruff, dunlin, greenshank, ringed plover, shelduck.

Leave Ely northwards from the Cathedral on the A10 but turn right in a quarter of a mile on to the B1382. Pass the Queen Adelaide, cross two level crossings, and after crossing the River Ouse turn right on to a track down the eastern bank. Pass under the railway and the beet settling pools are on the left. The black-headed gull colony is on the first lagoon.

THE OUSE WASHES   OS 135

When the Fenland south of the Wash was drained, large new cuts were dug to speed the flow of water to the sea. Even these, however, were liable to flood in winter and so 'washes' were created on all of the major rivers. Quite simply they consist of two high walls set some distance apart, usually less than a mile, with the river running between the banks. In times of flood the river is simply allowed to overflow in this limited region and not here and there over the entire Fenland. The Ouse Washes are the largest and have recently been the only ones to flood regularly, indeed the Nene Washes have been ploughed and put to agricultural use. Following the breeding of three rare species from the 1950's onwards various conservation organisations made discreet purchases of land in the area. In particular the RSPB together with the Ely Naturalists' Trust and the Wildfowl Trust have changed the very nature of the Washes. Both maintain reserves that are well worth visiting. While the Trust naturally concentrates on winter visitors and particularly the vast herds of Bewick's swans which it does its best to encourage with feeding, the RSPB devotes its energies to providing optimum conditions for black-tailed godwits and ruff to breed, with the odd chance of a pair or two of black terns. Sadly some of the wildness of the area disappeared as hides went up.

The Ouse Washes most often flood in February and March, though they attract wildfowl throughout the winter whenever there is water. The section between Welney and Pymore always floods first and is thus the first area that bird-watchers visit. Next to flood are the Welney–Denver and Mepal–Pymore sections, whilst the Earith–Mepal section only floods in the most exceptional circumstances. The whole provides a bird-watching locality 20 miles long by about threequarters of a mile wide. There is also an outlying area between Over and Earith that floods occasionally.

Wildfowl are the main attraction with Bewick's swan and pintail as the centrepieces. Up to one third of the total British population of this duck and over 800 Bewick's swans have been counted. Such numbers are often lost amongst the hordes of other wildfowl. Though surface feeding duck are most numerous, even sawbills are occasionally present in good numbers. Whooper swans are noted every year.

Should there be a freeze-up, the stretch of river between Denver and Wiggenhall provides excitement.

WINTER (When flooded, usually February–March): Bewick's swan, pintail, wigeon, teal, pochard, tufted duck, shoveler, golden plover, ruff, winter thrushes, short-eared owl.

SUMMER: black-tailed godwit, ruff, black tern, redshank, snipe, teal, gadwall, garganey, pintail, little owl, yellow wagtail, reed warbler.

The whole of the area can be worked from either eastern or western banks but crossing from one to the other is only possible where road bridges cross the river. In practice most watchers work the area from the western bank which is the first to flood. The best main road is the A10 between Cambridge and Kings Lynn and a start is made from this at Littleport. Each section is then dealt with in order of flooding, so that watchers keeping to the route as outlined will know that they have covered all the floods when they arrive at a dry area. It should be remembered that all fields are privately owned and are private shoots.

1. WELNEY–PYMORE (first to flood): turn westwards at Littleport on to the A1101. After 4 miles this turns northwards beside the Hundred Foot Drain and a large embankment. Turn left over the suspension bridge and continue across the Ouse Washes to Welney. Walk southwards between the two cuts on a high wall giving first class views over the Washes to the east. Walk 2 miles and return.

2. WELNEY WILDFOWL REFUGE (second to flood): as for section 1 but turn northwards on the east side of the Washes opposite Welney to Pintail House. The Warden will escort visitors to the observatory though Trust members may borrow a key. No visitors at all on Thursdays. Apply to the Warden in advance to make visiting arrangements. Limited accommodation is available.

3. RSPB–ELY NATURALISTS' TRUST RESERVE (second to flood): leave Welney on minor roads southwards to Manea. There are public hides at Purls Bridge. Permits are available from the RSPB between April and July for escorted visits.

4. MEPAL–EARITH (last to flood): leave Welney westwards turning left past the inn on to the B1100. After numerous right-angled turns, which should be taken left and right alternately, turn left at the B1098 and continue south to Chatteris. Turn left then right on to the A141, then quickly left again on to the B1050. In 1 mile turn left and follow a

narrow road to Sutton Gault. Park on western side of Washes and explore to the south along high embankment between cuts.

5. Return to Sutton, then B1381 to the southern end of the Washes, where the floods to the south can be seen from the A1123.

WICKEN SEDGE FEN   OS 135

This, a last small remnant of the ancient vegetation of the Fens, has been maintained by its owners, the National Trust, by delicate manipulation of the water level. The area is an impenetrable wilderness of sedges, reeds and thorn, intersected by wide rides along which visitors walk.

A mere of 10 acres was excavated on the neighbouring Adventurer's Fen in 1955, and the whole declared a sanctuary in 1957. The area is attractive at all seasons but principally in winter for duck, and in summer for breeding marsh birds.

WINTER: wigeon, shoveler, bittern, bearded tit.

SUMMER: great crested grebe, grasshopper warbler, long-eared owl.

The fen is reached from either the A142 westwards, or the A10 eastwards on to the B1085. The village of Wicken lies roughly half-way between these roads. At the western end of the village turn southwards for 300 yards down a track marked 'Wicken Fen'. A cottage on the left belongs to the warden who should be informed of arrival. Entrance is free but a key to the watch tower is worth the small fee plus the returnable deposit. This is an essential as it is the only way to see the mere.

WISBECH SEWAGE FARM   OS 124

The farm lies on the eastern bank of the River Nene some 5 miles downstream from Wisbech, across the river from Tydd Station (5 miles away by road). The sewage farm is of the older type, relying on natural evaporation and decay to do its work. Large lagoons have been created and, depending on pumping operations, one or other of these proves attractive to waders. Spring passage always brings something of interest and waders are continuously present from mid-July to mid-October. Rarities often include an American wader.

SPRING: wood and green sandpipers, spotted redshank.

AUTUMN: wood, green and curlew sandpipers, greenshank, spotted redshank, little stint, ruff.

Leave King's Lynn westwards on the A17 and turn southwards along an unclassified road that runs along the eastern bank of the River Nene from the Sutton Bridge swing bridge. After 1½ miles the road turns left and leaves the bank. A cinder track leads to the right after ½ mile.

Cheshire

MANCHESTER ORNITHOLOGICAL SOCIETY.

MID-CHESHIRE ORNITHOLOGICAL SOCIETY.

LIVERPOOL ORNITHOLOGISTS' CLUB.

SOUTH-EAST CHESHIRE ORNITHOLOGICAL SOCIETY.

MERSEYSIDE NATURALISTS' ASSOCIATION.

CHESHIRE BIRD RECORDING COMMITTEE.
This organisation produces the County Report.

CHESHIRE CONSERVATION TRUST.

READ: *The Birds of Cheshire*, T. Hedley Bell.

ALTRINCHAM SEWAGE FARM (Sinderland)   OS 101

Lies to the north-west of Altrincham on the edge of Carrington Moss
and is called Sinderland by local bird-watchers. At one time the farm
was known as one of the best places for inland passage of waders in
Britain but recent modernisation has reduced its attractiveness.
    SPRING AND AUTUMN: ruff, ringed plover, redshank, dunlin.
    Leave Altrincham northwards on the A56 to Manchester. Turn left
in a mile down Sinderland Lane to the works. There is a public road
through the middle of the farm and a public footpath along the southern
boundary.

DANE VALLEY   OS 111

The valley forms the boundary between Cheshire and Staffordshire some
5 miles south of Macclesfield and the same distance north of Leek. It is
a beautifully wooded valley both up and down stream from Danebridge,
near Wincle, an ideal starting point.
    SUMMER: dipper, redstart, pied flycatcher, tree pipit, grey wagtail, black-
cock, ring ousel, warblers.
    Leave Macclesfield southwards on the A523 and turn left on the A54

after 4 miles. After 3 miles turn right to Wincle and continue to Danebridge. Public footpaths follow the river up and down stream.

DEE ESTUARY AND HILBRE ISLAND
                              OS 100, 108, and 109: HT —0:17 Liverpool

The Cheshire–Flintshire border runs down the middle of the Dee Estuary,
and it divides what are undoubtedly the two best bird-watching localities
in the area between England and Wales, Shotton Pools, though on the
right bank of the Dee are in Flint, and the islands at Hilbre are in
Cheshire. The Dee at low tide is a huge shallow expanse 12 miles by 5
miles. Recent years have seen a considerable growth of salting along
the eastern bank and this will doubtless hasten the almost continuous
process of reclamation. Wildfowl are numerous here but are mainly
found in the upper estuary on the secure middle banks. They include
a flock of up to 1,000 pintail, which is but a fraction of previous
concentrations.
    During passage and winter the estuary is alive with waders, including
immense flocks of knot and oystercatcher as well as most of the other
species found regularly in Britain. At high tide most of the waders flight
to the islands at Hilbre which have become much used by bird photographers.
    Hilbre Island, Little Hilbre Island and Little Eye lie at the mouth of
the Dee just off the Cheshire shore. They have been the site of a bird
observatory and are now a reserve covering 5,750 acres. Though thronged
by tourists in summer, they are deserted for the rest of the year. Apart
from the waders regular species include divers, grebes, snow bunting,
gulls (including glaucous in many years) in winter; and skuas, shearwaters, gannet, fulmar, terns, auks and passerines on migration.
    Nearby on the mainland at West Kirby, the Marine Lake can hold
interesting duck in hard weather, while the Red Rocks promontory on
the north-eastern corner of the Dee is a good place for watching waders
and duck at high tide.
    WINTER: pintail, wigeon, shelduck, eider, knot, oystercatcher, godwits,
    purple sandpiper, divers, grebes.
    SPRING: waders, terns.
    AUTUMN: waders, terns, skuas, shearwaters, auks, gannet, passerines.
    Unless one is content to peer over miles of saltings there are very few
places around the Dee that are worth visiting and there are certainly
none to compare with the West Kirby–Hilbre area. The islands can be
reached from West Kirby across the mudflats at least three hours before
high water. It is best to walk to 'The Little Eye' (the smallest and
southernmost of the three) and then northwards along the rocks to the
main island. Permits are required only for the main island. Contact

Hoylake UDC, Hoylake, Wirral, Cheshire. For photographers Little Eye is recommended.

DELAMERE FOREST OS 109

Lying north of the Chester–Northwich Road, the Forest stretches for 4 miles west of the A49. Though the Forest is basically coniferous and is a favourite resort of crossbills during their periodic irruptions, areas of deciduous and mixed woodland occur, the largest being in the extreme north-western corner. The whole is Crown property with extensive Forestry Commission areas.

SUMMER: pied flycatcher, tree pipit, hawfinch, redstart, nightjar, long-eared owl, siskin, warblers.

Leave Chester eastwards on the A51 but fork left on to the A54 just before Tarvin. 1 mile after Kelsall fork left again on to A556. In 1¼ miles turn left at the crossroads with the B5152. Cross the railway at Delamere Station and turn left after 1 mile. Explore the forest along numerous tracks and paths, which are clearly marked, on either side of the road.

DODDINGTON MERE OS 110

The mere lies 5 miles south-east of Nantwich, next to the A51, is half a mile across and surrounded by private, open grassland. It is the only water in Cheshire with a regular flock of goosander.

WINTER: goosander, tufted duck, pochard, wigeon, shoveler, Canada goose, great crested grebe.

SPRING: Bewick's swan.

Leave Nantwich eastwards on the A51 and watch out for the mere on the right of the road after 5 miles. Fine views of the whole can be obtained from the road.

HOYLAKE–LEASOWE OS 100; HT —0:17 Liverpool

The villages lie on the north of the Wirral peninsula between the estuaries of the Dee and Mersey. Though overshadowed by the nearby Hilbre Island, this area of open foreshore has several attractions of its own. Waders of the usual varieties in winter and on passage, are augmented by skuas and terns in autumn, and by snow buntings and occasional shorelarks from November to March. This is the only regular haunt of these species in the county.

WINTER: knot, godwits, shorelark, snow bunting.

SPRING: waders, terns.

AUTUMN: knot, godwits, skuas, terns.

Hoylake promenade gives excellent views across 1½ miles of foreshore. It continues at its eastern end as a footpath and later as a wall to Leasowe.

LONGENDALE   OS 102

Longendale is the name of the hill area of Cheshire lying on the Pennines east of Stockport in the 'Panhandle' of the county. The area is mainly covered with rough grass and heather, part of which is a grouse moor. The valley itself has a series of reservoirs but like most high level waters they are generally bare in winter.

SUMMER: whinchat, ring ousel, curlew, golden plover, common sandpiper, red grouse, dunlin, twite, black-headed gull.

Leave Manchester eastwards on the A57. Turn left on to the A628 at Hollingworth and continue to Crowden, where one can join the Pennine Way. Great Crowden Brook is worth exploring.

MACCLESFIELD FOREST AND LANGLEY RESERVOIRS   OS 110

This is an area of mainly coniferous plantations, some 2 miles square, lying 3 miles south-east of Macclesfield. Immediately east of the village of Langley are three small reservoirs, two of which lie in the forest and are surrounded by trees. Wildfowl are regular in some variety. The forest is best worked in summer though the specialities can be seen in winter as well. The view from Shutlingsloe (1,659 feet) to the southeast is panoramic.

WINTER: goldeneye, wigeon, great crested grebe, blackcock, goldcrest.
SUMMER: blackcock, goldcrest, willow tit, redstart, golden plover, red grouse.

Leave Macclesfield southwards on the A523 but turn left to Langley on unclassified roads in the suburbs. In the centre of Langley fork left past the reservoir, then right alongside another, then turn left to the third. Public footpaths lead through the forest in various directions, but go south up to Shutlingsloe.

MERSEY ESTUARY   OS 109; HT +0:30 Liverpool

Near its mouth the Mersey is not only narrow and deep but flanked to both east and west by the industrial complex of Liverpool and Birkenhead. Further inland the river widens out and the industrial development is less dominating. The whole of this upper estuary empties out at low water leaving huge areas of mud along the southern bank. This coincides with the only area of fresh marshes on the Mersey. The Manchester Ship Canal acts as a barrier to casual disturbance.

Thousands of wildfowl are present in winter, including large but variable numbers of pintail. Bewick's swans and white-fronted geese (about a hundred) are more or less regular. Waders are present throughout the year in large numbers and the area of fresh marshes holds a wide range of the more usual migrant species.

WINTER: wigeon, pintail, shoveler, Bewick's swan, white-fronted goose, knot, curlew, short-eared owl.

SPRING AND AUTUMN: ruff, golden plover, curlew, knot.

Access to the estuary proper involves crossing the Manchester Ship Canal on to the 8 mile stretch of saltings and mud banks between the canal and the Mersey. Leave Chester on the A5116 to Moston and join the A41 westwards. After a little more than a mile, fork right on to the A5032 to Ellesmere Port. Pass under the railway bridge, turn right, and after passing over the Shropshire Union Canal, turn right again over railway lines on to the Ellesmere–Ince industrial road. Corridor Road turns off to the left to Stanlow Ferry (MSC). Permits must be obtained for any visit from the Manchester Ship Canal Co, 2 King Street, Manchester 3, and also from the Frodsham Wildfowlers' Club, if required during the shooting season.

ROSTHERNE MERE OS 101

Rostherne is the most famous of the Cheshire meres; it lies between Altrincham and Knutsford, and is threequarters of a mile by half a mile. It is of glacial origin and is deep, providing little food for the hordes of wildfowl that have made it famous. It is fringed by woodland, willow beds and stretches of reeds.

Rostherne Mere is of national importance as a refuge for wildfowl, indeed the 4,000 mallard that are found there form what is probably the largest regular flock in Britain (see Loch of Strathbeg). The Mere also acts as a large gull roost that reaches an annual peak of over 20,000 in mid-winter.

Passage periods often bring numbers of commic and black terns, while an interesting variety of birds breed.

WINTER: mallard, teal, wigeon, pochard, tufted duck, shoveler, Canada goose, great crested grebe.

SPRING: commic and black terns.

SUMMER: hawfinch, woodcock, reed warbler.

AUTUMN: commic and black terns, water rail.

Access to the area by permit is strictly controlled by the Nature Conservancy. Since 1962 the A. W. Boyd Memorial Observatory has been open to the public by permit. The Observatory is well equipped and gives first rate views over the Mere.

SANDBACH FLASHES   OS 110

This spot comprises four large sheets of water created by subsidence due to salt mining, surrounded by marsh and wet pasture. The area lies between Elworth and Elton Hall, 6 miles north-west of Crewe and 2 miles from Sandbach. A wide variety of species breed and the flashes are the best inland place in the county for wader passage.

WINTER: wigeon, pochard, goldeneye.

SPRING: waders, Bewick's swan.

SUMMER: redshank, common sandpiper, little ringed plover, great crested grebe, tufted duck, teal.

AUTUMN: green and wood sandpipers, greenshank, ringed plover, spotted redshank, little stint, curlew sandpiper, ruff.

The flashes are managed as a nature reserve by the Cheshire Conservation Trust, the British Soda Co Ltd, and Fodens Motorworks Ltd. Permits are neither issued nor necessary for ordinary bird-watching which is perfectly adequate from the maze of lanes in the area. Leave Middlewich southwards on the A533 alongside the Trent and Mersey Canal, continue straight on at this point and follow the unclassified road for 1 mile before turning left to the first of the flashes. Follow the OS for the other flashes.

There is access off the M6 near Sandbach.

TATTON PARK MERE   OS 101

The Mere lies in Tatton Park immediately north of Knutsford to the west of the M6 and within 2 miles of the famous Rostherne Mere. The area was bequeathed by the late Lord Egerton to the National Trust which, together with the County Council, runs the Hall and Park. The Mere is 1 mile long by a quarter of a mile wide and the south-eastern corner is bordered by a small mixed wood. Wildfowl are numerous and varied and black terns are regular double passage migrants. The Hall itself is worth a visit.

WINTER: mallard, wigeon, tufted duck, pochard, teal, shoveler, goldeneye, Bewick's swan, Canada goose, cormorant.

SPRING: black tern.

SUMMER: great crested grebe, tufted duck, teal.

AUTUMN: black tern.

Leave Knutsford northwards on the A50 and fork right on to the A5034 in 2 miles. Take the second on the right along the park boundary and enter by the northern entrance. Opening hours vary accordi g to the season but it is only open at weekends during the winter from 11 am till about dusk.

WEAVER ESTUARY
OS 109; HT +0:30 Liverpool

The estuary lies at the eastern end of the Mersey inlet and is closely linked to the best part of that estuary around the Ince Banks. It is now a feeder to the Manchester Ship Canal and is separated from the Mersey tideway by the Canal and the Weaver Sluices. The main attraction is wildfowl, especially on the 70 acres of Weston Marshes on the northern shore which are managed by the Merseyside Naturalists' Association as a reserve. Waders are usually present on passage at the Frodsham sludge lagoons.

WINTER: wigeon, smew, waders, short-eared owl.

SPRING: waders.

SUMMER: yellow wagtail, whinchat.

AUTUMN: golden plover, ruff, curlew, short-eared owl.

Leave Chester on the A56 to Frodsham. Pass under the railway bridge on entry and in 200 yards turn left on to the tracks across Frodsham Marsh bearing right to the Weaver. If necessary, inquire in the town as to the way to the marshes.

For access to the northern bank at Weston Marshes write to the Hon. Secretary, The Merseyside Naturalists' Association, 47 Woodsorrel Road, Liverpool 15.

Cornwall

CORNWALL BIRD-WATCHING AND PRESERVATION SOCIETY.
The Society represents a strong body of opinion in the south-west and is particularly active in the field of conservation. It owns two reserves, and conducts a series of research projects. The Ryves Memorial Prize is awarded in alternate years for original work in bird biology. It consists of books to the value of 20 guineas.

CORNWALL NATURALISTS' TRUST.
READ: *Bird Life in Cornwall*, B. H. Ryves.

CAMEL ESTUARY   OS 185; HT —1:00 Milford Haven

Flowing out on the north coast, with Padstow at its mouth, the Camel stretches inland for 8 miles to Wadebridge and is difficult of access, with the railway running along the southern shore. Fortunately the areas of sand near the mouth do not hold many birds, and at high tide most of the waders fly over Trewornan Bridge or to Burniere Point. Wildfowl include 100 whitefronts at Walmsley Sanctuary which is the property of the Cornwall Bird-Watching and Preservation Society. Though the Sanctuary covers only 42 acres the geese feed and roost in the area until they begin to roam more widely in February. Visitors are requested not to trespass on the reserve which is only successful because of the lack of disturbance. The area can be seen well from the road.

Waders are present in large numbers throughout the year and divers and grebes are noted annually.

WINTER: wigeon, shelduck, pintail, white-fronted goose, waders, divers, grebes.

SPRING: waders.

AUTUMN: godwits, grey plover, green sandpiper, spotted redshank, little stint, curlew sandpiper, ruff.

The mouth area can be seen from Padstow and Rock. Higher up, views can be obtained along the northern shore at Gentle Jane, alongside Dinham Creek from Tregena, and especially at Trewornan Bridge. For this point, leave Wadebridge eastwards on the A39 and after crossing the River turn left in half a mile on to the B3314. On the southern shore try the bridge over the railway north of Tregunna, 2 miles north-west of Wadebridge.

CROWAN RESERVOIRS   OS 189

These consist of three quite small pools near Camborne. Though the birds here are not numerous they are frequently interesting and occasionally rare. Waders in autumn are regular and a few duck and terns are frequently seen.

AUTUMN: green sandpiper, spotted redshank, greenshank, ruff, duck, terns.

Leave Camborne southwards on the B3303 to Praze-an-Beeble. Turn left on the B3208 which runs between the reservoirs in 1 mile.

FAL ESTUARY   OS 190; HT at Falmouth

The estuary stretches inland 8 miles to Truro. The main channel is deep with little foreshore and birds are concentrated in the side creeks that are like a series of small estuaries. The best are Devoran Creek, Tresillian River, Truro River and the Fal itself up to Ruan Lanihorne. All four are highly tidal and expose a good deal of mud. Though nowhere very wide their twisting nature makes it very simple for the birds to fly quickly out of sight when disturbed.

Wildfowl are not numerous though brent geese are occasionally present. Waders are frequent on passage though black-tailed godwits and greenshank winter on the Tresillian and the Fal.

WINTER: wigeon, teal, pintail, shoveler, merganser, black-tailed godwit, greenshank.

SPRING: waders.

AUTUMN: black-tailed godwit, green sandpiper, spotted redshank, greenshank, curlew sandpiper.

The best access points are:

1. DEVORAN CREEK: leave Falmouth on the A39 and after 5 miles the road runs alongside the creek. Continue and take the first right to Devoran and alongside the tidal area to Penpoll.

2. TRURO RIVER: leave Truro southwards on the unclassified road running along the eastern side of the river to Malpas.

3. TRESILLIAN RIVER: leave Truro southwards on unclassified roads to St Clement. Keep left past the church and continue alongside the river for 2 miles to Tresillian.

4. RIVER FAL: leave Truro eastwards on the A39 and half a mile past Tresillian fork right on to A3078. After 4 miles turn right at Tregony on to an unclassified road to Ruan Lanihorne. Keep right at the church and view from the road in half a mile. Take a maze of by-roads to Ardevora, 1 mile west-south-west of Ruan Lanihorne.

GULL ROCKS, HOLYWELL   OS 185

Gull Rocks lie offshore at Penhale Point near Holywell 3 miles south-west of Newquay. The Rocks are mainly noted for the mixed colony of auks.

SUMMER: guillemot, razorbill, puffin.

Leave Newquay southwards on the B3075. After 4 miles the main road turns sharp left while an unclassified road goes right. Take the road and continue through Cubert to Holywell. Turn left in the village towards Penhale but fork right over the bridge out toward Penhale Point. Finish on foot and observe the Rocks, preferably with a telescope.

HAYLE ESTUARY   OS 189; HT —1:20 Milford Haven

The estuary is on the north coast near St Ives, and is bordered on the eastern side by Hayle and the A30. The mud flats are little more than half a mile long and a quarter of a mile across with a small growth of salt marsh.

The Carnsew Basin is separated from the main channel and is the regular haunt of Slavonian grebes in winter. The narrower eastern arm is worth a look but often more rewarding are the artificial waters at its head. Sometimes a high tide swamps the land at the head of the main estuary toward St Erth.

Winter waders include an occasional common sandpiper and autumn passage brings a host of others, many of which use the pools at the eastern end. All can be seen at close range and at this time the Hayle is one of the best places for waders in the county.

WINTER: Slavonian grebe, wigeon, pintail, grey plover, common sandpiper, ruff.

AUTUMN: godwits, green sandpiper, spotted redshank, little stint, curlew sandpiper, greenshank, ruff.

The main vantage point is the A30 which runs alongside the main part of the estuary. St Ives is nearby, and an autumn holiday watching here and at St Ives Island could be rewarding.

HELL'S MOUTH TO GODREVY POINT   OS 189

This is one of the most beautiful stretches of cliff coastline in Cornwall and is owned by the National Trust. Though the 5 miles of cliffs from

Portreath to Godrevy Point are worth attention, this stretch involving Navax Point is the best. There are buzzards in the woods immediately south of Portreath.

SUMMER: razorbill, guillemot, raven, buzzard.

A track runs around the area making an excellent walk of about 3 miles. Leave the B3301, half a mile north of Gwithian on the north side of the Red River. A track runs away to the left out to Godrevy Point. The path to Hell's Mouth is about 1 mile further on along the B3301.

THE LOE POOL, HELSTON   OS 189

The pool is on the western side of the Lizard peninsula and is the largest inland water in Cornwall, covering 150 acres. It is separated from the sea by a shingle bar and is fed by the River Cober. The head of the pool is a marshy, reedy area that holds many species and the mixed hanging woods are an added attraction. Though a variety of birds can be found, duck in winter are the major attraction.

WINTER: teal, wigeon, shoveler, pochard, tufted duck, goldeneye, gadwall.

Leave Helston southward on the A394 and at the edge of the town take the B3304. After 1½ miles two tracks lead off to the left into the Penrose Estate. Access along these roads, which give excellent views of the pool, is during the pleasure of the Estate. No access off the roads is permitted.

LYE ROCK   OS 174 and 185

An area of high cliffs on the north coast near Tintagel. The main attraction other than the beautiful scenery is the large breeding colony of auks, including what is probably the largest puffinry in Cornwall.

SUMMER: puffin, razorbill, guillemot, buzzard.

Leave Tintagel northward on the B3263 and park in Bossiney. A footpath at the north end of the village leads to Bossiney Haven and along the cliff edge.

MARAZION MARSH   OS 189

Situated north of Mount's Bay, 2 miles east of Penzance, this marsh is one of the richest habitats in Cornwall. It is a submerged forest that is now a fresh marsh with reeds and shallow pools, and certainly a most attractive spot to any trans-Atlantic migrant. It is enclosed in a triangle formed by the main Penzance railway, the coast and the A394 along it, and the village of Marazion.

Passage waders are excellent both in spring and autumn, and almost anything else can, and does, turn up here. Divers and grebes are regular in winter and in particular both Slavonian and black-necked grebes are present.

WINTER: Slavonian and black-necked grebes, divers.
SPRING: garganey, waders.
SUMMER: reed warbler, stonechat.
AUTUMN: jack snipe, wood sandpiper, ruff, rarities.

Leave Penzance eastwards on the A30 and after 2 miles bear right at Longrock on to the A394. Pass over the railway and drive along the shore road. Park and view the marsh over the stone wall, there is no general entry.

PENZANCE   OS 189

As the point of departure of the *Scillonian* many watchers look eagerly around the harbour before setting out for Scilly. Mount's Bay itself is a good area for sea birds in winter with divers, especially great northern, and grebes being continuously present. Nearby Posandane holds numbers of waders and interesting 'flava' wagtails, while the Extension Pier is a regular high tide haunt of purple sandpipers.

WINTER: great northern diver, Slavonian grebe, scoter, velvet scoter, eider, goldeneye, purple sandpiper.
AUTUMN: divers, grebes.

The best vantage points are the harbour walls in Penzance itself, or near the monument just south; and the shore path which crosses the railway 1 mile east of the town on the A30.

ST AGNES HEAD   OS 185 and 189

On the north coast near St Agnes and south of Perranporth. The main attraction are the breeding sea birds.

SUMMER: kittiwake, razorbill, guillemot, raven.

Leave Redruth northwards on the A30 and turn westward at the junction with the B3277 to St Agnes. Continue straight on past the Church on to the unclassified Beacon Drive. After 1 mile, and opposite St Agnes Beacon, turn right out to Newdown's Head. Walk along cliff top to St Agnes Head. Wear stout footwear, there are adders in the area!

ST IVES ISLAND   OS 189

This is the headland that protects the harbour and resort of St Ives. There are no dramatic cliffs, and there is free access for the thousands of summer tourists, yet it is undoubtedly the best place on the Cornish mainland for sea bird passage. Leach's and storm petrels are regular in autumn, and Manx shearwaters are numerous and include some of the Balearic race. Sooty shearwaters are usually noted, and Sabine's gulls from America are annual visitors.

WINTER: divers, Slavonian grebe.

SPRING: sea birds.

AUTUMN: Leach's petrel, storm petrel, Manx and Balearic shearwaters, sooty shearwater, Arctic and great skuas, kittiwake, Sabine's gull.

An easy walk from St Ives. Access is general, except to the Coastguard Station.

THE ISLES OF SCILLY   OS 189

The islands lie 28 miles west-south-west of Land's End and are fully exposed to the rigours of the Atlantic. Yet the mildness of their climate and especially the bland winters have made them famous as producers of early flowers. Five islands are inhabited: St. Mary's, Bryher, Tresco, St Agnes and St Martin's. From a bird-watcher's point of view only St Mary's, Tresco, and St Agnes are really worth spending a holiday on, and of these, St Mary's is so much the better served by transport services that the general watcher need look no further. Of the uninhabited islands Annet is outstanding but many others are worth attention during the summer. The Western Rocks hold razorbills, and Gorregan has a small colony of guillemots and kittiwakes, these birds also breed on St Helen's. Annet, however, has large breeding colonies of storm petrel, Manx shearwater, common and Arctic terns, puffin and gulls.

St Mary's has a wealth of birds but is best during passage periods, and rare herons are annual. All of the beaches hold waders, and the rough marsh immediately east of Hugh Town is interesting.

Tresco has the Great Pool which attracts waders, holds a trans-Atlantic migrant at least once a year, and is the best area in Scilly for wildfowl. The woodland areas are larger than anywhere else in Scilly.

St Agnes, once the site of an attractive bird observatory, is as good as anywhere in Britain for seeing unusual birds, American waders and gulls, and heavy movements of sea birds in autumn.

The best sea-watching spot on the islands is Horse Point, St Agnes, but the best sea birds are seen from the *Scillonian* between Hugh Town and Penzance. Regulars include sooty shearwater, storm petrel, gannet, Sabine's gull, phalaropes, and skuas.

SPRING: turnstone, sanderling, whimbrel, herons, shearwaters, gannet, warblers, chats.

SUMMER: Manx shearwater, storm petrel, kittiwake, puffin, razorbill guillemot, gulls.

AUTUMN: waders, warblers, chats, flycatchers, firecrest, sooty shear-water, phalaropes, skuas, Sabine's gull.

The passage to Scilly is by RMMV *Scillonian* and RMMV *Queen of the Isles*, from Penzance, regular sailings and connections with overnight trains from London make it possible to be in Scilly 12 hours after leaving Paddington. There is also a BEA helicopter service from Penzance during the season, connecting with air services from other cities.

Launches connect with steamer services to all inhabited islands and also run from island to island at frequent intervals.

NOTE: the sea crossing can be very rough.

READ: *Birds of the Isles of Scilly*, H. M. Quick.

TAMAR LAKE   OS 174

The lake, on the Devon-Cornwall border, is a 50 acre reservoir lying about 400 feet up in the hills behind Bude. Its attractiveness to wildfowl led to its declaration as a reserve in 1950. There are records of geese, wild swans, unusual duck and a few waders and terns are regularly present in autumn.

WINTER: teal, wigeon, shoveler, pochard, tufted duck.

AUTUMN: waders, terns.

Join the A39 near Bude and continue northward to Kilkhampton. Turn right on to the B3254 and in half a mile continue on an unclassified road to Thurndon. Turn left to the reservoir.

Derbyshire

DERBYSHIRE ORNITHOLOGICAL SOCIETY.
The Society holds regular indoor and field meetings and publishes an excellent report and a monthly bulletin.

DERBYSHIRE NATURALISTS' TRUST.

DOVEDALE   OS 111

Dovedale lies in the limestone district north of Ashbourne and is a deep valley cut into the 1,000 foot plateau. The beautiful stream is bordered by natural or semi-natural ash woods. The usual upland valley bird population includes a host of warblers and chats.

SUMMER: dipper, wheatear, redstart, tree pipit, wood and other warblers.

Leave Ashbourne northwards on the A515 and turn left to Dovedale after 1 mile. There is a car park and access is by footpaths northwards. A large part of Dovedale belongs to the National Trust. Watchers should continue past Dovedale to Milldale, Beresford Dale and Wolfscote Dale all of which hold interest.

GOYT VALLEY   OS 111

The valley lies north-west of Buxton. The river has its origins in Goyt's Moss and falls 1,000 feet in 4-5 miles to Taxal, south of Whaley Bridge. A walk down the valley, or a drive, gives a succession of habitats from gritstone moorland through deciduous woodlands to farmland. Fernilee Reservoir is over 1 mile long and a further reservoir is in process of construction to the south.

SUMMER: curlew, golden plover, red and black grouse, ring ousel, grey wagtail, dipper, kingfisher, redstart, whinchat, wheatear, warblers, tree pipit.

Leave Buxton westwards on the A53. Fork right on to the A54 and then right again on to A537. Immediately turn right and in a quarter of a mile right once more. Turn left on to Goyt's Moss. This sounds difficult but is straightforward with the OS. Walk (or drive) down to Goyt's Bridge and take the footpath along the edge of the reservoir, down through the woodland to Taxal. The surrounding land is private.

LATHKILL DALE   OS 111

Lathkill Dale lies 2 miles south of Bakewell and is a typical example of a Derbyshire dale. It is heavily wooded along both banks and is not as frequented by tourists as Dovedale.

SUMMER: dipper, grey wagtail, redstart, wheatear, warblers.

Access is either up the dale from Alport, or down from Monyash. For the upward trek leave Bakewell southwards on the A6 and turn right after 2 miles on to the A524. After threequarters of a mile turn right to Alport. A footpath leads off to the right.

OGSTON RESERVOIR   OS 111

The reservoir lies 5 miles east of Matlock, has natural banks and covers 200 acres. There is a small duck population and Bewick's swans are regular each winter. Waders are noted in autumn in small numbers and there is a trickle of black terns.

WINTER: teal, wigeon, tufted, pochard, Bewick's swan.

AUTUMN: great crested grebe, little grebe, waders, black tern.

Leave the A61 westwards at the White Bear Inn to Stretton. Keep left following the B6014 to the official car parks from which the reservoir can be seen. Further views from the road along the south-western edge past Woolley.

STAUNTON HAROLD RESERVOIR   OS 120 and 121

Situated on the Leicestershire border, the reservoir covers 200 acres, and was flooded in 1963. Though the population does not appear to have settled down yet there is already evidence of sizeable numbers of winter wildfowl.

WINTER: wigeon, pochard, tufted duck, goldeneye.

SUMMER: great crested grebe.

AUTUMN: little grebe, migrants.

Leave Derby southwards on the A514 and turn southwards on the B5006 at Ticknall. Take the first on the left and bear left all the way to the car park. There is another public viewing spot at the other end.

THE TRENT AND NEWTON SOLNEY   OS 120

The meandering River Trent is joined by the equally meandering and oxbowed Dove just north of Newton Solney. The wet pasture is usually flooded soon after Christmas and the area then becomes one of the major haunts of wildfowl in the county. There are a few geese most winters and both wild swans are annual in small numbers.

WINTER: wigeon, teal, tufted duck, goosander, goldeneye, pintail, smew, geese, whooper and Bewick's swans, snipe, jack snipe, dunlin.

Leave the A38 between Derby and Burton on Trent at its junction with the B5008. Continue through Willington and stop near the River Trent. Walk along the southern bank up stream to Newton Solney. Many fishermen on Sundays.

Devonshire

DEVON BIRD WATCHING AND PRESERVATION SOCIETY.
The Society holds quarterly meetings in Exeter and Plymouth and publishes a thrice yearly magazine, *Devon Birds*. Field meetings are held in all parts of the county and research includes participation in national enquiries.

DEVON TRUST FOR NATURE CONSERVATION.

READ: *The Naturalist in Devon and Cornwall*, Roger Burrows.

AXE ESTUARY   OS 177; HT +0:25 Dartmouth

Roughly half way between Sidmouth and Lyme Regis on the south Devon coast, the Axe is a tiny estuary a mile long and a quarter of a mile wide. Winter wildfowl and waders are never numerous but autumn brings both godwits, ruff and spotted redshank (both occasional in winter). There is, however, always the possibility of rarities at this site, spoonbill and little egret have occurred on several occasions.

WINTER: wigeon, teal, golden plover, dunlin.

SPRING: waders.

AUTUMN: green, wood and common sandpipers, godwits, ruff, spotted redshank, rarities.

Leave the A35 5 miles west of Lyme Regis southwards on the B3172 to Axmouth. View from the road south of the village all the way to the bridge at the mouth.

BERRY HEAD   OS 188

Berry Head is the promontory that forms the southern part of Torbay, and lies a mile east of Brixham. With its lighthouse, coast-guard station and car park, it is a typical seaside tourist spot.

SUMMER: razorbill, guillemot, kittiwake, fulmar.

Leave Brixham eastwards on unclassified roads to Berry Head.

CHAPEL WOOD, SPREACOMBE, BARNSTAPLE   OS 163

This attractive wooded valley is an RSPB reserve containing most of the common woodland birds. Ravens and breeding buzzards are usually to be seen. Though the reserve covers only 13 acres, it is well worth a trip.

SUMMER: marsh tit, willow and garden warblers, buzzard, raven.

Access is by permit only (no charge) from the Honorary Warden, Mr C. G. Manning, Sherracombe, Raleigh Park, Barnstaple, Devon. Please restrict all correspondence to requests for permits only. Mr Manning will give full details of route and access with permit (S.a.e.).

DARTMOOR NATIONAL PARK   OS 175 and 187

Dartmoor Forest covers an area of over 50,000 acres. It is surrounded by a ring of common land that is known as the Commons of Devon, covering another 50,000 acres. The Dartmoor National Park includes all of this plus another area at least equally large making a grand total of 233,600 acres. Yet, in spite of its vastness, the habitats that it offers are limited, and a visitor can cover them all quite quickly if he so wishes. A great deal of the moor can be seen and explored by car but the advantage lies with those who are willing to do a certain amount of foot slogging. This should not, however, be undertaken lightly. The moor is notorious for its fogs and any inexperienced mountain walker should seek the companionship of an expert before venturing off the metalled roads.

The habitats of Dartmoor are as follows:

1. The open moor with heather, ling, etc., dominant, interrupted by the high Tors with their granite caps.

2. The high level 1,000 feet plus pedunculate oak woods at Wistman's Wood and Piles's Copse at Black Tor Beare.

3. The swift running streams in the wooded valleys.

4. The Forestry Commission's often quite extensive coniferous plantations.

5. The reservoirs.

6. The surrounding rolling countryside with wooded valleys.

On the open heath red grouse, curlew and wheatear are the most interesting birds. Lower heaths hold stonechats and whinchats in appropriate places. The high level oak woods are mere remnants with sparse bird life. The streams are an important focus for all of Dartmoor's birds. High up they are used by ring ousel, then lower by dipper and grey wagtail.

The Forestry Commission's plantations, especially those round Burrator and Fernworthy Reservoirs, at Soussons Down and Bellever, are good. The bird population varies greatly according to the stage of development of the woods, being most interesting when they are at little more than head height, when a mixture of heath and woodland birds can be found. The reservoirs at Burrator and Fernworthy hold a few wildfowl in winter, and, surrounded by pine woods, they make a pleasant setting for summer bird-watching.

The surrounding countryside, especially along the swift flowing rivers, is extremely beautiful and attractive to many species. Woodland holds both redstart and wood warbler, as well as forming possibly the most densely occupied buzzard area in Britain.

SUMMER: buzzard, raven, red grouse, curlew, wheatear, ring ousel, whinchat, stonechat, redstart, grey wagtail, dipper.

One is free to roam over a huge area of the central section, i.e. Dartmoor Forest proper, though some 30,000 acres mainly in the north-west are used for military training. Ranges are indicated by notice boards and white posts with two red bands. They must not be entered when red flags are flying from prominent positions, and firing times can be obtained from local Post Offices and Police Stations.

In the north leave Okehampton on the A30 westwards and park after 1½ miles near Fowley. Explore the woods along the West Okement River and follow that stream uphill to the high level oakwood at Black Tor Beare. Bear left across open ground to High Willhays for red grouse and continue northwards to Yes Tor and then to West Mill Tor. Strike northwards to pass Okehampton Camp to metalled road across railway. Turn left and walk on the southern side of the river back to original bridge near Fowley.

This hard walk should not be undertaken other than by experts and then in good weather when the military ranges are clear.

For the Two Bridges area: (a) Walk northwards up the West Dart River 1½ miles to Wistman's Wood. Venturing any further along this valley involves entering the military area. (b) Leave Two Bridges northwards on the B3212 after 2 miles pass the pine plantations on the right. At the end of these turn right to Bellever where there is a Youth Hostel and explore, especially southwards along the East Dart River.

The A362 that leaves the A30 at Whiddon Down, 8 miles east of Okehampton, and runs south-eastwards to Moretonhampstead is the best way of starting for the Fernworthy Reservoir area. Leave the A362 westwards to Chagford and follow a maze of lanes up to the southern side of Fernworthy.

Dartmoor lies on the A384 between Two Bridges and Ashburton and is a delightful spot and really only the beginning of the valley oakwoods that stretch almost unbroken downstream to Buckfastleigh. There are walks through the woodland which is National Trust property from Holne.

For Burrator Reservoir leave the A386 at Yelverton on to the B3212 and take the third on the right outside the town to Burrator.

READ: L. A. Harvey and D. St Leger-Gordon, *Dartmoor.*

EXE ESTUARY OS 176; HT +0:25 Dartmouth

The tidal stretch of the River Exe between Exeter and Exmouth is over a mile wide for most of its 5 mile length, providing several square miles of mud flats at low tide. The intertidal area extends to the stone of the railway embankments that line both shores. Since 1934 the western half has been a sanctuary, now known as the Exe Estuary Bird Sanctuary, extending over 1,000 acres.

The fresh marshes at Exminster hold wildfowl, including a few white-fronted geese most years. The lower estuary holds most interest, with duck dominant, though a flock of 100 dark-bellied brent geese regularly associates with them. A large variety of other species is noted and black-necked and Slavonian grebes are present.

Waders are plentiful at all seasons with a winter population including both godwits, spotted redshank, greenshank, and a few purple sandpipers at Exmouth, and about a hundred sanderling on Dawlish Warren.

Waders and terns are often numerous in autumn and occasional skuas are noted.

WINTER: brent goose, wigeon, pintail, shoveler, merganser, shelduck, goldeneye, eider, scoter, godwits, turnstone, grey plover, ruff, spotted redshank, greenshank, avocet, Slavonian and black-necked grebes.

SPRING: waders, terns.

AUTUMN: godwits, turnstone, ringed plover, whimbrel, common, green and wood sandpipers, greenshank, little stint, curlew sandpiper, terns, skuas.

Leave Exeter, or avoid it by taking the A38 round its eastern side, and turn left on to the A379. Turn left to Powderham, and at the church there is a very wet tunnel under the railway which gives views of the foreshore. A gate on the left leads to a level crossing (footpath) over the railway and on to the sea wall.

Further south, at Starcross, park off the main road and look for signs 'To Pier and Exmouth Ferry' in the centre of the village next to the Courtney Arms Hotel. Cross the railway, and walk to the end of the pier for excellent views in all directions.

Further south still, follow signs to Dawlish Warren and park in car park. Continue on foot across the Warren and out on to the sand spit for views up the estuary and out to sea.

Views on the eastern bank can be had by leaving Exeter eastward on the A35 and turning right at Clyst St Mary on to the A377. Take unclassified roads signposted Lympstone. Turn westwards under the railway and view estuary at several points. Views can also be obtained from Exmouth at the point and from the promenade.

HOPE'S NOSE   OS 188

The eastern tip of the peninsula that holds Torquay, Devon's largest seaside resort. It is thronged during the summer season but still holds the largest kittiwake colony in Devon with over 150 pairs. There are also late summer records of sea birds offshore in suitable weather (usually a wind with a southerly element).

WINTER: purple sandpiper, turnstone.
SUMMER: kittiwake, sea-birds.

The area is readily accessible from Marine Drive, Torquay.

KINGSBRIDGE ESTUARY   OS 187 and 188; HT +0:06 Plymouth

This is the southernmost estuary in Devon and, in spite of its large size seems to have been somewhat neglected by bird-watchers.

Wildfowl are usually very numerous, either on the upper part of the main channel or on Frogmore Creek. Waders include the usual species though more reports would be welcome.

WINTER: wigeon, teal, shelduck, goldeneye, waders.
AUTUMN: waders.

The central part of the estuary is certainly difficult to see but satisfactory views of the highest part can be obtained from the A379 between Kingsbridge and Charleton, a distance of some 1½ miles. The upper part of Frogmore Creek can be seen from the bridge and northern bank at Frogmore 1½ miles east of Charleton on the A379. It is also possible to get long views of the main channel from Blanksmill Bridge on the western shore between Kingsbridge and Salcombe.

LUNDY FIELD STATION AND BIRD OBSERVATORY   OS 163

Lundy Island lies in the Bristol Channel 11 miles north of Hartland Point. It is 3 miles by half a mile and is surrounded by granite cliffs rising to 450 feet. The top is mostly grass and heathland apart from the cultivated area in the south-east, and Millcombe which contains trees and shrubs. In spite of the blanketing effect of large land masses to north and south, the island receives an interesting collection of migrants, including a fair number of rarities.

SPRING: ring ousel, corncrake, warblers, chats.

SUMMER: Manx shearwater, guillemot, razorbill, puffin, fulmar, kitti-wake, raven, buzzard.

AUTUMN: migrants, short-eared owl, Lapland bunting, warblers, chats, flycatchers.

Visitors to the observatory must be members of the Lundy Field Society and a small charge is made for hostel-type accommodation, all enquiries to the Accommodation Officer, A. J. Vickery, 4 Taw View, Bishops Tawton, Barnstaple. Bookings for the hotel or one of the cottages must be made through the Resident Agent, Manor Farm Hotel, Lundy, Bristol Channel, via Bideford, Devon. Access is by MV *Lundy Gannet*, Mr A. Bealey, Tadworthy, Northam, Bideford; or during the summer season by Campbell's Steamer from Ilfracombe.

PLYM ESTUARY
OS 187; HT at Plymouth

The Plym forms the eastern boundary of Plymouth. Though this small estuary, 1½ miles by a quarter of a mile, lies within 3 miles of the huge Tamar complex, is has a distinct avifauna. Unlike most estuaries low tide is good, at high tide the waders flight to roost on the Saltram meadows to the south.

WINTER AND AUTUMN: golden plover, knot, black-tailed godwit, red-shank.

The main Exeter to Plymouth road, the A38, passes alongside the estuary as it enters Plymouth. (See Map.)

SCABBACOMBE HEAD
OS 188

The headland lies 3 miles south of Brixham and 2 miles east of Dartmouth on the south Devon coast. Because of the awkwardness of access, the surrounding area has remained relatively unspoilt and there is a small colony of breeding sea-birds.

SUMMER: kittiwake, razorbill, guillemot, fulmar, cormorant.

Follow the coast road (A379) to Hillhead 4 miles south of Paignton. Fork left on to the B3205 and after threequarters of a mile turn left on to unclassified roads to Scabbacombe Sands. A footpath leads from the Sands to Scabbacombe Head.

SLAPTON LEY
OS 188

Slapton Ley lies on the south Devon coast 5 miles south of Dartmouth and is part of a private nature reserve and the site of a bird observatory and field centre. The Ley itself stretches for 2½ miles from north to south and is divided into Higher and Lower Leys. The former is almost completely overgrown by reed, while the Lower Ley is open water and a

major haunt of winter wildfowl. Both are separated from the sea by the
50 yards of Slapton Sands along which runs the A379. The back slope
of this shingle bar is in part overgrown with black thorn and other bushes
which provide cover for a host of migrants including very respectable
numbers of rarities for a mainland area. Such rarities are mainly biased
towards marsh species but have included some bluethroats. The adjacent
part of Start Bay is frequented by sea birds at all seasons. In winter
numbers of sea duck include parties of eider, while the area is one of
the best in the county for divers.

Slapton is a magnificent place and the variety of its habitats ensures
first class bird-watching at all seasons.

WINTER: tufted duck, pochard, goosander, gadwall, eider, divers,
buzzard, raven.

SPRING: terns, waders, passerine migrants.

SUMMER: duck, sedge and reed warblers, buzzard.

AUTUMN: terns, gulls, waders, passerine migrants including rarities.

The A379 between Dartmouth and Kingsbridge provides some of the
finest bird-watching 'from the road' in the country.

The Ley area is a nature reserve covering 430 acres, under the strict
control of Slapton Ley Field Centre, from whom permits can be obtained.
The Centre offers a variety of courses including courses on birds. Groups
or individuals can follow their own programmes of field activities. An
observation cabin is operated on a part time basis by the Devon Bird
Watching and Preservation Society and provides accommodation for
four residents at a time.

START POINT AND PRAWLE POINT   OS 188

This area lies on the farthest south point of Devon where the county
bulges out into the English Channel. It is this geographical factor, more
than any special habitat, that makes the spot attractive. The birds are
almost exclusively migrants and a large variety of species have been
noted. Pre-eminent are sea birds in autumn with suitable weather. The
lighthouse at Start Point doubtless attracts many birds at night and
makes this a better point to watch for nocturnal migrants.

SPRING: migrants.

AUTUMN: migrants, passerines, Manx and Balearic shearwaters, gannet,
fulmar, guillemot.

The nearest big towns are Dartmouth and Kingsbridge which are
connected by the A379. Between the coastal Slapton Ley and Kingsbridge
are Frogmore, Chillington and Stokenham and roads south from the
villages lead to Prawle Point via East Prawle, and to Start Point. There
is a car park at Start Point.

TAMAR ESTUARY
OS 186 and 187; HT +0:16 Plymouth

The Tamar estuary is the large river system that enters the sea at Plymouth excluding the Plym Estuary. In the north the Tamar and Tavy estuaries can be worked from the peninsula between the two, while the southern pair includes St John's Lake and the Lynher River which are worked from the peninsula that ends in Torpoint. The two areas have roughly comparable numbers of wildfowl though the Tavy-Tamar sometimes holds 20-30 white-fronted geese, and their favourite resort at Weirquay is also a good vantage point for the famous avocets that regularly winter. The freshwater reservoir at Lopwell (40 acres) is worth a look for duck. The waders include wintering black-tailed godwit (150) usually on the Tavy.

WINTER: wigeon, teal, black-tailed godwit, avocet, turnstone, oyster-catcher.

AUTUMN: whimbrel, turnstone, spotted redshank, bar-tailed and black-tailed godwits, greenshank.

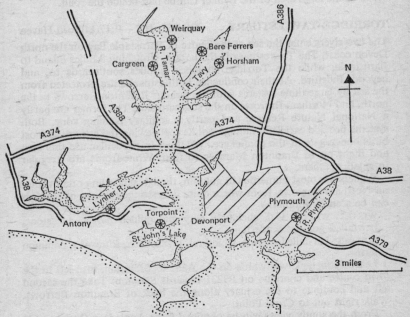

Tamar-Tavy-Plym: showing main access points to an area that holds several interesting species in winter. Notable are the avocets of Cargreen-Weirquay

1. NORTHERN GROUP: Leave Tavistock westwards on the A390 and turn left on to unclassified roads after 2 miles, signposted Bere Alston. Watch for further signposts for Bere Ferrers. To view from the southern shore, leave the A386 westwards north of Crownhill on to a maze of narrow lanes signposted Maristow. Watch out for signpost to Horsham on left. Turn down narrow lane, later becoming a rough track to the estuary.

For the Tamar follow signposts from either Bere Ferrers or Bere Alston to Weirquay, but you will probably have to ask the way. If the whole object of the trip is to see avocets, it is best to pay the toll (10p per car) across the Tamar Bridge to Saltash. Leave on the A374 but watch for A388 on outskirts, and turn off at Carkeel to Botus Fleming, where turn right to Cargreen. View from quay at half tide.

2. SOUTHERN GROUP: Leave Plymouth on the Torpoint Ferry. At Torpoint turn left along Marine Drive, right at the end and then first left to the road overlooking St John's Lake.

Continue westwards on the A38 and stop soon after Antony where views of the large area of the Lynher can be had beside the road.

TORRIDGE–TAW ESTUARY OS 163; HT —0:17 Milford Haven

The two rivers enter the sea at the centre of Barnstaple Bay on the north Devon coast. The Taw estuary is the largest, stretching 8 miles inland to Barnstaple, while the Torridge stretches 4 miles southwards to, and beyond, Bideford. At their confluence both estuaries are protected from the sea by large dune systems with the famous Braunton Burrows to the north, and Northam Burrows on the southern side. The former are partly a National Nature Reserve and partly a military training zone. Both systems provide excellent vantage points for viewing the estuary as most birds congregate at the confluence. Wildfowl in particular use this area and flight on to Braunton Marshes to feed. White-fronts are irregular in small numbers.

Waders are most numerous in autumn, though sanderling often winter on Northam Burrows, from where quite interesting numbers of seabirds can be seen in autumn.

WINTER: wigeon, teal, shelduck, grey and golden plover, turnstone, bar-tailed godwit, sanderling.

AUTUMN: bar-tailed godwit, whimbrel, greenshank, kittiwake, common tern.

Leave Barnstaple westwards on the A361 to Braunton, turn left in the town centre and continue on B3231 towards Saunton. Take the second left and continue to the estuary along the back of Braunton Burrows. Walk right out to Crow Point.

From the south, views can be obtained from Appledore Quay, and B roads and a track lead out to Northam Burrows.

WARNING: keep well clear of Braunton Burrows when the red flag is flying indicating military training.

WEMBURY
OS 187

Wembury lies at the eastern corner of Plymouth Sound. The main attraction, apart from the beautiful scenery around Wembury Village and the cliffs to the east, which are visited by fulmars, is the large area of inter-tidal rocks and foreshore. This is the haunt of one of the largest flocks of turnstones in Devon and a regular place for purple sandpipers. Chiffchaff and firecrest occasionally winter.

WINTER AND AUTUMN: turnstone, purple sandpiper, waders, cirl bunting, divers, buzzard, chiffchaff, firecrest.

Leave the A379 east of Plymouth southwards at Elburton on to a maze of unclassified roads to Wembury Point. Park at the top and walk down the hill turning left down a steep footpath roughly opposite the entrance to HMS *Cambridge*. Keep clear of the area on the right towards the point which is the Royal Navy's gunnery station.

WOODBURY COMMON
OS 176

This is one of the largest of a group of commonlands lying between the Exe Estuary and the Somerset–Dorset border. Other commons in the same area are Colaton Raleigh, Bicton and East Budleigh, but Woodbury is certainly the most attractive to birds. A large area of heath and scrub provides habitats for the usual heathland species.

SUMMER: stonechat, nightjar, red-backed shrike, tree pipit, redstart, buzzard.

Leave the A35 southwards on the B3180 8 miles east of Exeter at the Halfway Hotel. After 3 miles the B3179 joins on the right from Woodbury. Park here and explore along the roads and on numerous tracks.

YEALM ESTUARY
OS 187; HT +0:12 Plymouth

A small estuary about 4 miles east of Plymouth. The main flats are in the upper estuary and hold moderate numbers of wildfowl.

Waders include the usual species, though greenshank often winter. Kitley Pond, an area of fresh water at the head of one of the estuary's arms, is attractive to birds and strictly private.

WINTER: wigeon, teal, shelduck, redshank, greenshank.

AUTUMN: waders.

Leave the A379 southwards at Brixton where a signpost clearly states 'unsuitable for lorries'. Continue past brick works to Steer Point. The quay on the eastern side gives excellent views over the estuary.

Dorset

The Bird Report for Dorset is included in the Natural History section of the *Proceedings* of the Society, and is produced by the Dorset Bird Report Committee which co-ordinates ornithological field work in Dorset. Surveys undertaken by them on a number of species of special interest have contributed greatly to our knowledge of the status and distribution of birds which appear to be becoming less common.

DORSET NATURALISTS' TRUST.

READ: *The Naturalist in Central Southern England*, Derrick Knowlton.

ABBOTSBURY SWANNERY   OS 178

Situated at the western end of Chesil Fleet, the Swannery itself dates back to at least the fourteenth century, since when the swans have been protected by the landowners. Recent growth of the number of birds has caused a limit of eight hundred to be introduced, which is thought to be about the optimum.

SUMMER: mute swan, common and little terns, ringed plover.

WINTER: divers, long-tailed duck, merganser, smew, short-eared owl.

Leave the A35 southwards at the western end of Martingtown, 3 miles west of Dorchester. Follow signposts to Abbotsbury. Take the southward turning to the Swannery, half a mile away. There is an entrance fee and one can walk around the pens, the botanical gardens and along the beach as far as the Dragon's Teeth. Closes mid-September. For winter watching leave Abbotsbury westwards on the B3157 and turn left after ¾ mile to Chesil Beach. Walk eastwards along the beach.

ARNE HEATH   OS 179

The extensive heathland that once covered such a vast area of Dorset has been disappearing at an alarming rate. Thus National Nature Reserves have been established at Studland and Hartland, and in 1966 the RSPB established its Arne Heath Reserve covering 740 acres. Arne lies on a peninsula jutting into Poole Harbour from the south and is mainly covered with heather and gorse, though there are some stands of Scots pine. The most important species is the Dartford warbler, at present at a very low ebb, and doubtless the Society hopes that what it has already done for the bearded tit it can repeat for this elusive warbler.

WINTER: wildfowl, waders.

SUMMER: Dartford warbler, nightjar, stonechat, reed and grasshopper warblers.

Access April to August every Saturday, Sunday, Wednesday and Thursday (members free). Two parties 10.30 and 14.30. A nature trail is always open. Obtain permits in advance from RSPB. The china clay industry threatens ruin to this invaluable site.

BROWNSEA ISLAND   OS 179; HT at Poole

Brownsea is the largest island in Poole Harbour 1½ miles long by three-quarters of a mile wide. Its 500 acres include heath, woodland, lake and marsh. It is owned by the National Trust who have leased the northern half to the Dorset NT as a nature reserve. About 180 species have been identified on Brownsea since 1962, about 50 of which breed. It is the lagoon and marsh area that provide the most interesting bird-watching. At passage periods the lagoon holds large numbers of waders, especially at high tide when it forms one of the major roosts for the Harbour. Winter population of waders includes good numbers of both godwits, a few green sandpipers, and occasional avocet.

WINTER: wigeon, shelduck, pintail, godwits, grey plover, turnstone, green sandpiper, spotted redshank, avocet.

SUMMER: terns, nightjar, heron, woodcock, sedge warbler.

AUTUMN: wood sandpiper, whimbrel, greenshank, godwits.

Access is by boat from Sandbanks Ferry and Poole Quay to the quay on the Island. Private boats may land on the south shore (excluding the Castle Beach) and at the western end of the island only. Boats are also available, though less regularly, from Shell Bay and Rockley Sands. There is a landing fee. Access to the reserve is restricted to guided tours starting near the church on Wednesdays, Thursdays and Saturdays, at 11.15 am and 2.45 pm. There is a public hide near the quay equipped with a telescope. Children are half price.

BURTON BRADSTOCK   OS 177

East of the village, the build-up of shingle that eventually becomes Chesil Bank has created Burton Mere. It is now drained and completely over-grown by reeds, except for a few muddy areas at the eastern end. Inland the land rises steeply reaching over 500 feet within a mile. The tangle of bushes and trees behind the Mere holds the most exciting birds at migration times but is awkward to work. Migration, both nocturnal and diurnal, is very good considering that the area is not a promontory. Diurnal movements are marked in October with large numbers of finches, skylarks, thrushes, etc., coasting westwards.

SPRING: migrants, stonechat, whinchat, wheatear.

SUMMER: sedge and reed warbler, buzzard.

AUTUMN: chats, flycatchers, warblers, finches, skylark, thrushes.

Find the B3157 coastal road between Bridport and Weymouth. One mile west of Beacon Knap past a scattering of houses on the seaward side, is a track across Burton Common. This leads to the beach. Alternatively, walk along the beach from Burton Bradstock.

POOLE HARBOUR   OS 179; HT at Poole

The Harbour is a huge natural inlet lying immediately west of the Bournemouth–Poole conurbation. It is much used by the public as a holiday ground for sailing and more recently, water skiing. This has reduced its attractiveness as a breeding area and to a lesser extent, to passage migrants, though the improvements at Brownsea are some compensation.

Most duck concentrate in the north-eastern part of the Harbour and all three species of divers and all four species of grebe are regular, with Slavonian and black-necked often quite numerous. These species are often found in Poole, Studland and Shell Bays as well as the Harbour.

In winter black-tailed godwits outnumber bar-tailed; other species include the odd common sandpiper and occasional avocet.

WINTER: wigeon, shelduck, pintail, shoveler, scaup, merganser, golden-eye, smew, divers, black-necked grebe, Slavonian grebe, black-tailed and bar-tailed godwits, turnstone, common sandpiper.

SPRING: waders, terns.

AUTUMN: divers, grebes, wildfowl, whimbrel, spotted redshank, black-tailed and bar-tailed godwits, greenshank, knot, little stint, sanderling, terns.

Access to this vast area is at several points:

1. At South Haven Point, and along the edge of Brands Bay access via Toll (see Studland Heath) from south.

2. The Shore Road on the north side of the Ferry, the Blue Lagoon and Harbour Yacht Club are all good in winter.

3. Rockley Sands caravan site.

PORTLAND HARBOUR – FERRYBRIDGE   OS 178

Situated south of Weymouth where Chesil Beach joins the Isle of Portland; Ferrybridge refers to the general area at the eastern end of the fleet and includes a small area of inter-tidal sand and mud that regularly attracts small numbers of waders, terns and gulls. It does, however, produce more than its fair share of rarities and unusual species, including little gull, and is best during migration periods.

Portland Harbour is mainly known as a haunt of sea-duck, all three divers and Slavonian grebe.

WINTER: (at Portland Harbour) merganser, eider, scoter, divers, Slavonian grebe.

SPRING AND AUTUMN: (at Ferrybridge) waders, gulls, terns, little gull.

Leave Weymouth southwards on the A354 signposted Portland. Cross the Ferrybridge and park in car park on right overlooking the inter-tidal area. Views of Portland Harbour can be obtained from here by crossing the railway and sitting on the Harbour wall.

See Map, page 75.

PORTLAND BILL   OS 178

The headquarters of Portland Bird Observatory and Field Centre. By virtue of its geographical position jutting some 6 miles out into the Channel the area receives large numbers of migrants of all types. Small dry stone-walled fields and thorny hedges support the odd arable crop. The obelisk at the Bill makes an admirable shelter for the excellent sea-watching and regular species include Manx and Balearic shearwaters.

The commoner chats, warblers and flycatchers pass through in large numbers, and an unusual migrant is the occasional Dartford warbler. Rarities in recent years have included great reed, aquatic, olivaceous, subalpine, Bonelli's and yellow-browed warblers, while melodious and icterine warblers, and tawny pipits are annual.

Almost any other rarity can and does turn up and well over 2,000 birds are ringed annually.

WINTER: wildfowl, auks, divers, grebes, purple sandpiper.

SPRING: scoter, auks, divers, waders, gulls, chats, warblers, flycatchers.

AUTUMN: Manx and Balearic shearwaters, fulmar, gannet, scoter, velvet scoter, kittiwake, little gull, terns, auks, chats, warblers, flycatchers, rarities.

Leave Weymouth southwards following signs to Portland on the A354. The observatory is situated in the Old Light on the left a quarter of a mile before the Bill and the main areas for passerines are the fields on the right of the road.

Portland Bird Observatory and Field Centre is open from 1st March to 31st October and at other times by arrangement with the resident Warden. It is the 'Hilton' of bird observatories. Accommodation in six small dormitories and an evening meal is available at peak periods. Bookings must be made in advance.

All correspondence and booking to The Warden, Portland Bird Observatory and Field Centre, Old Lower Light, Portland, Dorset.

PURBECK CLIFFS   OS 179

These cliffs are formed of the same limestone as the Isle of Portland, and lie to the south of Poole Harbour. Rising to 400 feet within a quarter of a mile of the sea, they are amongst the most spectacular on the south coast. Breeding sea birds are the main interest between St Aldhelm's and Durlston Heads. Sea-watching can be very good and black redstarts winter.

WINTER: black redstart.

SPRING: divers, scoter, gannet.

SUMMER: guillemot, razorbill, puffin, kittiwake, cormorant, shag, raven, fulmar.

AUTUMN: firecrest, black redstart.

Leave Swanage southward to Durlston Head where birds nest near the lighthouse. Take the cliff path westwards past the lighthouses for a 5 mile walk to St Aldhelm's Head. There are several paths and tracks leading inland at various points as 'escape routes' but St Aldhelm's is almost the best part.

RADIPOLE LAKE AND LODMOOR   OS 178

Both lie in Weymouth and are separated by only half a mile of the Melcombe area of the town. Radipole is the estuarine backwater of the River Wey and its water level is artificially controlled. It was declared a sanctuary in 1948 and now consists of a series of inter-connected lagoons and a large reed bed. Lodmoor is a low lying area of rough grazing intersected by dykes and very liable to flooding. The creation of rubbish dumps on the area has reduced its attractiveness though it still holds birds and has a long list of rarities to its credit.

Wildfowl numbers in what is virtually a town park are remarkable, and waders are outstanding at migration times.

Terns are numerous at Radipole with black terns being almost continuously present in autumn. The lake is also one of the most consistent haunts of the little gull in England.

SPRING: waders, terns, garganey.

SUMMER: sedge, reed and grasshopper warblers.

AUTUMN: little ringed plover, sandpipers, spotted redshank, greenshank, little stint, terns, black tern, little gull, rails and crakes.

Lodmoor lies to the north of the coastal A353 out of Weymouth.

For Radipole pass under a small bridge at the north-western end of

the boat basin on to a roughly asphalted area for views over lagoons.
Continue along path between gorse for passerines and reed beds.
See Map.

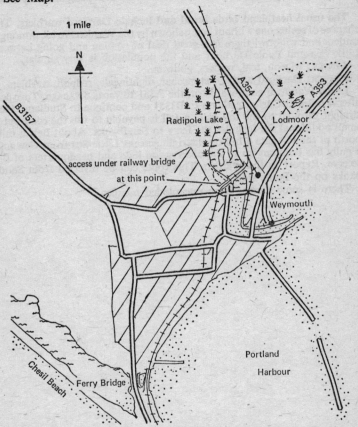

Radipole Lake, Lodmoor and Portland Harbour: outstanding urban bird-watching on all
sides of Weymouth

STUDLAND HEATH   OS 179

The Heath lies on the south side of Poole Harbour, and was declared a
National Nature Reserve in 1962, covering 429 acres. Though the various

heath plants, especially heather, are dominant, the reserve includes dunes, marsh and woodland and the freshwater lagoon of Little Sea. This wide variety of habitat leads to a wealth of bird life in a comparatively small area.

The usual heathland birds breed and include Dartford warblers. The chances of seeing one without being shown by the Warden are nil. Amongst waders and wildfowl there is a great deal of coming and going between Little Sea and Poole Harbour and the population is very similar.

WINTER: wigeon, teal, waders, godwits.

SUMMER: Dartford warbler, stonechat, nightingale, redpoll, warblers.

Leave Wareham southwards on the A351 towards Swanage. Turn left after 4 miles at Corfe Castle on to B3351 and continue to Studland. Pass straight through to the toll gate, a toll is payable to use the road but a small additional fee includes the ferry to Sandbanks. About half a mile north of the toll gate a hill on the right screens Little Sea from view and a gully has been cut up to the observation hide and headquarters of the reserve. Report to the Warden. This route can be reversed from Sandbanks on the Poole side.

There is some danger from unexploded missiles.

Essex

The Society is active and publishes a full and interesting report, including short papers and notes, as well as a bulletin. It organises indoor and field meetings and holds the only permits for the two big reservoirs.

ESSEX NATURALISTS' TRUST.

READ: *A Guide to the Birds of Essex*, Robert Hudson and Geoffrey A. Pyman.

ABBERTON RESERVOIR   OS 162

Lies 4 miles south of Colchester, the same distance north of the Blackwater Estuary, and is England's number one reservoir. Its 1,240 acres is spread over an area of 4 miles by 1 mile, and it was completed in 1940. Threequarters of the 12 miles perimeter is concrete banked and the depth of water varies down to 50 feet. Such a huge expanse so near the Essex coast was bound to attract wildfowl, but the Abberton numbers are often staggering. The following maxima have been recorded, usually in October–November: mallard 4,000, teal 12,000, wigeon 5,000, pintail 450, shoveler 1,300, pochard 3,800, tufted 600, goldeneye 350, goosander 85, smew 90, mute swan 450. Among the more erratic but nevertheless reasonably regular visitors are Bewick's swan, white-fronted goose, gadwall and, outstandingly, red-crested pochard. Birds of this species regularly occur but were labelled 'escapes' until quite recently; the majority are now accepted as wild birds.

Almost any wader is liable to turn up on passage. Many can be found away from the reservoir along the nearby Roman River valley, if it is flooded at the right time. Other passage migrants include good numbers of commic and especially black terns. Almost anything can turn up here.

WINTER: wigeon, pintail, shoveler, pochard, tufted duck, goldeneye, goosander, smew, Bewick's swan, white-fronted goose, gadwall, red-crested pochard, scaup, grebes, divers.

SPRING: whimbrel, black tern, garganey.

AUTUMN: red-crested pochard, garganey, greenshank ruff, common, Arctic and black terns, hirundines.

Access to the reservoir banks and surrounds is restricted to a number of officers of the Essex Bird Watching and Preservation Society. Members of this Society can usually gain access by arranging a visit with the Society's Chairman or Secretary.

Quite large areas of the reservoir can be seen from roads and a great many bird-watchers never bother to enter. Leave Colchester southwards on the B1026. After 5 miles, an iron gate on the left, set back from the road, gives views over a quite large area. A further threequarters of a mile south is the main bird-watching causeway. Continue southwards and after 1 mile the B1026 turns sharply left; at this point an unclassified road leads northwards signposted Layer Breton. In half a mile this leads to another causeway across the stretch with natural banks. There is a small heronry nearby.

ARDLEIGH RESERVOIR   OS 149

Created in the late 1960's, Ardleigh Reservoir is perfectly sited some 3 miles south-west of the Stour Estuary and 5 miles north-east of Colchester astride the main A12. It is a natural banked reservoir and, though narrow and subject to considerable disturbance, it has an interesting population of the common duck and other aquatic species. The extreme west (separated from the main reservoir body by the A12) is heavily overgrown and shallow and a likely haunt of crakes, rails and snipe. The main water level varies considerably and there are normally great crested grebes, dabchicks and a variety of duck breeding. On passage most of the 'fresh' waders put in an appearance.

WINTER: mallard, teal, tufted duck, pochard, gadwall, snipe.
SUMMER: great crested grebe, little grebe, yellow wagtail, sedge warbler.
PASSAGE: greenshank, redshank, common and green sandpipers.
Leave Colchester northwards on the A12 and cross the reservoir after 5 miles. Be careful not to park on the main road.

BLACKWATER ESTUARY   OS 162; HT —0:05 Sheerness

The estuary is 10 miles by 2 miles and is considerably deeper than its neighbour the Stour. It is an important estuary from a wildfowl point of view and is noted for brent geese. These birds usually congregate on the northern shore at Goldhanger and around Osea Island, and number over a thousand at each site. Wigeon and shelduck are the most numerous duck and sea-duck congregate at the mouth.

Waders are well represented and include the usual estuarine species with autumn additions of both godwits. High tide is important when watching waders flighting to roost on the Gore Saltings or Osea Island.

WINTER: brent goose, wigeon, shelduck, teal, pintail, shoveler, waders, short-eared owl.

AUTUMN: whimbrel, redshank, godwits.

1. Leave Maldon northwards over the bridge to Heybridge. Turn right and then right again on to the B1026 to Goldhanger in 2½ miles. Take the first lane on the right past the village down to the sea wall. Walk eastwards to the point.

2. Leave Maldon southwards on the B1018 and turn left after 5 miles at Latchingdon and Snoreham, signposted Lower Mayland. Continue round many bends to Steeple and turn left at the far end of the village towards Stansgate Abbey Farm. Park and join sea wall where convenient. View Steeple Creek and walk eastwards to Ramsey Island.

3. View Bradwell Creek, etc., by walking westwards from Bradwell Waterside (see Bradwell).

BRADWELL BIRD OBSERVATORY   OS 150; HT —0:20 Sheerness

The Observatory was established in 1954 at the mouth of the River Blackwater on the southern shore near the Dengie Flats area. Bradwell is an ideal centre for exploring the estuary and the flats from St Peters to Holliwell Point.

Waders are numerous and a first class variety is noted in autumn, good numbers are caught and ringed. Other species include snow bunting and twite and brent geese in winter.

Spring and autumn bring numbers of passerine migrants, including the regular chats, warblers and flycatchers, and larger numbers of thrushes and goldcrests.

WINTER: brent goose, grey plover, turnstone, snow bunting, twite.

SPRING: waders, migrants.

SUMMER: oystercatcher, black-headed gull.

AUTUMN: grey plover, turnstone, whimbrel, sanderling, curlew sandpiper, little stint, goldcrest, snow bunting, twite, thrushes.

Leave the A127 at Nevendon northwards on to the A132. In 2 miles pass through Wickford and continue to A130. Cross this on to B1012 and continue on B1010, B1020 to Southminster. Then B1021 to Bradwell on Sea.

Spartan accommodation provided at the Observatory. Write to A. B. Old, Bata Hotel, East Tilbury, Essex.

CANVEY POINT   OS 162; HT —1:25 London

In spite of its proximity to the heavily built up Canvey Island, the point is well situated in the Thames Estuary for migrating terns and skuas but has other attractions. It is often a good place to watch for the brent geese that use the Leigh marshes, and other wildfowl. Waders are often numerous.

WINTER: brent goose, wigeon, shelduck, waders.

AUTUMN: grey plover, turnstone, redshank, ringed plover, terns, skuas.

Leave the A13 at Great Tarpots southward to South Benfleet. Turn right, pass the station, cross Benfleet Creek and continue through Canvey. At the road's end continue half a mile on foot to the point.

DENGIE FLATS   OS 162; HT —0:41 Sheerness

Between the Rivers Blackwater and Crouch lies a huge expanse of rough grazing, intersected by an intricate maze of dykes and streams. Between Bradwell and Burnham stretch 16 miles of sea wall making one of the most daunting bird-watching walks in the country. The area is wonderful for wildfowl with dabbling duck especially numerous. Wigeon (3,000+) and brent geese (2,000) are dominant and this area with Foulness and the Blackwater forms the headquarters of the latter species in Britain; they belong almost exclusively to the black-bellied form (*Branta bernicla bernicla*).

Waders are numerous on the fields and mud flats and hen harrier and short-eared owl are frequent in winter. High tide visits are essential.

WINTER: brent goose, wigeon, teal, shelduck, golden plover, knot, curlew, grey plover, hen harrier, short-eared owl.

SPRING AND AUTUMN: waders.

For route to the area, see Bradwell. Access is awkward and is probably best achieved from Eastlands Farm at Bradwell, then south along the sea wall to Sandbeach outfall, returning over the fresh marshes via Glebe Farm.

Alternatively, leave Burnham eastwards before the Station and follow the metalled road to East Wick. Continue through Coney Hall to the sea wall at the mouth of the Crouch: walk eastwards to Holliwell Point and beyond.

For the really hardy, with warm and waterproof clothing and sustenance; arrive Bradwell and walk all round to Burnham on Crouch – 16 miles of sea wall.

EAST TILBURY – MUCKING   OS 161; HT —1:03 London

This area lies just across the river from the better known Cliffe marshes in north Kent, and doubtless draws many of its birds from this area. Duck are drawn by the narrow strip of saltmarsh that flanks the coast for several miles and waders too are numerous. Green sandpipers are found in the moat surrounding Coalhouse Fort.

WINTER: wigeon, pintail, shelduck, waders, short-eared owl.

AUTUMN: greenshank, common and green sandpipers, short-eared owl.

Leave the A13 east of Gray's Thurrock, 1 mile after it crosses the A128, southwards on to unclassified roads to East Tilbury. Continue straight through to Coalhouse Fort. A gate on the left before the Fort leads to the sea wall. Walk northwards and use pill boxes as hides to watch duck on a rising tide.

FOULNESS   OS 162; HT —0:34 Sheerness

Foulness lies on the Essex coast within 15 miles of Southend and is fully occupied by the military authorities as a firing range and access is strictly controlled. The Maplin Sands are currently threatened with development as London's third airport.

The main wildfowl of the area are brent geese (4,000), numbers of waders at high tide are the largest in Essex and greenshank occasionally winter. High tide visits are essential.

WINTER: brent goose, wigeon, oystercatcher, grey plover, curlew, bar-tailed godwit, knot, short-eared owl, hen harrier, merlin, snow bunting, twite.

AUTUMN: oystercatcher, grey plover, bar-tailed godwit, whimbrel, turnstone, wood and green sandpipers, spotted redshank, greenshank.

Positively no entrance without a permit which is not granted for casual bird-watching, but only for valuable field work like duck-counts. Try Second Permanent Under Secretary of State, Ministry of Defence, Whitehall, SW1. It is possible to look over the creeks near Havengore Island which is a favourite resort itself without a permit.

Leave Southend eastwards on the A13 and turn left 2 miles from the city centre on to the B1017 to Great Wakering. Leave left at the end of the village on to the unclassified road to Foulness.

HANNINGFIELD RESERVOIR   OS 161

Situated 6 miles south of Chelmsford and though over-shadowed by the more famous Abberton, is ranked sixth among England's top wildfowl reservoirs. Completed in 1954, it covers 870 acres and is further from the coast than Abberton. There are large numbers of wildfowl in winter and both gadwall and garganey are present in spring and autumn and often breed.

In autumn there is a build up of little grebes (300) and black-necked grebes are regular.

Waders of a great variety are present on passage, when almost every visit produces something of interest. Terns, including occasional Arctic, breed and black and commic are present in autumn.

WINTER: teal, wigeon, shoveler, pochard, tufted duck, goldeneye, smew, divers, grebes, dunlin.

SPRING: waders, black tern, garganey.

SUMMER: terns, garganey.

AUTUMN: little ringed plover, whimbrel, wood, green and common sandpipers, spotted redshank, greenshank, little stint, curlew sandpiper, ruff, commic tern, black tern, garganey.

Permits to enter are available only to members of the Essex Bird Watching and Preservation Society and can be obtained from one of several officers. Members should contact the Secretary.

Good views of the reservoir can be obtained from public roads. Leave Chelmsford southwards on the A130. After some 6½ miles turn left, signposted West Hanningfield, turn left in the village and view in 2–300 yards at the end of the dam where a hill drops down southward. Continue southwards but watch out for a pool on the left for passage waders. Bear right and view on right, and again half a mile further opposite entrance to the Hall. Continue taking right hand turns at two T junctions to near Whitelilies Farm, where quite close views can be obtained.

SOUTHEND PIER   OS 162; HT —0:10 Sheerness

This is without doubt the least likely locality to be included in a bird book, yet because of its position at the mouth of the Thames Estuary, and its exceptional length, well over a mile, it is an ideal place to watch for migrants in autumn. Though gulls, waders, duck and even brent geese can be seen at other times of the year, September is the month for this locality. The main species are terns and skuas and some large movements of both have been noted.

AUTUMN: terns, skuas.

Centre of Southend from the promenade. Now being restored at a cost of half a million pounds and soon to boast a labour saving railway.

TOLLESBURY   OS 162; HT —0:27 Sheerness

A village on the northern shore at the mouth of the Blackwater. The area is a maze of mudflats, creeks, saltings, dykes and fresh marshes. In autumn it is full of waders of all descriptions, and minor rarities do turn up.

Wildfowl are better in winter, especially sea duck on the estuary. Unlike most similar areas, there are attractions in summer. Duck breed on Old Hall marshes and downstream there are common terns and black-headed gulls on Great Cob Island. There is also the second largest heronry in Essex.

WINTER: waders, merganser, eider, goldeneye, wigeon, twite, snow bunting.

SUMMER: garganey, shoveler, tufted duck, pochard, black-headed gull, heron, water rail, collared dove.

AUTUMN: whimbrel, bar-tailed godwit, spotted redshank, greenshank, knot, short-eared owl.

Leave the A12 1 mile north of Kelvedon eastwards on the B1023 to Tollesbury. Pass straight through the village, bearing right and taking the second left as far as the old railway track. Park and walk along this to the estuary and sea wall. Turn left out to Shinglehead Point and continue along wall back to Tollesbury.

For Old Hall Marshes leave Tollesbury northwards, there is only one road of any substance, and watch for track on right in 1 mile. Follow this out to sea wall and continue to Great Cob.

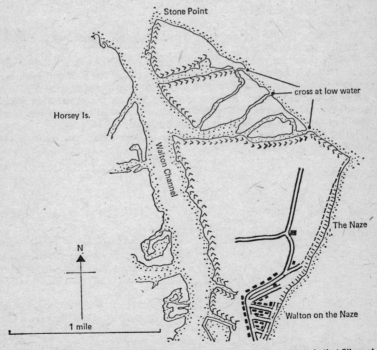

Walton on the Naze: the route out to Stone Point involves crossing channels that fill up at high tide. The return route should be exactly the outward route back to the mainland, but then westwards to Walton Channel

WALTON ON THE NAZE
OS 150; HT —0:09 Harwich

Situated on the coast immediately north of the resorts of Clacton and Frinton. The area that concerns the bird-watcher is the Naze to the north of the town, the saltings out to Stone Point, and the huge tidal complex of Hamford Water.

The Naze is well positioned to receive migrants and the bushes along the cliff path are always worth searching. Waders and wildfowl are the specialities with brent geese and various sea duck outstanding. Horsey Island holds a flock of feral greylag geese. The only purple sandpipers on this coast frequent the broken sea wall, twite and snow bunting are winter visitors to Stone Point, and sea watching for skuas can be lucrative.

WINTER: brent goose, scoter, merganser, goldeneye, shelduck, eider, curlew, grey plover, bar-tailed godwit, purple sandpiper, snow bunting, twite, short-eared owl.

SUMMER: black-headed gull, common and little tern.

AUTUMN: grey plover, godwits, green sandpiper, greenshank, curlew sandpipers, skuas, chats, warblers.

Follow the main roads to Clacton, but leave the A133 at Weeley on to the B1033. This runs to Frinton and then becomes the B1336 to Walton. Follow the main street northwards and park near the cliff edge. Follow the cliff footpath. Watch for purple sandpipers on the broken sea wall, and twite and waders on the marshes. Cross the tidal creeks at low tide (making sure of your return) out to Stone Point.

Leave Walton on the B1034 to Kirby le Soken but turn right in 1½ miles to Kirby Cross.

Gloucestershire

Both Societies are strong and active with indoor and field meetings. The N. Glos. NS publishes a monthly journal, and the *Gloucestershire Bird Report* which covers the whole County. The Bristol Naturalists' publish the *Bristol Bird Report*.

COOMBE CANAL AND POOLS   OS 143

The fields around this disused canal are liable to extensive flooding and are often under water for several weeks, autumn and winter. The canal runs between the main Gloucester and Tewkesbury Road, A38, and the River Severn to the west. Wildfowl include up to 150 white-fronts and when the water level is low waders are frequently present.

WINTER: wigeon, teal, pintail, shoveler, white-fronted goose, waders.

AUTUMN: waders.

Coombe Hill lies at the junction of the A38 and the A4019 from Cheltenham. Immediately opposite the A4019 a track leads off westwards to the canal. Permission should be obtained from the cottage at the end, and access is along the towpath.

FOREST OF DEAN   OS 142 and 156

A National Forest Park covering some 25,000 acres. The area has been forested since time immemorial and the birds represent as complete a hardwood woodland community as can be found in any part of the British Isles. The whole area, 8 miles by 6 miles, is worthy of exploration, though the area in the south-west is the most attractive.

Notable is a large population of pied flycatchers which are not generally viewable by the public. More widespread are the usual woodland warblers and amongst the specialities are sparrowhawk, buzzard, red-backed shrike and woodlark.

The woodland streams attract a large bird population, the area around Parkend is very good and is favoured by Crossbills during irruptions.

SUMMER: buzzard, sparrowhawk, nightjar, red-backed shrike, dipper, raven, wood and grasshopper warblers, pied flycatcher, redstart, woodlark, siskin, hawfinch.

The Forest lies between the rivers Severn and Wye, and between the A4136 to Monmouth and the A48 to Chepstow. Access is generally unrestricted with the exception of the pied flycatcher experiment which is being undertaken by the Forestry Commission, from whom permission must be obtained to view.

The Parkend area is best reached from the A48. Turn north at Lydney on the B4234, NOT the B4231. After 4 miles turn left on the B4431 and explore the area to the south.

Local newsagents sell guide books to the area, of which the *Wye Dean Tourist Guide* is the best. Various pamphlets showing the Ramblers' Association waymarked paths are also available.

Several local inns provide bed and breakfast and there is the Forestry Commission's Christchurch camping site.

FRAMPTON GRAVEL PITS   OS 156

These are a series of deep gravel pits set in a landscape of woods, scrub and agricultural land, lying a mile east of the Severn. They form the most important standing water in the county and a large variety of birds is noted annually. The main attraction is winter wildfowl, including the rarer species, though the rarities list includes bearded tit, little gull and grey phalarope.

WINTER: gadwall, tufted duck, shoveler, pochard, smew, goosander, goldeneye.

SPRING AND AUTUMN: black tern.

Leave the A38 westward on to the B4071 towards Frampton-on-Severn 3 miles north of Slimbridge. The main entrance to the pits is on the left before the village. Access is unrestricted to members of the North Gloucestershire Naturalists' Society and Dursley Society carrying their membership cards.

FRAMPTON SANDS   OS 156; HT +0:45 Avonmouth

The sands are closely linked to the New Grounds of the Wildfowl Trust and access is restricted between September and March to keep disturbance to a minimum. During the winter only the commoner waders are found though in spring and autumn there is an extensive passage of a number of species, including spotted redshank. The adjacent meadows and dykes hold green sandpiper and ruff.

Together with the New Grounds, Frampton Sands is the best place in Gloucestershire for waders. The tideway here is a mile wide and the mud is extensive.

WINTER: waders, gulls, geese.

SPRING AND AUTUMN: whimbrel, godwits, spotted redshank, curlew, green and wood sandpipers, sanderling, greenshank, white wagtail.

Leave the A38 westward on to the B4071 2 miles north of Cambridge. After 1½ miles turn left into Frampton on Severn and continue straight through the village for 1 mile. Turn right towards the Church but then left to Splatt Bridge, whence the river can be reached on foot. The Wildfowl Refuge lies to the south, and between September and March no access southward beyond the Frampton breakwater is allowed. Northward towards Fretherne is usually permitted but is not of special interest.

GUSCAR ROCKS, RIVER SEVERN OS 156; HT +0:25 Avonmouth

The rocks lie just off the northern shore of the Severn Estuary half way between the new South Wales Motorway Bridge and the Severn Railway Bridge. The rocks stand out above a huge expanse of sandy mud at low tide and are the haunt of many species of waders and up to 2,000 wigeon.

WINTER AND AUTUMN: dunlin, knot, turnstone, wigeon.

Leave the A48 threequarters of a mile south-west of Alvington, signposted southwards to Plusterwine. Continue on footpath to the sea wall and turn right opposite the rocks.

THE NEW GROUNDS, SLIMBRIDGE OS 156

The New Grounds lie on the south-east bank of the Severn and extend for some 3 miles north-east of the Severn Railway Bridge. The 1,250 acres of enclosed pasture and high salt marsh plus the huge area of sand-flats is managed as a wildfowl refuge by the Wildfowl Trust.

The Trust, formerly the Severn Wildfowl Trust, was established by Peter Scott in 1946 close to the refuge and to the Berkeley New Decoy, which was built in 1843. A large series of ponds has been excavated and numerous enclosures house the best and largest collection of wildfowl in the world. A unique contribution to conservation was made at Slimbridge with the building up of a captive flock of néné or Hawaiian geese that held over half of the world's population of this all but extinct species before a number of birds were sent to Hawaii and released. As a safety measure against endemic disease, separate collections have been set up at Peakirk in Northamptonshire and elsewhere.

The Trust not only manages these collections, which are open to visitors, but it is leading the way in wildfowl conservation in a realistic alliance with the Wildfowlers' Association of Great Britain and Ireland,

and has a number of research workers actively engaged on the scientific study of wildfowl. It has carried out the large-scale ringing of ducks and geese in its two decoys, by means of rocket-netting and on expeditions to the Arctic breeding grounds. The ringing of swans has been encouraged by the Trust and perhaps as many as one in four mute swans in the country now carries a ring.

The Trust's grounds prove attractive to a huge range of birds, especially duck, which fly in from the estuary to feed. The white-fronted geese on the Dumbles usually build up to 1,000 by Christmas and may number 4,000–5,000 in the new year. All other species of British geese have occurred here, including lesser white-front in most years. A flock of several hundred Bewick's swans winter here, spending part of each day in one of the enclosures. Observation hides have been constructed along the sea wall overlooking the Dumbles and the geese can be seen from two tower hides. There is also a hide accessible to all visitors overlooking the pond in the Rushy Pen frequented by the wild Bewick's swans.

Waders, too, benefit from the lack of disturbance and on both passages there are good collections of birds. Collared doves are regularly present, being attracted by the free grain; and peregrines are seen most winters.

RESIDENT: waterfowl collection, collared dove.

WINTER: white-fronted goose, Bewick's swan, wigeon, shoveler, pintail, gadwall, waders, peregrine.

SPRING AND AUTUMN: grey plover, whimbrel, godwits, green and wood sandpipers, spotted redshank, greenshank, little stint, ruff, turnstone.

Leave the A38 threequarters of a mile south of Cambridge, signposted Slimbridge and follow signs to Wildfowl Trust. Admission is daily from 9.30, times of closing varying according to season. Members only are admitted up to 12 noon on Sundays, and they may take a guest without charge. A tropical house provides a home for hummingbirds and other exciting exotics – there is a small extra charge for admission. Meals and refreshments are obtainable in the restaurant in the Trusts' grounds.

READ: *Annual Report of the Wildfowl Trust*, and *The Story of the Wildfowl Trust;* both obtainable from the Trust's Bookshop.

NEW PASSAGE   OS 156, HT +0:13 Avonmouth

At this part of the Severn Estuary the narrow mud flats are backed by spartina beds and a strip of saltings. There are a few small pools and the whole can be viewed from the sea wall. The New Passage Hotel is a good vantage point and the adjacent inlet is a particularly good spot. A variety of wader species is regularly present including ringed plover, sanderling and turnstone, but during migration periods whimbrel and common sandpiper can be seen along with green sandpiper and greenshank in autumn. Good flocks of dunlin flight at high tide.

WINTER: dunlin, turnstone, sanderling, curlew.

SPRING: whimbrel, common sandpiper.

AUTUMN: whimbrel, common sandpiper, greenshank, green sandpiper.

Leave the M5 westwards at exit 17 to East Compton and continue on the B4055. Join the B4064 to New Passage Hotel. The area of major attraction lies to the north. If the rifle range is in use a ¼ mile detour is necessary.

SOUTH CERNEY GRAVEL PITS   OS 157

These pits form the most extensive collection of gravel pits in the county, lying some 3 miles south of Cirencester, and 1 mile west of the A419. There is a good range of breeding birds, while winter brings numbers of wildfowl. Migration is not outstanding but odd waders, black terns, etc., turn up.

WINTER: wigeon, pochard, tufted duck, grebes.

SUMMER: great crested grebe, kingfisher, sedge and reed warblers.

Leave Cirencester southwards on the A419, and after 1 mile turn right on to an unclassified road direct to South Cerney village. Access is down the lane beside the bus shelter almost opposite, and is by permission of the owners, Edwin Bradley & Sons, Okus Quarries, Swindon.

TEWKESBURY   OS 143

The Severn Ham is an area of damp open grassland lying between the rivers Severn and Avon. Little more than a mile long and half a mile wide the whole area can be easily explored but visitors should be careful of hay crops and of disturbing anglers.

SUMMER: corn bunting, curlew, yellow wagtail, reed warbler.

Arrive in Tewkesbury from the south on the A38. Pass the Abbey and turn left at once, this road then runs along beside the Avon and a footbridge crosses over into Severn Ham beside Abel Fletcher's Mill.

WYE VALLEY   OS Tourist Map Wye Valley

The Wye runs in a beautiful wooded valley forming the boundary between Gloucestershire and Monmouthshire. The woods are interrupted here and there by steep limestone outcrops producing a dramatic effect. There is a good variety of breeding birds.

SUMMER: dipper, grey wagtail, raven, buzzard, warblers.

The best arrangement is to park at one bridge, walk to the next, cross and walk back. There are bridges at Bigsweir, west of St. Briavels, at Brockwear, near Tintern, at Chapel Hill (foot only) and Chepstow.

Hampshire

AVON FLOODS
OS 179

After leaving its upland origins, the Avon meanders over a wide floodplain with numerous oxbows and divisions into two channels. Around Harbridge and Blashford, it regularly floods its banks in winter and these, together with the extensive gravel diggings at the latter, are one of the most important wildfowl haunts in the country. Dabbling duck are found on the floods with a flock of 500+ white-fronted geese. Diving duck are found on the pits.

WINTER: teal, wigeon, shoveler, white-fronted geese, pochard, tufted duck.

Leave Ringwood northwards on the A338 and take the third on the right which is a cul de sac. A footpath at the end leads through the gravel pits. Views of others from the A338. Continue to Blashford where a track leads left down to the flood area. At Ibsley, 1¾ miles north, turn left to Harbridge and observe floods from the road. All of the area is private and permits must be obtained from the Somerley Estate Office. Trespassers are doing bird-watching a great deal of harm at this site.

CHRISTCHURCH HARBOUR
OS 179; HT —0:17 Poole Bridge

This is the first area of open foreshore east of Bournemouth. The Harbour, though comparatively small, has quite large mudbanks with areas of saltings and shingle, but is disturbed by sailing in summer. Stanpit Marsh is a local nature reserve of Christchurch Borough Council, covering 112 acres. It consists of saltings, tidal mud, fresh pools, reed beds and water meadows. In autumn all of the usual waders are present in small numbers and the gorse bushes sometimes hold interesting passerine migrants.

Better for these species is Hengistbury Head on the southern side of the Harbour which has been the headquarters of the Christchurch Harbour Ringing Group since 1956. Sea bird movements can be good.

WINTER: dunlin, divers and grebes, scoter.

AUTUMN: little stint, curlew sandpiper, sanderling, skuas, auks, terns, yellow wagtail, sedge and reed warblers, passerine migrants.

From Christchurch a public footpath on the east side of Town Bridge over the Avon leads to Stanpit Marsh. A ferry from Mudeford runs across to Hengistbury Head. Beach chalets are available at the Mudeford end of Hengistbury from the Christchurch Corporation, but these must be booked well in advance.

GILKICKER POINT
OS 180

Situated at the entrance to Portsmouth Harbour, immediately south of Gosport. The area lies alongside some golf links and is prominently marked by the old fort that is now used by Trinity House. Gilkicker is essentially a migration watch point both for sea birds and passerines. The most interesting season is autumn though spring can be very good if weather conditions are right. In October visible migration of finches, skylarks, etc., is often dramatic.

SPRING AND AUTUMN: skuas, eider, merganser, divers, grebes, chats, warblers, finches, skylark, etc.

Leave the A27 at Fareham, southwards on to the A32 to Gosport. Fork right on entering the town to Stokes Bay. Walk along the shore to the point.

THE GINS AND NEEDS OAR POINT
OS 180 and New Forest Tourist Map

At the mouth of the Beaulieu River on the western bank, the area consists principally of a shingle bank stretching out into the mouth of the river, an older shingle bank with grass and scrub, a tidal creek between the two, and a series of shallow pools protected by the sea wall. There is additionally the low mud-covered Bull Island, that can be reached at low tide.

The whole area is justly famous for the numbers of waders that it attracts, notably spotted redshank, for which the area represents the main haunt in Britain. It is also the site of the first breeding of the Mediterranean gull in Britain.

WINTER: wigeon, shoveler, spotted redshank, greenshank, black-tailed godwit, golden plover, turnstone.

SPRING: bar-tailed godwit, spotted redshank.

SUMMER: black-headed gull, Mediterranean gull, sandwich and common terns.

AUTUMN: spotted redshank, greenshank, black-tailed godwit.

Leave the main A35 on the northern side of Lyndhurst between Bournemouth and Southampton, and take the B3056 southward to Beaulieu. Turn right in the village on to the B3054 and then left in a quarter of a mile on to a minor road towards Bucklers Hard. Keep left after 600 yards and right after 1 mile. Turn left down the edge of a copse after turning sharp right at St Leonards. Follow this past the farm towards the shore and park where a track leads off to the left towards Needs Oar Point.

Access is by permit only and the area is well wardened by the Hampshire and Isle of Wight Naturalists' Trust.

KEYHAVEN AND PENNINGTON MARSHES
OS 180 and New Forest Tourist Map

These marshes form the central section of the coastline between Hurst Castle Spit and the Lymington River. A series of lagoons at Pennington

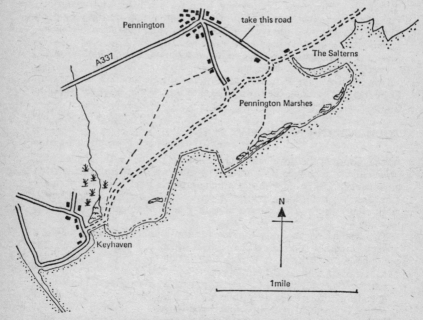

Keyhaven and Pennington Marshes. This area attracts a wide variety of species especially waders in autumn

lie just inside the sea wall, and on the seaward side there are large areas of saltings. The sea wall separating the two provides an ideal vantage point and a comfortable walk of either 3 or 5 miles from Pennington. The pools are amongst the best in the county for waders in autumn.

SUMMER: common tern, black-headed gull.

AUTUMN: green and wood sandpipers, little stint, greenshank, ruff.

Leave the A337 half a mile south of Lymington, left to Keyhaven. See map.

LANGSTONE HARBOUR AND FARLINGTON MARSHES
OS 181; HT +0:06 Portsmouth

Langstone Harbour is a vast area of inter-tidal mud and salting. Winter brings hordes of wildfowl and waders with the flock of brent geese (up to 900) being the largest on the south coast. They may be seen from Hayling Island at high tide or from Farlington at other times. The flock of up to 30 black-necked grebes is especially important.

Waders are very numerous and form an almost solid mass of birds on the high tide roosts on Baker's and South Binness Islands. Dunlin reach 15,000 in the Harbour and there is also a large roost of this species on Portsmouth Airfield. Greenshank usually winter in very small numbers and black-tailed outnumber bar-tailed godwits. Passage is more important at Farlington Marshes, where an area of fresh marsh extends into the Harbour for a mile from the northern shore.

The area of grazing is drained by a stream which ends in a muddy reed-fringed lagoon where some of the rarest waders have been noted. The thorn bush area in the north is worth a look for passerine migrants at appropriate seasons.

The concentration of gulls at Eastney sewage outfall regularly includes extreme rarities and held an Iceland gull, 2 Mediterranean gulls, a little gull and a Sabine's gull in one recent year.

WINTER: brent goose, wigeon, teal, shelduck, merganser, goldeneye, long-tailed duck, bar-tailed and black-tailed godwits, grey plover, oystercatcher, greenshank, knot, sanderling, divers, grebes, black-necked grebe, short-eared owl.

SPRING: godwits, whimbrel, sandpipers, garganey.

SUMMER: grey plover, bar-tailed godwit, terns.

AUTUMN: grey plover, whimbrel, green, wood and common sandpipers, greenshank, little stint, spotted redshank, godwits, ruff, short-eared owl, passerines.

1. Farlington Marsh is a nature reserve of the Hampshire and Isle of Wight NT and is of free access. See map. At low tide and with gumboots one can walk out over North Binness and Long Island for a period of six hours to obtain excellent views over the main channel.

2. Leave the A27 at Havant southwards on to Hayling Island. Continue to South Hayling and turn right into Station Road, pass the station, follow on to Park Road and then turn right into North Shore Road. A fence at the end is navigable at the left end on to a path running along the Harbour wall.

3. The Harbour mouth can be reached on either side and there is a ferry from Portsea to Hayling for walkers. Do not neglect Eastney sewage outfall.

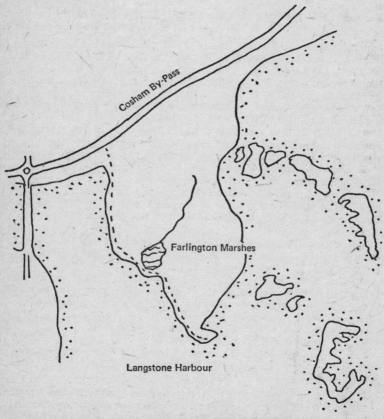

Langstone Harbour and Farlington Marshes: directly accessible from the new motorway North of the harbour: adequate verges, lay-bys, and good bird watching from the road.

NEW FOREST

The Forest lies between Southampton Water and the Hampshire Avon and is not, as is commonly thought, the result of William the Conqueror removing farmers to make a hunting ground. The Royal Forest covers 64,707 acres, of which 2,000 acres are permanently enclosed and private, and 16,000 acres which are free of common rights as long as they remain enclosed. There remain some 45,000 acres of permanent common, of which 5,000 acres is woodland. There is an additional area of 6,000 acres abutting on to the Forest provided by a ring of 22 other commons, making a grand total of 51,000 acres of commonland.

The underlying rocks are basically sandy and give rise to heather scenery with occasional large areas of gorse, bracken, scrub and rough grass. The woodlands are mainly mixed and vary enormously in age. Quite large areas of old oak and beech forest exist, while more recent plantings include areas of Scots pine.

A wonderful range of breeding birds includes crossbills, a few pairs of siskin and a small colony of firecrests. The Forest is the stronghold of the Dartford warbler in Britain but numbers are at present very low and the birds are hard to find in 144 square miles.

It has been said that the New Forest is generally a disappointment bird-wise, but though a day trip can miss all the specialities, one needs only a fair amount of luck and persistence for a truly wonderful day, week, or month.

SUMMER: woodcock, wood warbler, nightingale, goldcrest, redstart, crossbill, redpoll, hawfinch, grey wagtail, hobby, sparrow hawk, buzzard, stonechat, nightjar, Dartford warbler, red-backed shrike, woodlark, curlew, redshank, snipe, wheatear.

The whole of the Forest area merits attention and, in particular, the status of the Dartford warbler and red-backed shrike is under constant inquiry. There are three Forest Nature Reserves where access is restricted to the trackways and rides; at Bramshaw (525 acres), Mark Ash (226 acres) and Matley and Denny (2,577 acres).

If there is no time to explore and find areas of your own the following are worth a visit – but there are many other good spots:

1. Drive from Brockenhurst across Rhinefield to enter the varied but huge woodland area near Rhinefield Lodge. Continue on the A35 and cross directly into the Knightwood Oak area, through Mark Ash and out on to the A31.

2. Of the heaths, Beaulieu is amongst the best. The northern half west of the B3054 between Beaulieu and Dibden is good; and in the south the area west of Crockford Bridge can be so.

3. The Beaulieu Road area on the Lyndhurst–Beaulieu Road, B3056, especially on the south side next to Denny Wood.

4. The north-western heaths north of the A31 out to Dockens Water and Broomy Inclosure.

At all times be careful of ponies on the road. There are hundreds of accidents every year.

Camping is permitted from mid-March to mid-October but permits must be obtained before setting up camp from the Forestry Commission, Red Lodge, Lyndhurst, Monday–Friday. Camping Offices at Hollands Wood (A337); Queens House Grounds, Lyndhurst (off A35); Marlpit Oak (off B3055); Shave Green, Cadnam (A337); Ashurst (A35) and Stoney Cross Airfield (off A31), issue permits on Friday evenings, Saturdays and Sundays during the season.

NEWTOWN MARSH, ISLE OF WIGHT   OS 180

The marsh was formed when the sea wall was breached by gales in November 1954, 130 acres are now flooded at high tide. This is an excellent area for wildfowl and waders, including a good wintering flock of black-tailed godwits, and the occasional wintering greenshank.

WINTER: teal, wigeon, shelduck, black-tailed godwit, greenshank.

SPRING: waders.

SUMMER: black-headed gull.

AUTUMN: golden and grey plovers, greenshank, little stint, ruff.

Leave the A3054 6 miles west of Newport and turn right to Newtown. In the village turn left and continue as far west as possible, a footpath from here crosses on to the sea wall. For the eastern end of the wall, access is through Town Copse (National Trust). See map.

PORTSMOUTH HARBOUR   OS 180; HT at Portsmouth

Though at first sight Portsmouth Harbour appears as huge and as attractive as Langstone Harbour, it is so heavily used by shipping and so encircled by urban development that it has been ornithologically neglected. Most of the waders that occur in Langstone are present, and roost on Pewit Island and the saltings of Horsea Island. Wildfowl mainly arrive with hard weather.

WINTER: curlew, redshank, grey plover, bar-tailed godwit, wigeon, teal, goldeneye.

SPRING AND AUTUMN: curlew, grey plover, godwits.

Leave the A27 at Portchester, southwards to Portchester Castle and view estuary. There is a public footpath along part of the eastern side of this peninsula. Views can be obtained westwards from the Cosham–Portsea Island Bridge, and southwards from the A27 at Paulsgrove at low tide.

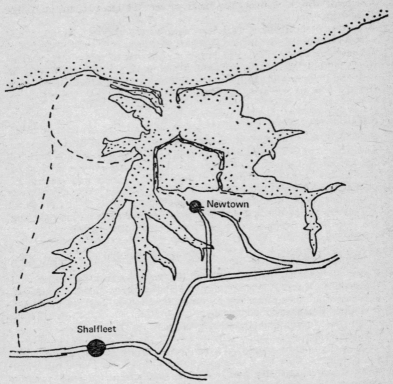

Newtown Marshes, Isle of Wight: formerly enclosed, the broken banks now provide public footpaths and ideal view points over the whole of Newtown Marshes

ST CATHERINE'S POINT, ISLE OF WIGHT OS 180

This is the southernmost point of the Isle of Wight and consists of farmland with rough uncultivated areas of undercliff. Its interest lies in its geographical position jutting into the Channel, though its power of collecting migrants is less than Portland or Dungeness. The wealth of cover also scatters migrants. Sea watching can be rewarding and big days bring shearwaters, duck, divers and waders, the commoner nocturnal migrants are sometimes plentiful and diurnal movements are heavy in October.

SPRING: divers, gannet, sea-duck, scoter, warblers, chats, and fly-catchers.

AUTUMN: shearwaters, Balearic shearwater, gannet, Arctic skua, warblers, chats, flycatchers, finches, thrushes.

Leave the coastal A3055 at Niton southwards to the undercliff. The rough land at the Point is private but the public are allowed to stray at will, and there is a footpath along the cliff top. A small band of watchers run the area as a ringing station.

SELBORNE
OS 169

The village is on the B3006 between Alton and Petersfield. It is celebrated as the home of Gilbert White who wrote its *Natural History* and founded the science of ornithology. The beech hanger to the south is reached by the famous zig-zag path made by the White brothers and tea can be obtained at The Wakes Museum.

SUMMER: wood warbler, warblers, goldcrest.

Leave Alton on the B3006 to Selborne. The Wakes is on the right and the path to the Hanger starts just past the Selborne Arms.

SOWLEY POND
OS 180 and New Forest Tourist Map

The pond lies about half a mile from the coast, between Lymington and the Beaulieu River. It is entirely private and is surrounded by woodland. It is important as a refuge for wildfowl, especially in hard weather when it seldom freezes over completely.

WINTER: wigeon, teal, shoveler, pochard.

SUMMER: heron, common tern.

Leave Lymington eastwards over the toll bridge (small fee) and turn right along by the river round to South Baddesley. In 1 mile turn right and follow round to the pond which is visible from the road over the fence.

TITCHFIELD HAVEN AND HILL HEAD
OS 180

The area lies on the Solent between Gosport and the Hamble River, and consists of two branches of the River Meon flowing through freshwater marshes. Though there is a public footpath along the lesser stream, the whole area is private and is strictly maintained as a sanctuary. The winter population includes large numbers of wildfowl with black-tailed godwit (500) and the usual waders. Hill Head is an exciting place for a sea watch in autumn, when the usual terns are often joined by roseate. The marshes themselves are excellent at this time and regularly hold a variety of 'fresh' waders with black terns frequently present.

WINTER: wigeon, teal, shoveler, black-tailed godwit, turnstone.

SPRING: black tern, whimbrel.

SUMMER: sedge and reed warblers, roseate and black terns, black-tailed godwit, green and wood sandpipers, ruff, rarities.

Leave the A27 at Titchfield on to the B3334 to Stubbington, turn right to Hill Head. At the shore turn right to the Harbour Bridge. The public footpath up the western stream starts on the western side of the main stream some 150 yards past the bridge. Dr C. Suffern meets all comers every Saturday and Sunday, except from 25 March to 1 May, at the Bridge at 10.30 am and leads a walk along the eastern (private) side, returning by about 12.30 pm. He is the only person permitted to do this and thus provides a unique service to his fellow ornithologists. Though no notice need be given, it would be courteous to drop Dr Suffern a card at Hook Cottage, Hook with Warsash, Hants, noting one's intention to be present. In bad weather he may not be able to come.

The best place for a sea watch is at Meon shore where the public footpath up the Meon begins to the west of Hill Head.

Herefordshire and Radnorshire

HEREFORDSHIRE ORNITHOLOGICAL CLUB.
The Club holds a regular programme of indoor and field meetings and is active in the preservation and welfare of birds. It is particularly keen to attract junior members.

HEREFORDSHIRE AND RADNORSHIRE NATURE TRUST.

CLIFFORD WYE (Hereford)   OS 141

This is a stretch of the River Wye about 3 miles downstream from Hay. It is low lying and frequently holds quite interesting collections of wildfowl in winter, including goosander and Bewick's swan.

WINTER: teal, wigeon, goldeneye, goosander, Bewick's swan, dipper, willow tit.

Leave Hay eastwards by A438 and stop in 3 miles at Clifford. Drop down to the disused railway line, walk along westwards, cross it and go down the Wye bank eastwards.

HAUGH WOOD (Hereford)   OS 142

The wood lies on the steeply rising ground on the east side of the Wye below Hereford. This large area of mixed woodland is owned by the Forestry Commission, and the National Trust owns 17½ acres along the roadside. It rises to over 600 feet and has an interesting and varied bird population.

SUMMER: woodcock, nightjar, nightingale, grasshopper warbler, wood warbler.

Leave Hereford eastwards on the B4224 to Mordiford and take the second left towards Woolhope. This climbs up to Haugh Wood. Many tracks and paths lead off to north and south. There is a permanent nature trail on the north side of Fownhope Road.

LUGG MEADOWS (Hereford)   OS 142

The meadows border the River Lugg to the north-east of Hereford, just before it joins the Wye. They are divided into Upper and Lower Meadows and lie north and south of the A465. In winter the meadows flood and wildfowl are plentiful. A few waders including jack snipe occur most years.

WINTER: wigeon, teal, pintail, shoveler, pochard, waders.

Leave Hereford on the A465 or A438 and stop at Lugg Bridge, there is a path along the river bank.

RADNOR MOORS (Radnor) OS 141

Radnor Moors lie in the huge area between Kington, Builth Wells and Penybont and rise to 2,000 feet. The area is rather bleak moorland and there is surprisingly little afforestation. Red grouse are widespread and other upland species can be seen.

SUMMER: raven, buzzard, red grouse, wheatear, whinchat, ring ouzel, merlin, dipper, grey wagtail.

The whole area is surrounded by main roads and intersected by numerous minor roads. Perhaps the best is from Kington to Gladestry and then south-westwards via Newchurch, Bryngwyn, Rhosgoch, Llanbedr and Llan Bwchllyn Lake. But exploration is necessary.

WIGMORE (Hereford) OS 129

On the A4110, 3 miles south of its junction with the A4113 and 8 miles east of Knighton. The area has three main attractions, the Wigmore Rolls, a large area of mainly coniferous forest to the west of the village, the winter floods along the Teme on either side of Criftin Ford Bridge, and the ground north of Wigmore village. The latter holds sizeable flocks of duck, and the woods hold the usual breeding species but are particularly attractive in winter. During irruption years they are a favourite haunt of crossbills.

WINTER: wigeon, teal, siskin, redpoll.

SUMMER: teal, Canada goose, curlew, redshank.

Leave the A4110 just south of Wigmore westwards on to an unclassified road through the forest. Take the track going eastwards nearly opposite the cemetery, but beware of deep ditches. Leave Wigmore northwards to Adforton and just before the village turn right. Keep right in half a mile to Criftin Ford Bridge and the River Teme.

Hertfordshire

BERKHAMSTEAD & NORTHCHURCH COMMONS   OS 160

The two commons lie 6 miles north-west of Hemel Hempstead. A large
part of the area belongs to the National Trust. Open rough heathland
is mainly dominant in the south, while the northern part consists of
mixed woodland. The variety of species found here is typical of southern
heathlands and woodlands and the winter population includes large
numbers of fieldfares and redwings.

SUMMER: woodcock, nightjar, grasshopper warbler.

WINTER: redpoll, brambling, fieldfare, redwing.

Leave the A41 north-eastwards from either Berkhamstead, on unclassified roads, or from Northchurch on the B4506.

BRAMFIELD FOREST   OS 147

The Forest is 4 miles north-west of Hertford and is one of the most
productive areas of woodland in the county. It is owned by the Forestry
Commission and is mixed deciduous and conifers. There is a wealth of
woodland species in summer and redpolls are often present in huge
flocks in winter when great grey shrikes are almost regular.

WINTER: redpoll, great grey shrike.

SUMMER: nightjar, long-eared owl, turtle dove, warblers, grasshopper
warbler, redpoll.

Leave Hertford northwards on the A602 and turn left on the outskirts
to Bramfield. 1 mile past the village, and in the forest, a wide path leads
off to the north-east.

NORTHAW GREAT WOOD   OS 160

Situated 2 miles north-east of Potters Bar, near Cuffley. It covers 750 acres of mainly oak wood but with some pine plantations. The wood is the county stronghold of the redstart, and nightingales are usually present in good numbers. The commoner woodland species breed, and redpolls occur in large flocks in winter.

WINTER: redpoll.

SUMMER: redstart, nightingale, warblers, lesser whitethroat, wood warbler, tree pipit, hawfinch.

Leave Potters Bar northwards on the A1000. Turn right after 2 miles on to the B157. Stop in 1½ miles where several well defined footpaths leave the road on the left. No limitations on access.

TRING RESERVOIRS   OS 159

The waters consist of Marsworth, Startops End, Tringford and Wilstone Reservoirs, lying 2 miles north of Tring and were created in the early years of the last century to serve the Grand Union Canal. They were built on the site of old marshes and relics of marsh flora are retained around their edges. They were made ornithologically famous by the breeding of little ringed plover in 1938, the first in Britain, and are now a National Nature Reserve. Wildfowl are quite numerous and waders are good on autumn passage. Black and commic terns are noted on both passages with sometimes large numbers of the former, and there is a small gull roost in winter.

WINTER: teal, wigeon, shoveler, pochard, tufted duck, goosander, gulls.

SPRING: waders, black terns.

SUMMER: great crested grebe.

AUTUMN: ringed and little ringed plovers, green and common sandpipers, greenshank, little stint, curlew sandpiper, black and commic terns.

Leave the A41 between Tring and Aylesbury northwards on the B489 at Aston Clinton. There are footpaths covering most possible views of all the waters.

Huntingdonshire

HOUGHTON GRANGE BIRD CLUB.
The Club is the most active ornithological group in Huntingdonshire
and holds a regular programme of field and indoor meetings. It acts as
organiser for all BTO enquiries in the county and issues a regular Bulletin.

HUNTINGDONSHIRE FAUNA AND FLORA SOCIETY.

BEDFORDSHIRE AND HUNTINGDONSHIRE NATURALISTS' TRUST.

GRAFHAM WATER   OS 134

Also known as Diddington Reservoir, this is England's largest man-made
lake covering 2½ square miles. It was officially opened in 1966 but birds
were present in the winter 1965-66. Grafham has now become one of
the richest bird lakes in England. In winter its sheer size makes it difficult
to work – waves lash the shore like a miniature sea. But there are large
numbers of surface feeding duck to be seen. In spring black terns are
often present for a week or more.
   WINTER: pintail, tufted duck, pochard, Bewick's swan.
   SPRING AND AUTUMN: black tern, redshank, greenshank, common
sandpiper.
   Leave the A1 westwards at Buckden 3 miles south-west of Huntingdon,
and follow signs to the many car park vantage points.

LITTLE PAXTON GRAVEL PITS   OS 134

Between the A1 and the River Ouse 5 miles south of Huntingdon. The
pits vary in age and offer a variety of habitats, the southern-most supporting a strong growth of sedges and willows.
   WINTER: wildfowl.
   SUMMER: sedge warbler.
   Leave the A1 at Little Paxton eastwards. The pits lie to north and
south in threequarters of a mile and footpaths lead northwards alongside
the largest open water.

MEADOW LANE GRAVEL PITS, ST IVES   OS 134

The pits lie south-east of St Ives, 5 miles east of Huntingdon. There are a series of pits covering 200 acres and varying from current workings to mature, reed fringed lakes. Diving duck are notable and migrants are numerous and interesting.

WINTER: diving duck.

SPRING AND AUTUMN: migrants, waders.

The road to the railway station in the south-east of St Ives passes under a railway bridge. Follow this but do not turn right to the station. At the far end a footpath to Holywell passes several pits. Permission to enter from St Ives Sand & Gravel Co. Ltd.

MONKS WOOD   OS 134

Monks Wood lies 6 miles north of Huntingdon and is a National Nature Reserve covering 387 acres and the site of Monks Wood Experimental Station. A wide variety of woodland species breed.

SUMMER: woodcock, grasshopper warbler.

Leave the A1 eastwards 2 miles north of Alconbury. Access is by permit from the Nature Conservancy, 60 Bracondale, Norwich. NOR58B Norfolk.

WOODWALTON FEN   OS 134

The Fen lies east of the A1 between Peterborough and Huntingdon and has been maintained as a reserve by the Society for the Promotion of Nature Reserves since 1919. It was declared a National Nature Reserve covering 514 acres in 1954. Though the main interests are aquatic plants and their associated insects, there is an interesting variety of breeding marshy birds.

SUMMER: sedge and grasshopper warblers.

A public footpath crosses the area northwards from Church End, but visitors are recommended to obtain a permit from the Nature Conservancy, 60 Bracondale, Norwich, NOR58B, Norfolk. Leave the A1 eastwards on the B1090 or B660 5-8 miles north of Alconbury.

Kent

READ: *The Birds of Kent*, James M. Harrison (2 vols): *The Birds of the North Kent Marshes*, E. H. Gillham and R. C. Homes.

BOUGH BEECH RESERVOIR   OS 171

Lying in the Weald to the south-west of Sevenoaks and directly west of Tonbridge this newly-created reservoir lies on the Kent-Sussex border though its water is destined to be drunk in Surrey. Though still in the settling down period the lake has created quite a reputation for itself in south-east London and the outer suburbs. Part has already been made a reserve of the Kent Trust for Nature Conservation and both fishing and sailing are banned at the eastern end. There are additional plans to create an island to encourage nesting birds.

Though naturally a great area for wintering birds Bough Beech is equally good at other seasons. Ospreys are more or less regular on passage and there are interesting records of breeding waders. Great crested grebes breed as do tufted duck and heron. Regular migrants include black tern (whiskered tern has been recorded) and most of the fresh-water waders such as green sandpiper, greenshank, black-tailed godwits, etc. Most of these congregate on the muddy area east of the causeway where a pectoral sandpiper has appeared. The surrounding land boasts a fair cross section of the birds that one would expect to find in south-eastern England.

WINTER: gadwall, pintail, shoveler, goldeneye, goosander, smew, shelduck, pochard, tufted duck.

PASSAGE: osprey, black tern, green sandpiper, spotted redshank, greenshank, curlew sandpiper, little stint, ruff, wheater, garganey.

SUMMER: redshank, woodcock, heron, little grebe, great crested grebe, willow tit, grasshopper warbler, tufted duck.

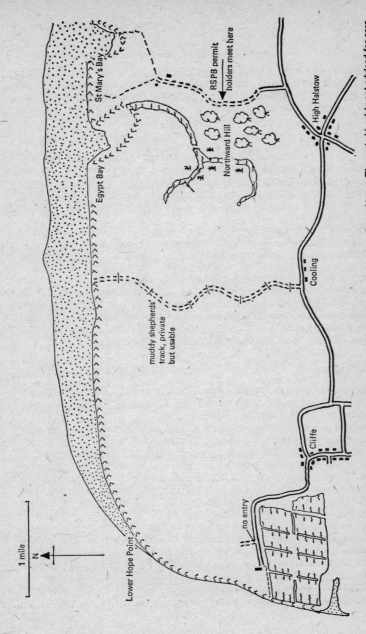

1 mile

N

Lower Hope Point

muddy shepherds'
track, private
but usable

St Mary's Bay

Egypt Bay

Northward Hill

RSPB permit
holders meet here

High Halstow

Cooling

Cliffe

no entry

North Kent Marshes, Cliffe–High Halstow: showing the three major access routes and the ease of round tours. The central track is not advised for cars

Leave the old Tonbridge-Sevenoaks road (A21) westwards on the B2027. Past Chiddington turn northwards sign-posted Ide Hill. Keep left after 1 mile and that road crosses the end of the reservoir at Winkhurst Green which is well signposted.

CLIFFE   OS 172; HT +0:10 Sheerness

Cliffe lies at the western end of the north Kent marshes where the huge area of mud to the east narrows as the Thames turns southward. Though originally an area of rough pasture the extraction of clay for the cement industry has resulted in a series of flooded pits near the sea wall. These are a favourite resort of diving duck and hold exceptionally large numbers in hard weather.

Waders occur on the meadows, together with various predators and black terns frequently fly upstream at Lower Hope Point in autumn.

WINTER: tufted duck, pochard, scaup, merganser, pintail, smew, grebes, divers, waders, snow bunting, short-eared owl.

SPRING AND AUTUMN: waders, black tern, garganey.

Leave the A2 1 mile after its junction with the M2 at Strood, left on to the A289. After 1 mile turn left on to the B2000 to Cliffe. Pass straight through the village and turn left at the bottom. Bear right along a rough concrete road out to pits. Park near Coastguard Cottages and continue on foot beside pits to the sea wall. Walk northwards.

DUNGENESS   OS 184; HT —0:14 Dover

Dungeness has been a famous natural history site since the last century and is at present part RSPB reserve, part Dungeness Bird Observatory, and also the site of a Nuclear Power Station.

Dungeness is a shingle promontory jutting out into the Channel between Hastings and Folkestone, the shingle is some 18 feet thick and only barely above high tide mark. The area is a mass of ridges each of which represents a past beach with slacks between them in which most of the vegetation grows. These masses of gorse and brambles are attractive to the migrants which are concentrated by the geographical situation of the 'Ness. The RSPB reserve, covering 1,233 acres has the only two areas of natural water, the Open Pits, in the entire peninsula.

The main attraction is the migrants and the Observatory is thronged through spring and autumn by students of bird migration. The bushes harbour a variety of birds over 6,000 of which are caught annually. They include large numbers of the commoner chats, flycatchers and warblers as well as the rarer autumn visitors such as bluethroat and melodious warbler, and the true vagrants like Radde's, Pallas' and dusky warblers. Sea watching for migrants is usually good.

Dungeness is not dead in summer. It is the only breeding resort of the common gull in England, stone curlew breed on the shingle, and black redstarts on the power station. At all seasons the gravel pits at Denge Marsh are worthy of inspection. Terns and tufted duck breed and black terns are common on passage.

WINTER: wigeon, teal, scoter, divers, grebes.

SPRING: wheatear, warblers, scoter, skuas, auks, gannet, waders.

SUMMER: common and herring gulls, common tern, wheatear, stone curlew, black redstart, ringed plover.

AUTUMN: chats, flycatchers, warblers, bluethroat, melodious warbler, skuas, scoter, gannet, Mediterranean gull, little gull, black tern, common, Arctic and roseate terns, rarities.

Leave Rye eastwards on the A259 and turn right in 1 mile to Camber Sands. Continue to Lydd and take the ring road to Dungeness. At Dungeness avoid forking left to the pub and keep right towards Old Light. The end cottage is the Observatory.

For the RSPB reserve parties meet the Warden at Boulderwall Farmhouse, but check this when applying for permit to the RSPB. At present they are only organised between 1st April and 1st September on Saturdays and Wednesdays.

Spartan accommodation is available at the Observatory.

GREATSTONE   OS 184

The village lies on the eastern side of the Dungeness peninsula, and has an open sandy beach usually referred to as the Lade Sands. The area is best known for its collection of waders and in particular for the sanderling that are present through most of the year. At high tide, waders flight to nearby Lade Pits. Little terns are often numerous in spring.

WINTER: sanderling, oystercatchers, redshank.

SPRING: sanderling, bar-tailed godwit, greenshank, little tern.

SUMMER: common tern, collared dove.

AUTUMN: sanderling, greenshank, godwits, terns.

From Dungeness take the coastal road past Lydd-on-Sea and watch out for the birds just past Greatstone.

From New Romney take the road signposted Littlestone and turn right in the village along the shore.

HERNE BAY PIER   OS 173; HT —0:25 Sheerness

The pier is noted as a good place for an autumn sea watch and is worth a visit in August and September. If there is no passage there will probably be some waders about and in late autumn knot reach a maximum of 2,000.

AUTUMN: skuas, kittiwake, terns, waders.

Leave Canterbury northwards on the A291 to Herne Bay. The pier, almost 1 mile long, is obvious.

HIGH HALSTOW AND EGYPT BAY   OS 172; HT +0:05 Sheerness

This is the central area of the North Kent marshes and probably the best for those searching for large numbers of birds. The water meadows attract up to 1,500 white-fronts in the new year, and the fleets are used by wildfowl and passage waders. The foreshore, here over 1 mile wide, is the most attractive habitat. On a rising tide huge numbers of duck and waders are moved within range of the sea wall and concentrations occur particularly in Egypt and St Mary's Bays. The area also boasts the woodland of Northward Hill, which, though being primarily known for the large heronry (usually over a hundred nests) also holds the commoner woodland species.

WINTER: white-fronted goose, wigeon, pintail, shoveler, shelduck, knot, curlew, redshank.

SPRING: whimbrel, garganey.

SUMMER: shelduck, heron, long-eared owl.

AUTUMN: green and wood sandpipers, greenshank, little stint.

Leave the A2, 1 mile after its junction with the M2 at Strood, left on to the A289. In 2 miles join the A228 and after 4 miles turn left towards High Halstow. Take the first on the right, Decoy Hill Road, and halt where gate bars the way to motor vehicles. Turn right past the gate to St. Mary's Bay. Turn left on sea wall to Egypt Bay.

About half-way along Decoy Hill Road is the entrance to Northward Hill which is an RSPB reserve of 131 acres. Access is by free permit which is obtainable in advance from the RSPB – Wednesday and Saturday.

MEDWAY ESTUARY   OS 172; HT +0:05 Sheerness

The estuary is over 8 miles by 5 miles and is at first sight a somewhat daunting area. Innumerable creeks divide the basin into a maze of mud banks and saltings that at high tide become almost as many islands. To add to the confusion walls are breached and fresh marshes become tidal, while other areas are being reclaimed. Luckily the bird population is rather concentrated and it is possible to see most of what is present from three stops and a long walk. The outstanding areas are all on the south shore between Ham Green and Chetney, and include Greenborough and Barksore.

The wildfowl population is now recognised as being of major international importance. Waders are sometimes exceedingly numerous and varied with maxima usually reached in autumn.

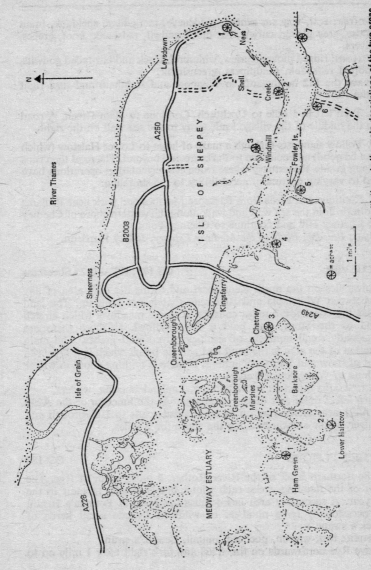

The Medway and Swale showing the main access points. The numbers correspond with those in the main descriptions of the two areas

WINTER: teal, wigeon, pintail, goldeneye, merganser, shelduck, brent goose, grey plover, curlew, bar-tailed godwit, redshank, knot, grebes, divers.

AUTUMN: ringed plover, curlew, whimbrel, black and bar-tailed godwits, spotted redshank, sandpipers, greenshank.

Leave the M2 northwards to Wigmore and Rainham and turn right on the A2.

1. Turn left in 1 mile to Upchurch. Continue to Ham Green. A road in the middle of the village leads away to the sea wall on the right.

2. Follow signposts through a maze of lanes to Lower Halstow (which can be good) and continue to Barksore and beyond. The road then runs along beside the estuary where extensive reclamation operations have led to varying degrees of accessibility to the shoreline.

3. Continue eastwards from Barksore Marshes and park near Bedlams Bottom. Join the sea wall and walk along the western shore of Chetney to Chetney Hill and continue to Chetney Point.

READ: *Breeding Birds of the Medway Estuary*, Jeffery Harrison.

RECULVER   OS 173; HT —0:25 Sheerness

Reculver lies on the north Kent coast and forms the only area of any size between Whitstable and Ramsgate that is not built up. The land behind the coast for 2 miles consists of water meadows which stretch inland to the Stour, and hold a few wildfowl. Offshore there are occasionally small numbers of seaduck, divers and grebes. The main attraction of the area is the sand and shingle beach which is a favourite haunt of snow and Lapland buntings. If there is nothing about in winter continue to Westgate for waders.

WINTER AND AUTUMN: snow bunting, Lapland bunting, waders.

Turn left 2 miles east of the roundabout at the junction of the A299 and A291 near Herne Bay on to unclassified roads to Hillborough and Reculver. Walk eastwards along the shore for 2 miles.

ROTHER FLOODS   OS 184

On the northern bank of the River Rother, 3 miles north of Rye. The extent of the flooding varies each winter but is usually greatest in the new year. A secondary area lies 4 miles upstream at Potman's Heath. The occasionally large numbers of wildfowl include small herds of Bewick's swans.

WINTER: teal, wigeon, pochard, pintail, Bewick's swan.

Leave Rye northwards on the A268 and fork right after 1 mile on to the B2082. This crosses the Rother in 2 miles and footpaths lead from the bridge in both directions along the northern bank. Continue past Wittersham and turn left to Potman's Heath. On the far side of the bridge a footpath leads half right and joins a track, turn right to another bridge.

SANDWICH AND PEGWELL BAYS   OS 173; HT +0:20 Dover

The two bays form the entrance to the Stour estuary on the east Kent coast between Ramsgate and Deal and are ideally situated to receive continental migrants. This led to the establishment in 1961 of the Sandwich Bay Bird Observatory. Though passerines are of importance the area is well provided with inter-tidal sand which becomes rather muddier near the mouth of the Stour in Pegwell Bay. Behind the sand and dunes lie the noted Sandwich Golf Links and between them and the river are areas of fresh marshes, the northern parts of which are attractive to migrant waders.

Wildfowl are not of great importance though both wild swans occur every year as do parties of white-fronted and brent geese. Divers and grebes frequent Pegwell Bay. Open shore waders are very plentiful in winter and passage is usually excellent.

WINTER: curlew, bar-tailed godwit, knot, redshank, golden plover, teal, swans, divers and grebes, hen harrier, snow bunting.

SPRING: waders, passerines, terns, rarities.

AUTUMN: whimbrel, green and wood sandpipers, greenshank, little stint, ruff, passerines, rarities.

Take the A256 or A257 to Sandwich. A toll is payable if coming southwards from Ramsgate. Leave eastwards on unclassified roads towards Sandwich Bay. Then:

1. Turn left on foot after 1 mile towards the Golf Club buildings and take the track off to the left just before the entrance. Continue and bear right towards the shore across the links or along the river bank out towards Pegwell Bay.

2. Continue straight on, paying the toll, to Sandwich Bay Estate and the Observatory at No. 1 Bungalow, Old Downs Farm. As an alternative to the above it is possible to walk northwards to Pegwell Bay along the beach.

Sandwich Bay Bird Observatory offers hostel type accommodation.

SHEPPEY AND THE SWALE
OS 172; HT —0:05 Sheerness at Harty Ferry

The Isle of Sheppey and the Swale channel forms a vast area of prime bird-watching on the north coast of the county. Intending visitors should note carefully which side of Kingsferry Bridge they wish to work (both are exceedingly attractive) as from Shell Ness to Seasalter is 3 miles direct and about 30 by road. The Swale is bordered by large mudflats on both banks especially near the mouth and above Fowley Island. The area forms one of the best for waders in the county and is the winter resort of up to 15,000 knot. Bar-tailed godwit, 500, and grey plover, 1,000, are more plentiful in late autumn, but are also present in winter.

Behind the protective sea walls are expanses of rough grazing intersected by dykes and fleets. These form the main haunts of wildfowl in the area, especially on the Sheppey shore. Sea duck are mainly found at the eastern end of the Swale off Shell Ness, and both white-fronted and brent geese are regular.

Freshwater waders are numerous in autumn and though they can be found on many fleets and marshes, Windmill Creek is the best.

Other birds in the area include as good a collection of predators in autumn and winter as one would find anywhere in southern England and a passage of skuas off Shell Ness in autumn.

WINTER: knot, bar-tailed godwit, oystercatcher, grey plover, turnstone, white-fronted and brent geese, wigeon, pintail, shoveler, merganser, eider, goldeneye, scoter, hen harrier, merlin, short-eared owl.

SPRING: green sandpiper, spotted redshank, garganey.

AUTUMN: black-tailed and bar-tailed godwits, grey plover, wood, green and curlew sandpipers, spotted redshank, greenshank, little stint, marsh harrier, skuas.

The route from London follows the A2 and the M2 at least as far as its junction with the A429. Thereafter a decision must be made between the various sites and access points. Access is as follows:

1. SHELL NESS: Leave the M2 at A249 signposted Sheppey and continue over Kingsferry Bridge (always worth a stop and a look at the Swale) to a roundabout at A250. Follow signposts to Leysdown and continue straight through until a gate with 'Private' notice bars the way. Walk directly to the sea across rough ground. Along this beach is a huge gathering of waders at high tide, with wildfowl offshore.

Turn southwards and walk along the beach to Shell Ness Reserve for more waders, but do not pass beyond the block house.

2. HARTY FERRY: A road southwards between Leysdown and Eastchurch is signposted 'Ferry Inn'. Turn down and continue for 1 mile before turning sharp left over Capel Fleet. This is always worth investigating for duck and autumn waders. The road then runs parallel to the fleet for another mile before turning right and then right again down to the Ferry Inn, for waders, duck and white-fronts. Walk eastwards.

3. WINDMILL CREEK AND DUTCHMAN'S ISLAND: Three walks allow access. Leave the A249 eastwards one mile north of Kingsferry Bridge on tracks through Elmley to the Dam. Or leave the A250 150 yards east of 'The Greyhound' in Brambledown and walk southwards to the rubbish tip. Or from Herty Ferry westwards along the sea wall.

4. MURSTON: Leave Sittingbourne on the A2 eastwards to Bapchild, turn left and follow unclassified roads to Little Murston and then walk to the sea wall. The adjacent reed marsh with bearded tits is a Kent Trust reserve.

5. CONYER: Leave the A2 at Teynham northwards on unclassified roads to Conyer. Continue past the inn and walk round works along the sea wall on the western side next to the creek. Turn eastwards past Fowley Island, a favourite haunt of mergansers.

6. SOUTH HARTY FERRY: Leave the A2 to Faversham town centre. Leave westwards on an unclassified road to Oare and continue to Ferry. Turn westwards from here to Fowley Island.

7. THE SOUTH OAZE: Take the M2 to its present southern end and junction with the A2, continue on to the A299 but turn first left on to B2040 and first right to Goodnestone, then continue to the sea. A path behind the inn runs westward on to the sea wall and gives excellent views of the huge foreshore which is in process of being declared a reserve.

8. SEASALTER: Continue eastwards along the coast road after No 6 or leave the A299 (a continuation of the M2) left at Fox's Cross to Seasalter. Westwards lies the coast road to Graveney, and across the railway in the town centre and eastwards a footpath. Both provide waders at high tide.

STODMARSH OS 173

Stodmarsh lies in the Great Stour valley some 4 miles downstream from Canterbury. Though doubtless always a marshy area it owes its real value to subsidence caused by the nearby coalmining activities at Chislet. An area of open water covering 500 acres, and an even larger area of reed beds has been created providing the largest fresh-marsh in Kent. The marsh is bisected by a wall running from the village to the river bank from which all the birds can be seen. In winter the valley further down is liable to flood near Grove Ferry and this area with the water at Stodmarsh is a great attraction to wildfowl. At the very end of the season in March there is an influx of garganey, often over 100. Much of the area is a National Nature Reserve affording protection to the Savi's warblers that have been here for a number of years.

WINTER: wigeon, teal, shoveler, pochard, pintail, gadwall, wild swans, hen harrier.

SPRING: ruff, garganey, marsh harrier.

SUMMER: bittern, bearded tit, shelduck, sedge, reed and Savi's warblers.

AUTUMN: migrants, hirundines, wagtails.

Leave Canterbury eastwards on the A257 and turn left after 1½ miles, on to unclassified roads to Stodmarsh. In the village turn left past the Red Lion at a tiny triangle of green down a farm track. Keep right, and after 300 yards turn right along a bank, across a dyke, and then left along the Lampen Wall from which views can be obtained over the whole area.

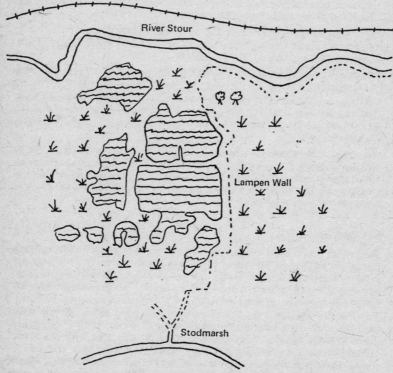

Stodmarsh: many watchers walk all the way to Grove Ferry relying on public transport for the return journey. Do not park at the entrance to the lane leading to the marsh

THORNDEN WOOD

This is one of a series of woods near Canterbury that include Blean Woods, which are a National Nature Reserve, Church Wood, Denstead Wood, Challock Forest, Lyminge Forest and Gosley Wood, all of which are worth attention.

Thornden is a mixed wood and this doubtless adds to its attractions. The usual woodland species are present plus a few specials including an abundance of nightingales.

WINTER: redpoll, siskin.

SUMMER: woodpeckers, warblers, wood warbler, grasshopper warbler, redstart, nightingale, redpoll.

Leave Canterbury on the A290 and turn right after 1 mile. Turn left after threequarters of a mile at T junction and in 1½ miles fork right into Thornden Wood. A great many birds can be seen from the road, but explore paths and tracks.

YANTLET CREEK AND ALLHALLOWS

This area forms the eastern third of the marshes that stretch from Lower Hope Point to the Isle of Grain. The area is basically grazing marshes intersected by dykes and fleets and separated from Grain by the tidal Yantlet Creek. Grain is now spoiled from an ornithological point of view by the huge BP refinery that occupies the southern half. A sluice has been constructed across the Creek leaving almost a mile non-tidal. The Thames foreshore to the north is over 1 mile wide and forms the most important habitat for waders and duck. Stoke Fleet lies immediately north of the A228 at Stoke level-crossing; and Stoke Lagoon lies on the north side of Yantlet Creek where it is non-tidal. The Fleet is heavily overgrown with reeds and harbours duck, water rail, etc., while the Lagoon is superb for freshwater waders in spring and autumn.

The main tidal area is the mouth of the Creek where waders assemble at high tide. Peak numbers are found on autumn passage but birds are present throughout the winter. The Cliffe-Halstow section is more favoured by wildfowl than Allhallows, though white-fronted geese, 300, are usual.

WINTER: ringed plover, grey plover, curlew, bar-tailed godwit, redshank, knot, white-fronted goose, wigeon, pintail, water rail.

SPRING: waders, black tern.

SUMMER: redshank, reed and sedge warblers, garganey.

AUTUMN: bar-tailed godwit, grey plover, knot, greenshank, spotted redshank, sandpipers, little stint, ruff, black tern.

Leave the A2 1 mile after its junction with the M2 left on to the A289 and in 2 miles join the A228. Stop at the level-crossing threequarters of a mile past Lower Stoke and park. The following walk crosses private land but the owners usually raise no objection providing gates are closed, etc.

1. Walk northward alongside the disused railway track to a gate on the left which leads to the northern side of Stoke Fleet. Inspect for snipe, warblers, rails, etc. Return the same way.

2. From Lower Stoke take unclassified roads to Allhallows, pass through the village to the disused station (now a grocery) and park. Walk to the sea wall, turn right to Yantlet Creek – high tide roost on far shore. Follow sea wall along the Creek past the sluice and continue till wall leaves on the right past Stoke Lagoon.

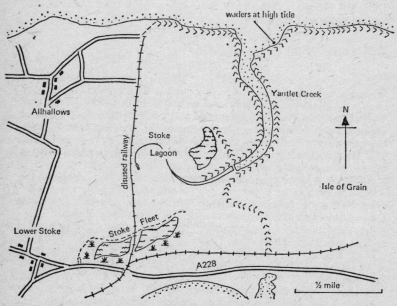

Yantlet Creek: the best approach is from Allhallows eastwards along the Thames, and the best spot Stoke Lagoon

Lake District (Cumberland and Westmorland)

DUDDON ESTUARY (Lancs)   OS 88; HT +0:03 Liverpool

An area of inter-tidal sand, 9 miles by 1½ miles, immediately north of Barrow-in-Furness on the Lancashire border. Above Millom and Askam both shores are lined with saltings. Wildfowl are not numerous but include several hundred pintail and occasional flocks of greylags. Waders are numerous with a wide variety on passage.

WINTER: wigeon, pintail, greylag goose, knot.
SPRING: waders.
AUTUMN: knot, turnstone, bar-tailed godwit, greenshank.
Access on both shores.

1. At Millom cross over the railway near the station and turn left, turn left again under a railway and follow a track down to the shore. A footpath from here leads along the back of the saltings.

2. Leave the A5093 3 miles north of Millom at The Green, turn right to Greenroad Station and continue to the shore.

3. Leave the A595 at Broughton-in-Furness southwards to Foxfield. A level crossing south of the station leads to the shore.

4. Leave the A595 1½ miles north of Askam westwards to Marsh Grange. Continue over the railway to Dunnerholme Ho. and to the shore.

KILLINGTON RESERVOIR (Westmorland) OS 89

The reservoir is 650 feet up 5 miles east of Kendal and is over a mile long. It holds a small number of wildfowl, some of which breed on the sheltered islands. The flock of up to a hundred goosander is outstanding.

WINTER: goosander, wigeon, teal.

Leave Kendal eastwards on the A684 and turn right after 6 miles towards Killington. The reservoir lies on the right after threequarters of a mile.

LAKELAND FELLS (Cumberland/Westmorland)

OS Tourist Lake District

The Fells lie at the heart of the Lake District centred on the Scafell area. Though noted for their beauty and as the centre of a National Park the Fells are not outstanding for birds, but do hold the bulk of breeding ravens and peregrines in northern England. Large numbers of the former gather at the top of Helvellyn. The usual upland species breed. The eastern fells are lonely and desolate and hold some of the more interesting species. Since the early 1970s golden eagles have returned to breed in Lakeland. Anyone fortunate enough to stumble across these birds should keep the information to himself.

SUMMER: buzzard, peregrine, wheatear, ring ouzel, pied flycatcher, redstart, warblers.

The bird-watcher need not venture to the tops for his birds but some climbing up screes may be necessary for ring ouzels. Otherwise the valleys are best and none better than Borrowdale. South of Keswick on the B5289 walk from the Bowder Stone southwards, up Stonethwaite Beck for delicious woodland. Continue to Seatoller and walk up to Seathwaite past excellent woodland and then up to Sty Head with wheatears all the way. Grasmere is another good centre and Easedale has most of the typical species including ring ouzel above Easedale Tarn.

Youth Hostels are ideally situated and other accommodation ranges up to the highest quality. No one should venture on to the hills unprepared and without *Wainwright's Guide* to the appropriate area. These Guides are available in local shops and are invaluable to walkers.

MORECAMBE BAY (Cumberland) OS 75; HT +0:37 Liverpool

The Bay forms the estuary of the rivers Waver and Wampool and lies on the southern shore of the Solway, 13 miles west of Carlisle. The Bay is about 2 miles square and is flanked on the south and east side by large expanses of salting. Geese are no longer regular and are usually pink-feet and the occasional barnacle. Wigeon are the dominant duck and there are variable numbers of sea-duck. Waders are numerous in winter, and on passage a wide variety of species appears.

Grune Point is an excellent migration centre and gathers numbers of interesting passerines as well as sea birds offshore.

WINTER: pink-footed and barnacle geese, wigeon, goldeneye, scaup, knot, bar-tailed godwit.

SPRING: bar-tailed godwit.

AUTUMN: greenshank, godwits, spotted redshank, ruff.

Access is awkward but can be accomplished at:

1. GRUNE POINT: leave Silloth northwards to Skinburness and walk to the Point.

2. ANTHORN: leave the B5307 at Kirkbride northwards to Whitrigg, turn left to Anthorn.

Both places demand telescope and high tide.

RAVENGLASS (Cumberland)   OS 88; HT +0:05 Liverpool

A local nature reserve of 583 acres, situated on the Drigg Dunes which bar the mouth of the River Esk on its northern shore. The reserve was established in 1954 to protect the breeding colony of black-headed gulls, (6-8,000 pairs) the largest in Britain. A variety of other species breed, including four species of tern.

Wildfowl in winter are not outstanding but divers are quite frequent and the commoner waders are numerous.

WINTER: wigeon, goldeneye, divers, knot, peregrine.

SPRING: waders.

SUMMER: black-headed gull, common, Arctic, Sandwich and little terns, ringed plover, merganser, shelduck.

AUTUMN: knot, turnstone, whimbrel, greenshank, bar-tailed godwit.

The best method for a casual visit is by boat from Ravenglass just off the coastal A595 with permission from Cumberland County Council, The Courts, Carlisle, Cumberland. The village provides excellent views over the major part of the estuary area.

ROCKCLIFFE (Cumberland)   OS 75 and 76; HT +0:37 Liverpool

A large area of salting and merse backed by water meadows protected by a sea wall. It lies between the mouths of the Esk and Eden, 6 miles north-west of Carlisle. Geese are the major winter attraction with up to 4,000 pink-feet dominant and 250 barnacles outstanding. Greylags number several hundred and there are a few Greenland white-fronts. Duck are quite numerous and waders are widespread. though not as numerous as on the Scottish shore.

WINTER: pink-footed, greylag, white-fronted and barnacle geese, wigeon, pintail, shoveler, waders, merlin, short-eared owl, peregrine.
SPRING: waders.
AUTUMN: knot, bar-tailed godwit, greenshank.

Leave Carlisle northwards on the A7 and after 2½ miles fork left on to the A74. Turn left to Rockcliffe and continue northwards and westwards to the old coaching house. Ask permission to cross to sea walls.

ST BEES HEAD (Cumberland)   OS 82

St Bees Head lies 2 miles south of Whitehaven. The high red sandstone cliffs are one of England's notable sea-bird breeding stations.
SUMMER: guillemot, razorbill, black guillemot, puffin, kittiwake, fulmar, raven.

Leave Whitehaven southwards on the B5345 and turn right after 1½ miles to Sandwith. Follow unclassified roads as far as possible out to an OS height point 415, east of Tarnflat Hall. A footpath from here leads to the coast half a mile north of the North Head, and the cliff edge footpath runs all the way round to South Head.

SIDDICK POND (Cumberland)   OS 82

This water lies immediately north of the industrial town of Workington and is surrounded by railways and colliery tips. It suffers great disturbance, especially during the breeding season, but still holds a variety of species. The southern end has an interesting reed bed and the pond is so close to the sea that there is a regular movement of duck and waders between the two. The water level varies a great deal and when a low level and passage season coincide there are usually good numbers of waders present.
WINTER: wigeon, shoveler, pochard, goldeneye, pintail, scaup, waders.
SPRING: waders, common tern.
SUMMER: sedge warbler, corn bunting, shoveler, tufted duck.
AUTUMN: duck, black-tailed godwit, ruff, green sandpiper, greenshank, common and Sandwich terns.

The pond can be watched from the A596 1 mile north of Workington at the northern end. Half of the pond adjacent to the road has been fenced off and incorporated in the Thames Paper Board Mill site. Care is being taken to preserve the amenity value as far as possible.

Lancashire

AINSDALE SANDS NATIONAL NATURE RESERVE   OS 100

The Reserve covers 1,216 acres of dunes and slacks immediately north of
Formby and overlaps slightly with the Southport Sanctuary to the north.
The habitats include the sea, the sandy shore, the dunes and slacks and
the extensive stands of Austrian pines. Numerous waders are found on
the comparatively narrow shore, and the dune slacks, notably Massam's
Slack in the south-west of the Reserve, have thickets of sea-buckthorn that
attract many breeding and migrant passerines. There is a good passage
of sea-birds.

WINTER: scoter, bar-tailed godwit, knot, sanderling, snipe, rails.

SPRING: waders, passerines, chats.

SUMMER: nightjar, long-eared owl, redpoll, shelduck, whinchat, warblers.

AUTUMN: godwits, sanderling, turnstone, auks, terns, Arctic skua,
passerines, visible migration.

Access is available by public and special reserve footpaths. In Formby
alight at Freshfield Station and walk up the road on the landward side
of the railway. This continues as a footpath and crosses the railway line
and is then known as Fisherman's Path. It runs through the Reserve and
the interesting Massam Slack to the shore.

Though outside the Reserve, there is a road to Ainsdale-on-Sea to the
north that is a favourite sea-watching spot.

ALT ESTUARY   OS 100; HT —0:21 Liverpool

The estuary lies between Liverpool and Formby near Hightown and is the only extensive area of mud between the Ribble and the Mersey. As a result it attracts more waders than the surrounding sand banks and has a good population of duck. Waders and terns often flock near the Altcar Rifle Range.

WINTER: wigeon, knot, turnstone, bar-tailed godwit.

SPRING: waders.

AUTUMN: green sandpiper, black-tailed godwit, spotted redshank, greenshank, terns.

Leave the A565 westwards on to the B5193 at Lady Green and turn right to Hightown. Cross the level crossing and continue to end of the street where a footpath leads to the estuary. The river can be crossed a quarter of a mile north of here and access south of the ranges is straightforward. A track leads southwards from the seaward side of the level crossing to the shore at Formby Bank.

BARROW DOCKS   OS 88; HT —0:09 Liverpool

Lying immediately south of Barrow, this is an excellent place for storm driven sea-birds and duck in hard weather. Cavendish Dock is probably the best.

WINTER: red-necked and Slavonian grebes, scaup, goldeneye, smew, wigeon.

Access to the docks is usually straightforward.

FAIRHAVEN-LYTHAM   OS 94; HT —0:04 Liverpool

Situated on the south-west corner of the Fylde at the mouth of the Ribble. The huge foreshore here is predominantly muddy and attracts a larger variety of waders than the St Anne's area. There are thousands of knot, black-tailed godwit number a thousand in autumn, and purple sandpipers are regular on the mussel beds. Thirteen species can usually be seen on a winter day. Snow buntings are regularly on the shore north of Fairhaven lake.

WINTER: knot, bar-tailed godwit, black-tailed godwit, purple sandpiper, dunlin, shelduck, snow bunting.

SPRING: waders.

AUTUMN: black-tailed and bar-tailed godwits, turnstone, knot, purple sandpiper, whimbrel, passerine migrants.

Straightforward access from promenade, but for a quick look, park at Fairhaven Lake.

See Map.

FORMBY POINT   OS 100; HT —0:21 Liverpool

An extensive area of sand hills, slacks, pine woods, golf course and open shore. Though all of these hold interesting birds, it is the sea that is the main attraction throughout the year. Passage, especially autumn, brings numbers of waders, Arctic and other skuas and little gulls. The tobacco waste dump in the dunes is a haunt of passerine migrants and winter visitors.

WINTER: divers, goldeneye, scoter, velvet scoter, bar-tailed godwit, turnstone, sanderling, snow bunting.

AUTUMN: gannet, skuas, terns, gulls, ringed plover, bar-tailed godwit, spotted redshank, sanderling, passerines.

The roads past Formby and Freshfield Stations lead out to the sea.

FOULNEY ISLAND   OS 88; HT —0:05 Liverpool

Situated near Walney Island in the south-west of Lakeland, Foulney is a mile long sandy-shingle promontory stretching southwards parallel to Walney. It was declared a nature reserve by the Lake District NT in 1963. Breeding birds include over 1,500 pairs of the four commoner terns. The Rampside Sands on the eastern side are a haunt of waders, grebes, divers and wildfowl.

WINTER: merganser, scoter, velvet scoter, scaup, pink-footed goose, waders, red-necked grebe, divers.

SPRING: waders, scoter.

SUMMER: common, Arctic, Sandwich and little terns.

AUTUMN: waders, terns, skuas.

Leave Barrow southwards on the A5087 and on reaching the coast turn right to Rampside. Continue past the village out towards Roa Island. For access to the reserve, apply to the Lake District Naturalists' Trust.

FRECKLETON FLASH, FRECKLETON SEWAGE FARM AND CLIFTON MARSH   OS 94

A compact group of 'fresh' wader habitats on the north side of the Ribble, 6 miles west of Preston. The variety of rarities has included Temminck's stint, white-rumped sandpiper, Baird's sandpiper, buff-breasted sandpiper, dowitcher, semi-palmated sandpiper and pectoral sandpiper. Black terns are regular in autumn and wildfowl haunt the Flash.

WINTER: glaucous and Iceland gulls, ruff.

SPRING: waders.

AUTUMN: wood and green sandpipers, greenshank, curlew sandpiper, little stint, ruff, rarities, black tern.

The Flash can be reached along the sea walls from Freckleton village which continue past the sewage farm to Clifton Marsh. Permits for the sewage farm are available only in limited numbers and local watchers should enquire details of their society.

See Map on next page.

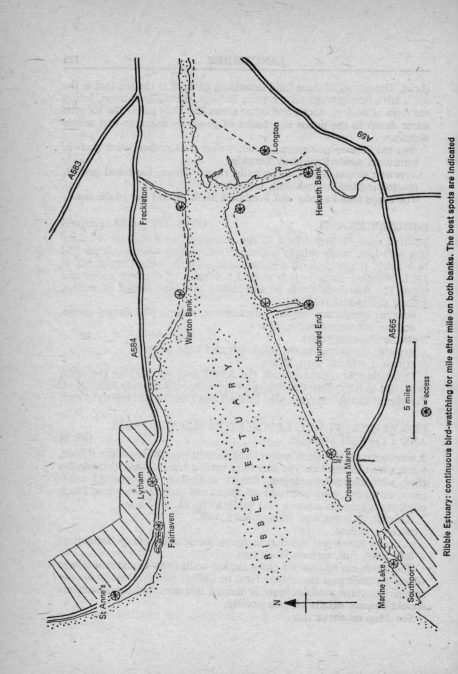

Ribble Estuary: continuous bird-watching for mile after mile on both banks. The best spots are indicated

HUNDRED END, HESKETH BANK AND CROSSENS POOL
OS 94; HT —0:25 Liverpool

Situated on the south bank of the Ribble between Southport and Preston. A vast expanse of inter-tidal foreshore is backed by large areas of salting and further areas of fresh marshes, separated by a sea wall. Though noted for the large wader roosts at Crossens Pool and Hundred End, the marshes with their dykes and flashes attract a good variety of 'fresh' waders.

WINTER: waders, short-eared owl, merlin.

SUMMER: common tern, black-headed gull.

AUTUMN: greenshank, spotted redshank, green sandpiper, little stint, ruff, grey plover.

Leave Southport northwards on the A565 and turn left at Crossens. Cross dyke and turn left along the bank out to Crossens Pool. Return or continue along bank to Marsh Farm and then to Hundred End. Leave Hundred End northwards along wall to Hesketh Out Marsh. Continue for 6 mile walk to Hesketh Bank Station. These walks fit in rather well with the railway stations at Banks and Hesketh Bank, with an 11-mile walk between them.

KEER ESTUARY
OS 89; HT +0:02 Liverpool

The estuary flows into Morecambe Bay just west of Carnforth and is the centre of one of the most extensive salting areas in the Bay. Greylag geese appear occasionally, and up to 4,000 shelduck congregate in this area in late summer prior to the autumn moult migration to the Heligoland Bight.

WINTER: wigeon, shoveler, pintail, waders.

AUTUMN: greenshank, spotted redshank, shelduck.

Leave Carnforth northwards on unclassified roads to Millhead. In half a mile turn left and in a quarter of a mile where the road turns sharp right, take track straight on over the railway. A footpath runs along the right bank to some slag heaps.

KENT ESTUARY
OS 89; HT +0:01 Liverpool

This is the central estuary of Morecambe Bay, lying to the north-west of Arnside. A railway viaduct divides the narrow 4 mile upper half from the wider, sandy area around Grange-over-Sands. Up to 300 greylag geese frequent the estuary on the saltings east of Arnside and on Meathop Marsh on the western shore.

WINTER: greylag goose, wigeon, teal, pintail, waders.

SPRING AND AUTUMN: waders.

The promenades at Arnside and Sandside on the south of the estuary provide good vantage points along the B5282. To view the northern shore and Meathop Marsh, which is a nature reserve of the Lake District NT leave Grange-over-Sands (several railway crossing points), eastwards on the B5277 and turn right on an unclassified road to keep to the coast after half a mile. This leads to Meathop, look south for geese, and 1 mile further crosses a brook. A footpath strikes half right here to a footbridge over a cut and alongside the estuary.

LEIGHTON MOSS   OS 89

Leighton Moss lies 4 miles north of Carnforth near the village of Silverdale. Though used for pasture for over 200 years, war-time neglect of the pumping station allowed the land to revert to marshland and it has now been leased by the RSPB. A central causeway, which is a public footpath, divides Leighton from Storrs Moss, though both are part of the reserve. Storrs has a larger area of open water in spite of its greater distance from the sea. Areas of willow scrub with some oak and birch give way to sedges along the moss edge, while reeds are the typical habitat over the greater part of the area. The Society has recently created shallow edges to attract waders. Amongst an outstanding collection of breeding birds, the bittern is the centre of attraction, though the reed warbler here reaches its farthest north.

Winter brings wildfowl with quite large numbers of water rails.
WINTER: shoveler, pintail, water rail, redpoll.
SPRING: black tern, marsh harrier, waders.
SUMMER: bittern, shoveler, pochard, grasshopper and reed warblers, lesser whitethroat.
AUTUMN: waders, black tern, marsh harrier, great grey shrike, redpoll.

Permits are available together with arrangements for the current season from the RSPB. The causeway begins near Silverdale Station on the road between Myers Farm and Yealand Storrs and lead eastwards. There is a public hide here giving good views over the reserve.

LEVEN ESTUARY   OS 88; HT +0:02 Liverpool

The estuary forms the north-western arm of Morecambe Bay and is divided into inner and outer estuaries by a railway viaduct. Waders are present at all seasons but are most numerous in autumn.
WINTER: wigeon, pintail, shoveler, goldeneye, scaup, merganser, waders.
SPRING: waders, shelduck.
AUTUMN: waders.

The area is difficult to work but the following are vantage points:

1. Leave Ulverston southwards on the A5087 to Bardsea. A path leaves the road to the east where it reaches the shore.

2. Leave Ulverston northwards on the A590 and turn right 200 yards past the canal. Follow unclassified roads to Plumpton Hall. A footpath leads to the shore and then left under the railway and out into the upper estuary.

LYTHAM-WARTON MARSH   OS 94; HT —0:04 Liverpool

The marsh lies on the Ribble Estuary eastwards from Lytham and is the most extensive area of salt marsh on the northern shore. Pink-feet are occasionally seen, as are most of the commoner wildfowl. Waders are especially good on passage.

WINTER: wigeon, pintail, shelduck, waders, merlin.

SPRING: waders.

AUTUMN: whimbrel, greenshank, curlew sandpiper, spotted redshank, black-tailed godwit.

Access is rather awkward but a footpath leads along the edge of the saltings and can be reached from Warton Bank, Freckleton Village, and beside the Customs' Building in Lytham. The latter is most straightforward and is a good vantage point for wildfowl watching at high tide.

MARTON MERE   OS 94

Marton is a small, natural, reed-fringed mere lying behind Blackpool at the base of a rubbish tip, and has been declared a nature reserve by the Corporation. In spite of the attention it receives from Blackpool's youngsters the mere is an excellent place for wildfowl (three species are usually present) and 'fresh' waders, large numbers of which pass through in autumn. A caravan park extends along the southern side and there are plans to landscape the area and convert it to a marina. Over a hundred and fifty species have been recorded and there are large seasonal roosts of wagtails and hirundines.

WINTER: wildfowl, jack snipe, corn bunting.

SPRING: waders, passerine migrants.

SUMMER: reed warbler.

AUTUMN: wildfowl, waders, passerine migrants, spotted crake.

In Blackpool go to the eastern side of Stanley Park. Turn off East Park Drive a hundred yards north of the junction with Lawson Road and follow a tarmac track over the rubbish tip.

MORECAMBE BAY   OS 89; HT +0:01 Liverpool

Morecambe Bay is the huge expanse of inter-tidal sand lying between Morecambe and Walney Island and is roughly 10 miles square. Counts of the birds of the area show it to be one of the most important wader sites in Western Europe. Over a hundred thousand oystercatchers have been counted on occasion.

Here we are dealing with the stretch of coast from Heysham to More-cambe and Hest Bank where the immediate offshore shoals are rather narrow. Notable in a rather poor collection of wildfowl (the sands are a good roost but provide little wildfowl food) are sawbills and sea duck between Morecambe and Hest Bank.

WINTER: merganser, goosander, long-tailed duck, smew, goldeneye, pintail, shoveler, bar-tailed godwit, knot, oystercatcher, divers.

SPRING AND AUTUMN: whimbrel, greenshank, turnstone.

Almost the entire length of this shore is flanked by the A5105. At the Heysham end follow minor roads out to Lower Heysham, where a foot-path runs along the shore. At Hest Bank cross the railway north of the station and walk northwards on a track along the edge of the saltings.

PENNINGTON FLASH   OS 101

Lies 1 mile south-west of Leigh and like most flashes is shallow with considerable emergent vegetation. It is a notable haunt of wildfowl and a few 'fresh' waders are noted in autumn when there are often black terns present.

WINTER: pochard, tufted duck, merganser, Bewick's swan.

AUTUMN: greenshank, ruff, black tern.

Leave Leigh southwards and turn right at Lowton Common. Just before the road turns sharp left in half a mile, turn right to the Flash. There are various routes over Aspull Common.

ST ANNE'S – SQUIRE'S GATE   OS 94; HT —0:04 Liverpool

This stretch of beach runs north of St Anne's pier on the south-west corner of the Fylde. The foreshore is sandy and stretches 3 miles into the Irish Sea, whereas south of Fairhaven the shore becomes increasingly muddy and attracts rather different species. Dominant in this stretch are winter concentrations of thousands of waders. Autumn brings large numbers of these species and terns into the area. With late autumn westerly gales, numbers of sea birds are blown on shore regularly, including shearwaters, skuas and Leach's petrels. At Squire's Gate the shore is only half a mile wide and sea duck, divers and grebes can be seen quite regularly in autumn and winter.

WINTER: sanderling, redshank, knot, bar-tailed godwit, oystercatcher, eider, scoter, divers, grebes.

SPRING: waders.

AUTUMN: common, Arctic, Sandwich and little terns, sanderling, knot, godwit, oystercatcher, Arctic skua, Leach's petrel, shearwaters.

The whole area can be seen from the foreshore which is of open access in many places.

SOUTHPORT – MARTIN MERE OS 94 and 100; HT —0:26 Liverpool

Southport is on the southern shore at the mouth of the Ribble but the area included here covers the town and Marine Lake, the sandbanks at the mouth of the estuary that have been a National Wildfowl Refuge covering 14,300 acres, since 1956, the 3,000 acres of now drained Martin Mere, and the huge expanse of low lying mosses between Lydiate-Hightown and Southport-Scarisbrick. Pink-feet are the main attraction with 5,000 in autumn and 3,000 in winter roosting on the sands and feeding at Martin Mere and the mosses. Other wildfowl in this vast area includes a regular number of sea duck on Southport Marine Lake, and Hesketh Park Lake in Southport holds a variety of duck that come to roost. The muddy area around the pier attracts good numbers of waders.

WINTER: pink-footed, barnacle and brent geese, wigeon, pintail, shoveler, merganser, goldeneye, whooper swan, bar-tailed godwit, knot.

SPRING AND AUTUMN: waders.

The Marine Lake, the Pier and Hesketh Park are within a short walk of the mainline station. Martin Mere and the mosses and geese marshes can be reached by a number of roads, though the best idea is to wait for them to flight by the shore at Marine Lake. The Wildfowl Trust opened a Refuge on 363 acres of marsh at Martin Mere in the summer of 1974. There is a waterfowl collection and geese viewing facilities.

WALNEY ISLAND   OS 88; HT —0:05 Liverpool

Situated at the south-west corner of the Lake District separated by only the narrow Walney Channel from industrial Barrow-in-Furness, to which it is linked by a bridge. The island is 8 miles long and the southern half has been declared a nature reserve by the Lancashire and Lake District NT. Breeding birds include the largest ground-nesting colony of lesser-black-backed and herring gulls in Europe, the southernmost breeding station of eiders in Britain, and a variety of other species. The area at the southern point together with Piel Island and Foulney is one the largest wader roosts in Lancashire and thousands of birds can be counted at high tide. The island is also used as a bird observatory with a Heligoland trap and fair numbers of passage migrants are ringed. Skuas and terns are regularly noted offshore in autumn, and eiders are present offshore in large numbers almost throughout the year.

WINTER: oystercatcher, knot, eider, teal, wigeon, shelduck, divers, grebes.

SUMMER: herring and lesser black-backed gulls, eider, oystercatcher, ringed plover.

AUTUMN: waders, terns, skuas, passerine migrants.

Straightforward from Barrow. Access to the reserve is by permit. Cottage accommodation on hostel lines is available to genuine naturalists.

WYRE–LUNE–COCKER   OS 94; HT —0:02 Liverpool

This area lies between the Fylde and Morecambe Bay and is overshadowed by both. The two large estuaries enter the sea through the same maze of sands some 8 miles apart and there is 16 miles between Lancaster at the head of the Lune and Poulten-le-Fylde on the Wyre. The only really attractive bird-watching area is the 4 miles between the mouth of the Lune at Glasson and the Pilling Sands which was declared a National Wildfowl Refuge in 1963. Several thousand pink-feet frequent the sands and regularly flight to the Cockerham-Winmarleigh area to feed. An occasional barnacle or brent will join them. Most of the duck are found on the Lune near Overton and on the south side at Condor Green and vast numbers of the more common waders occur off Fluke Hall, Pilling.

WINTER: pink-footed goose, wigeon, teal, knot.

SPRING AND AUTUMN: greenshank, knot, redshank.

The best place to see the geese is from the B5272 between Winmarleigh and Cockerham. Watchers are warned not to stray from the road. Other good points are the following:

1. Leave Cockerham northwards and turn left after threequarters of a mile out to Bank End. A footpath runs southward at Hillam to Pattys.

2. Leave the A588 at Condor Green westwards on the B5290 saltings on the right, to Glasson. View the Lune out near Fishnet Point.

3. Leave Morecambe southwards on the A589. At Heysham this road turns sharp right, continue straight here to Overton. Footpaths lead out to Bazil Point and back again further east along a track.

4. Leave Overton (3) westwards and turn left down the coast to Sunderland. A footpath leads to Sunderland Point.

Leicestershire and Rutland

BURLEY WOOD AND BURLEY FISH PONDS (Rutland)   OS 122

Situated 2 miles east of Oakham. The wood is mainly deciduous and holds the usual woodland species in good numbers. The Fish Ponds have been created along the course of one of the upper tributaries of the Welland. Both are maintained as sanctuaries.

WINTER: duck, great crested grebe.

SUMMER: woodland warblers, reed warbler.

Leave Oakham on the A606 to Stamford. Access to the grounds and to the Fish Ponds is by permit only. These can be borrowed from the Leicestershire and Rutland Ornithological Society and the Rutland Natural History Society by members only.

CHARNWOOD LODGE (Leics)   OS 121

Lies between Loughborough and Coalville and is a Leicestershire Trust for Nature Conservation Reserve. It covers a variety of habitats including moorland, woodland and heath.

SUMMER: warblers, grasshopper warbler, redstart, woodcock.

Access is for Trust members with permits only.

Charnwood Forest is a high heathland area dotted with small woods. It lies roughly between Coalville, Loughborough and Leicester and is in the main privately owned. Benscliffe Wood is worth investigating from the road without trespassing.

CROPSTON RESERVOIR, BRADGATE PARK & SWITHLAND WOOD (Leics)   OS 121

This group of outstanding habitats lies 5 miles north-west of Leicester. The reservoir is about threequarters of a mile long and holds a number of winter wildfowl including Bewick's swans. Bradgate Park holds some moorland-type birds and provides the best vantage point for seeing the reservoir. Swithland Wood has most of the commoner woodland birds.

WINTER: wigeon, pintail, tufted duck, pochard, goldeneye, Bewick's swan.

SUMMER: whinchat, redstart, woodcock, wood warbler.

AUTUMN: waders, black tern.

Leave Leicester westwards on A50 and watch for B5327 on the right in the suburbs. This leads to B5328 and a right turn to Cropston. The reservoir can be viewed from the road across the dam and from inside Bradgate Park the entrance to which lies on the left over the dam. The Park and Swithland Wood are open to the public.

EYE BROOK RESERVOIR (Leics)   OS 133

The reservoir is 3 miles north-east of Corby, and was created by damming the stream of the same name in 1940 and now covers some 400 acres. It is 2 miles by 1 mile and reaches a maximum depth of 40 feet. The natural banks and gently shelving sides provide excellent feeding for a great variety of aquatic species and for the brown trout which have made the reservoir a favourite haunt for fishermen. Other than for this sport the reservoir is strictly protected and ranked eighth best for wildfowl in England. An area of marsh-like habitat has been created at the northern end near the inlet and this attracts both duck and waders and is always worth close scrutiny. The Rutland (eastern) side has been extensively planted with spruce, pine and other trees, providing a sanctuary for smaller birds.

The main attractions are the winter wildfowl with wigeon reaching a peak of 1,500 in January–February. Pintail once reached 450. Divers and geese are irregular but are seen most winters, and up to 50 Bewick's swans are now regular.

Eye Brook is also the best place in Leicester and Rutland for wader passage. Terns are regular and black terns pass through in spring and autumn.

WINTER: wigeon, pochard, goldeneye, pintail, shoveler, goosander, great crested grebe, gulls.

SPRING: waders, black terns.

AUTUMN: wood and green sandpipers, ruff, greenshank, little stint, duck, little grebe, terns.

The reservoir can be viewed without leaving the public highway but members of the Leicestershire and Rutland Ornithological Society can enter the plantation and marsh if carrying their membership card. Leave the A47 southwards at Uppingham on the A6003 to Caldicote or take that road northwards from Kettering. Turn westwards 50 yards north of the level-crossing at Caldecote to Stoke Dry and the reservoir.

KNIPTON RESERVOIR AND BELVOIR FISH PONDS (Leics)   OS 122

The two waters are within 2 miles of each other, some 5 miles south-west of Grantham. Birds tend to move readily from one to another and they are thus treated together. Duck are sometimes numerous, and Canada geese are regular. There is a heronry at Briery Wood, Belvoir.

WINTER: wigeon, teal, tufted duck, pochard, Canada goose.

SUMMER: heron.

Leave Grantham south-westwards on A607 to Croxton Kerrial. Turn right to Knipton. Here turn left for Knipton Reservoir and right for Belvoir Fish Ponds. Knipton can be seen rather unsatisfactorily from the road but Belvoir is in a private park. Access to both is by permission from the Estate Office, Belvoir Castle, Grantham.

STANFORD RESERVOIR (Leics/Northants)   OS 132

Situated some 6 miles north-east of Rugby, it is 1 mile long with natural banks. Though not outstanding from the numbers point of view the water holds a wide selection of wildfowl, including a good flock of goosander. Summer birds include hirundines and wagtails and there is an autumn passage of waders and black terns.

WINTER: wigeon, shoveler, pochard, goosander, great crested grebe, cormorant.

AUTUMN: wood and green sandpipers, greenshank, black tern.

Leave Rugby eastwards on the A427 to Swinford. 1½ miles past here turn sharp right and then left down to the reservoir dam. Access is by permit, obtainable from Rugby Joint Water Board, 50 Albert Street, Rugby. Views can be obtained from the road at the eastern end. Take the Welford Road out of Kilworth and view from bridge in half a mile.

SWITHLAND RESERVOIR (Leics)   OS 121

Placed 2 miles south of Loughborough and only 2 miles from the Cropston-Bradgate area. The water is larger than Cropston but is interrupted by a railway causeway which crosses the southern half. Wildfowl are interesting and Canada geese breed and form sizeable flocks in autumn. The edges attract a few passage waders and wagtails.

WINTER: wigeon, teal, tufted duck, pochard, goldeneye, siskin, redpoll, brambling.

SPRING AND AUTUMN: Canada goose, waders.

Leave A6 between Leicester and Loughborough westwards at Mountsorrel. Take an OS map and navigate through a maze of turnings to the road running along the north-eastern edge and over the dam, this is open to the public. The southern end can be viewed from the unclassified road east of Swithland village.

Lincolnshire

BOSTON POINT & FREISTON DELPHS

OS 114; HT —0:04 King's Lynn

These two spots are both at the mouth of the Witham and 3 miles north along the Wash shore. A huge area of saltings lies to the west of the point and a vast area of shoals to the north and east. The point has concentrations of wildfowl in winter including brent geese which winter all along this coast to Freiston. Waders are numerous and the Delphs immediately behind the sea wall hold a variety of 'fresh' species. Skuas, etc., get blown in with northerly gales.

WINTER: brent goose, wigeon, scaup, shelduck, goldeneye, eider, bar-tailed godwit, knot, twite.

SPRING AND AUTUMN: green and wood sandpipers, godwits, knot.

Leave Boston south-eastwards on a maze of lanes to Fishtoft. Cross Nunn's Bridge and continue to the sea wall. Walk for 1 mile to Boston point. Return to Fishtoft, turn right to Freiston and then to Freiston Shore. Walk northwards along sea wall to Delphs.

See Map.

CHAPEL POINT AND PITS

OS 114

Lie at the southern end of the Roman Bank that protects the land against flooding, about 6 miles north of Skegness. The point is merely a convenient and good place to sea-watch, the pits lie to the north and occasionally hold grebes and sea duck, with 'fresh' waders in autumn. Passerine migrants can be exciting and included a bluethroat and red-breasted flycatcher within a week in one recent September.

WINTER: grebes, sea-duck, divers.

AUTUMN: wood sandpiper, greenshank, divers, fulmar, gannet, skuas, terns, kittiwake, auks, passerine migrants.

Leave Skegness northwards on the A52. Turn right to Chapel St Leonards after 6 miles and continue northwards to Chapel Point. Chapel Pits lie half a mile and 1 mile further north and can be seen from the road. They are a reserve of the Lincolnshire NT from whom permits can be obtained.

GIBRALTAR POINT   OS 114; HT —0:22 King's Lynn

Situated on the northern shore at the mouth of the Wash, 3 miles south of Skegness. It is a local nature reserve and the site of the Bird Observatory and Field Research Station. Though the emphasis is on migration winter brings numbers of divers and sea duck, while there is always a very large flock of snow buntings, and a few shore larks and Lapland buntings. On passage waders in great variety pass through and terns and skuas are noted offshore in some numbers. Passerines include chats, warblers and flycatchers, often in dramatic numbers. Almost anything can and does turn up.

WINTER: divers, sea duck, hen harrier, rough-legged buzzard, great grey shrike, oystercatcher, bar-tailed godwit, knot, shore lark, snow bunting, Lapland bunting.

SPRING: waders, chats, warblers.

SUMMER: little tern, ringed plover.

AUTUMN: pink-footed goose, whimbrel, bar-tailed godwit, green and wood sandpipers, spotted redshank, curlew sandpiper, ruff, commic and black terns, skuas, chats, warblers, flycatchers, rarities, diurnal migrants.

Leave Skegness southwards to Gibraltar Point. Accommodation is available on hostel lines at the Observatory.

See Map, page 139.

GRIMSBY DOCKS   OS 105

The docks are immediately north of the town at the mouth of the Humber. Though a hive of activity throughout the year they are of ornithological interest in winter when their calm waters offer a haven to sea birds.

WINTER: eider, scaup, long-tailed duck, smew.

Most of the outer docks can be seen from public roads and access is generally straightforward.

HOLBEACH   OS 124; HT —0:05 King's Lynn

This site lies on the south-western corner of the Wash, 8 miles north of Holbeach on the A151. As in other parts of the Wash, new land is constantly being taken from the sea and provides bird-watching of varying quality before it finally disappears under the plough. The main interest at Holbeach lies on the sea wall between Fotheringham House and Holbeach St Matthew and especially at the high tide roost of waders on Flushing Creek Wall. During spring tides waders are forced on to the fields behind the sea wall and have been caught by the Wash Wader Ringing Group with rocket propelled nets. The Flushing Creek wall is designed to funnel the tide and create a scouring action along the sea wall and has prevented the build-up of large areas of saltings at this point.

Vast assemblages of the commoner waders are the main attraction but 'fresh' waders are regular in some numbers in autumn on the numerous dykes. The only other species of interest are wildfowl with large numbers of duck and a November roost of pink-feet.

AUTUMN: knot, dunlin, grey plover, turnstone, bar-tailed godwit, green, wood and curlew sandpipers, little stint, greenshank, ruff, short-eared owl.

WINTER: knot, dunlin, grey plover, turnstone, short-eared owl, hen harrier, wigeon, pink-footed goose.

Leave the A17 at Chapelgate northwards on to the B1359. Leave this to the left after 2½ miles signposted Holbeach St Matthew. Continue through the village and along banks to a Police Notice liberally sprinkled with gunshot wounds. On foot northwards to the sea wall and then out past a wildfowler's barge to Flushing Creek Wall.

HUTTOFT SEA BANK AND PIT OS 105

The bank stands 5 miles south of Mablethorpe and was raised by the Romans to defend this low lying coast against invasion by the sea. In raising the bank, fresh water pits were created on the landward side. They attract a variety of species including wildfowl and waders on migration. This is one of the best places in the county for skuas with both Arctic and great occurring in autumn, and passage of other sea birds is often heavy.

WINTER: snow bunting, eider, long-tailed duck, red-throated diver.

SPRING: waders, terns, auks, garganey.

AUTUMN: garganey, pintail, goldeneye, merganser, golden plover, wood sandpiper, curlew sandpiper, ruff, Arctic and great skuas, kittiwake, gannet, divers, auks, black and commic terns.

Leave Mablethorpe southwards on the A52 and after 6 miles turn left at Huttoft Grange. In 1½ miles turn right to the bank and pit. There is a track to the shore at the south end of the pit. View from the road, the pit is private.

NENE MOUTH   OS 124; HT —0:07 King's Lynn

The name in fact refers to the Nene outfall cut which is an artificial waterway lying on the southern shore of the Wash. There is not really a great deal to see though waders can be exceedingly numerous at high tide. The area is often excellent during migration when black terns and skuas are often present. Passerine migrants are frequently found in the Old Lighthouse garden.

WINTER: dunlin, grey plover, turnstone.

AUTUMN: black tern, skuas, waders.

Leave the A17 at Sutton Bridge on the western side of the river. Take the more westerly road northward and not the one marked alongside the river. Turn right at King John's Farm, signposted Gedney Drove End, continue along the river bank to the Old Lighthouse. Park here and continue along bank having discreetly examined the garden for migrants.

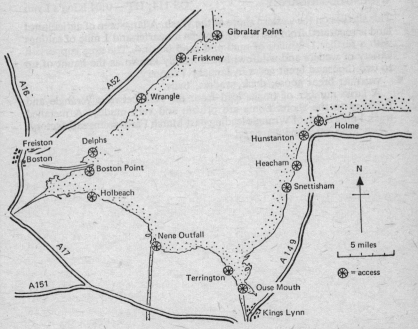

The Wash: showing the main access points. Only the four on the east coast and Gibraltar Point are worth visiting at all times. The other points are hightide specialities only

TETNEY HAVEN

OS 105; HT at Grimsby

This is the most extensive area of salting and foreshore on the Lincolnshire coast away from the Wash and lies 6 miles south of Grimsby. Northcoates Point is a good place for sea-watching. A wide variety of waders is seen on autumn passage and huge roosts of these species are noted in the new year.

WINTER: bar-tailed godwit, knot, dunlin, brent goose, merganser, snow bunting, Lapland bunting, divers.

SPRING: waders.

AUTUMN: wood and green sandpipers, spotted redshank, greenshank, curlew sandpiper, divers, skuas, terns.

Leave Grimsby southwards on the A1031 to Tetney. Turn left to Tetney Lock and walk along the south wall to Tetney Haven. Alternatively leave the A1031 north of Marsh Chapel eastwards to Horse Shoe Point.

WRANGLE-FRISKNEY

OS 114; HT —0:04 King's Lynn

This site lies on the western shore of the Wash. A large area of agricultural land is separated from the sea by between a quarter and 1 mile of saltings with a further 1–2 miles of mud and sand beyond. The area supports a variety of waders and wildfowl but is mainly known as the haunt of up to two thousand brent geese in January–February.

WINTER: brent goose, duck, waders, twite.

A large number of tracks lead from the A52 between Wrangle and Friskney to the shore. Some are private and very muddy. A metalled track 1 mile north of Wrangle leading past Marsh Farm seems satisfactory.

See Map on previous page.

London

LONDON NATURAL HISTORY SOCIETY.
The Society has a strong Ornithological Section. Field meetings for bird-watchers take place almost every Saturday and Sunday and include coach trips to anywhere within day or week-end range. The most ambitious of these is to the Scottish Solway for a long weekend. Indoor meetings are monthly and the *London Naturalist*, the *Bird Report* and a bi-monthly Bulletin are published. The Society covers the area within 20 miles of St Pauls.

READ: *Birds of the London Area*, Ed. R. C. Homes.

BARN ELMS RESERVOIRS   OS Tourist Map London

Barn Elms is rated tenth best for wildfowl in England and lies very close to central London alongside the Thames on the southern side of Hammersmith Bridge.

Duck are always present in large numbers in even the mildest winters and diving duck regularly reach four figures. At one time Barn Elms was 'the' London locality for smew but numbers in recent years have been very small and watchers looking for this species would be well advised to go elsewhere.

Other species of interest are terns, including black, on both spring and autumn passage, and usually an interesting trickle of the commoner waders. A small disused gravel pit behind the pumping station at the entrance end is often interesting.

WINTER: tufted duck, pochard, gadwall, wigeon, smew.

SPRING AND AUTUMN: black and common tern, waders.

On the southern side of Hammersmith Bridge turn eastwards at traffic lights along Merthyr Terrace. Access is strictly by permit only from Metropolitan Water Board, New River Head, Roseberry Avenue, EC1. Permits entitle holder to visit several London reservoirs. They are available only to *bona fide* watchers aged over 21. Some evidence of seriousness is required, viz. membership of London Natural History Society, BTO or RSPB.

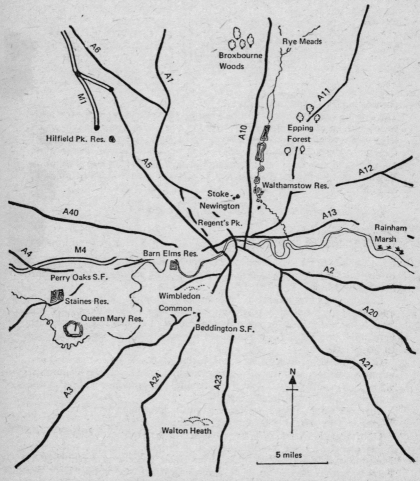

A6

M1

A1

Rye Meads

Broxbourne
Woods

A11

Hilfield Pk. Res. ⊛

A10

Epping
Forest

A5

Walthamstow Res.

A12

Stoke
Newington

A40

Regent's Pk.

A13

Rainham
Marsh

A4

M4

Barn Elms Res.

Perry Oaks S.F.

A2

Staines Res.

Wimbledon
Common

Queen Mary Res.

Beddington S.F.

A20

A3

A24

A23

A21

N

Walton Heath

5 miles

London Area showing position of best areas in relation to the main arterial roads. Note the huge area of reservoirs in the Lea Valley between the A10 and A11 are almost entirely of restricted access

BEDDINGTON SEWAGE FARM   OS Tourist Map London

The farm lies between Mitcham and Croydon in the south London suburbs. It is roughly 1 mile square and though of the old type it is slowly being altered, and there are rumours of complete modernisation. At present the principle habitats are the open flooded grass fields and the series of small sludge lagoons. The state of flood of the fields and the lagoons determines the frequency of waders, and when appropriate flooding coincides with migration a wide variety of species occurs. In winter the fields hold huge flocks of snipe and smaller numbers of jack snipe.

WINTER: snipe, jack snipe, short-eared owl, green sandpiper.

SPRING: waders.

SUMMER: yellow wagtail, snipe, redshank.

AUTUMN: waders.

Leave Mitcham Fair Green eastwards toward Croydon on the A236. At the first roundabout turn right. After 1½ miles the road forks near Hackbridge Station and a gravel track leads left at the fork to the farm. Access is by permit from Beddington Sewage Treatment Works, Beddington Lane, Croydon, CR0 4TH.

BROXBOURNE WOODS (Herts)   OS 160 and 161

This is a large area of old mixed deciduous woodland with new fir plantations and areas of open heath with bracken. It lies 2 miles west of Hoddesden, which is on the A10.

SUMMER: nightingale, nightjar, grasshopper warbler, woodcock, tree pipit, warblers.

Leave Hoddesden westwards at the important major fork on an unclassified road to Goose Green. There is a footpath through Highfield, Cowheath and Broxbourne Woods.

EPPING FOREST (Essex)   OS 161

The Forest lies on either side of the A11 between Buckhurst Hill and Epping. It is over 4 miles long and 1 mile wide and is of free public access. The trees are mixed deciduous including large areas of thorn, oak and the famous pollarded hornbeams. Redstarts are numerous and Epping is the London stronghold of this species.

SUMMER: redstart, nightingale, tree pipit, wood warbler, hawfinch, redpoll, grasshopper warbler.

Leave London on the A11 and explore on foot.

HILFIELD PARK RESERVOIR (Herts) OS 160

The reservoir is situated in the south-western corner of Hertfordshire just east of the Watford by-pass, and covers 115 acres. The main attraction is the large numbers of the commoner duck which make this the most important water in Hertfordshire. In winter a few smew are regularly present and gulls use the water as a roost, over 25,000 have been counted.

WINTER: pochard, wigeon, smew, goldeneye, goosander, gulls.

The reservoir lies just north of Watford on the A41. It can be seen from the main road and also from Dagger Lane along the southern boundary. A public footpath runs along the edge of Elstree Airfield and the reservoir.

PERRY OAKS SEWAGE FARM OS 160

The farm is immediately west of London Airport (Heathrow). Undoubtedly the main attraction is the passage of waders, particularly in autumn. Additionally there is a gathering of little ringed plovers in the second half of July, and green sandpiper and ruff in winter. Most autumns produce an outstanding rarity.

WINTER: ruff, green sandpiper.

SPRING: dunlin, ringed plover, little ringed plover.

SUMMER: black-headed gull, yellow wagtail.

AUTUMN: greenshank, redshank, ruff, sandpipers, little stint.

Pass London Airport on A4 and fork left on to B3378. Turn left on to B379 for a quarter of a mile to row of cottages on left near the entrance.

The areas of interest lie immediately inside the gate on the right where a bank encloses a large sludge lagoon, and further east, near the airport; reached by following the main track straight through. Access is by permit only from GLC, Dept. of Public Health Engineering, County Hall, SE1.

QUEEN MARY RESERVOIR (Littleton Reservoir) OS 160

For its size, 707 acres, this water holds a disappointing number of duck with only tufted at all numerous, but the species collection is often wide. The water is also a large gull roost with something over 20,000 birds coming in during December. Interestingly, only half of these birds are black-headed gulls which dominate every other London gull roost.

The reservoir has a very good collection of near-rarities most years and black terns in spring and autumn often bring more unusual terns with them. Rare grebes, gulls and wildfowl regularly turn up.

WINTER: goosander, goldeneye, wigeon, shoveler, gulls, rarities, grebes, sea duck.

SPRING AND AUTUMN: black tern.

With Compliments

RSPB

The Royal Society for the Protection of Birds
The Lodge, Sandy, Bedfordshire SG19 2DL
Sandy (0767) 80551

Take the A308 to Ashford. Stop at Charlton Road at the eastern corner of the reservoir and apply for entry to the building opposite the main gate, 50 yards down Charlton Road. Access is by permit only from the Metropolitan Water Board (see Barn Elms for permit details).

RAINHAM MARSH (Essex)   OS 161

The marsh lies on the northern bank of the Thames at Erith Reach below Dagenham. Though basically an area of water meadows they have been changed recently by the pumping of mud slurry dredged from the Thames into an embanked section, and the creation of a rubbish tip. The main attraction is the brackish pools of mud and the condition of these is largely dependent, like sewage farms, on the activities of the authorities involved, in this case the Port of London Authority. At passage periods gatherings of waders are often large and exciting. Little ringed plover are regular in both spring and autumn.

WINTER: duck, short-eared owl.

SPRING: little ringed plover.

AUTUMN: little ringed plover, sandpipers, spotted redshank, little stint, shelduck.

Take the A13 from central London through to Dagenham. Some 2 miles further fork right to Rainham Village and turn right in to Ferry Lane soon after the church. Continue for 1 mile to the factory area and then continue on foot along the riverbank to the marshes.

REGENT'S PARK   OS 160

The Park is in central London and at the present time a team of bird-watchers cover it almost every day of the year. In spite of being within a short bus ride of London's West End and surrounded by bricks and mortar, Regent's Park regularly boasts an annual species list about the hundred mark.

The best periods are spring and autumn passage when most of the commoner summer visitors to Britain are regularly recorded.

Diurnal migration is studied, especially in October, from the top of the adjacent Primrose Hill which gives wonderful views over the whole of London. A good range of species can be watched heading basically westerly on most October mornings soon after dawn. Passage is most obvious when the wind is from the north-west.

The best areas for migrants are the Sanctuary at the north-eastern arm of the lake and the woodland enclosures in the north-western corner of the Park.

SPRING: willow warbler, chiffchaff, whitethroat, lesser whitethroat, spotted flycatcher.

AUTUMN: pied flycatcher, redstart, wheatear, warblers, finches, thrushes, pipits, redpoll, tree sparrow, brambling.

There are many buses from central London to Baker Street and the Park is an easy walk from Baker Street underground station.

RYE MEADS SEWAGE PURIFICATION WORKS (Herts) OS 161

The works are situated between the rivers Lea and Stort immediately north of their confluence and cover an area of 263 acres. Though a varied range of habitats exist the most important are the effluent lagoons and the sludge drying beds and lagoons. The lagoons provide an area of about 58 acres of shallow water and it is doubtless this, as well as the geographical position, that makes the area so attractive to migrants.

Duck are present throughout the winter, and waders are frequent in small numbers on both spring and autumn passage. Breeding species include both sedge and reed warblers and a marsh-reed warbler that has coined the nickname 'mead' warbler because of its showing characteristics of both marsh and reed warblers (in fact aberrant reed warblers).

Rye Meads has a regular passage of both nocturnal and diurnal migrants with swifts and hirundines dominating. It is also the home of an energetic ringing group. The group ring c.5,000 birds per year and set the pattern of taking as much detail as possible of the bird in hand. A full set of measurements as well as weight is taken for every capture and weight is taken for every retrap. The results have been significant increases in our knowledge of the variation of the weights of migrants, particularly reed warblers and swifts.

WINTER: goldeneye.

SUMMER: sedge and reed warblers, little ringed plover, swift.

AUTUMN: swift, hirundines, waders, migrants.

Access is by permit only. The ornithological and scientific activity at the works is administered by the Rye Meads Ringing Group.

STAINES RESERVOIR OS 160

The 424 acres of the Staines reservoirs are rated ninth amongst English top reservoirs from a wildfowl angle. It is one of the most intensively worked areas in the country and one may expect to meet more bird-watchers along the central causeway than almost anywhere else. Sunday is 'the' day and though the attractions are seasonal, there is always someone else about.

Throughout the winter duck are present in large numbers and the variety is the best in the London area, the reservoirs are also a good place during passage periods when waders are regularly present in small numbers. Influxes of black terns in spring tend to be large and this species is regularly present in August. Both waders and terns have included some first rate rarities in recent years. Amongst the most interesting birds to be seen at Staines at any time of the year is the regular flock of black-necked grebes during August–October.

WINTER: smew, goosander, wigeon, shoveler, goldeneye, tufted duck, pochard.

SPRING: black tern.

AUTUMN: black tern, commic tern, black-necked grebe, little gull, rarities.

Take the A30 to the Bulldog, turn right (northwards) along B378 parallel to the reservoir bank and stop after half a mile at a footpath leading up to the causeway that divides the reservoirs. Alternatively, continue southward for 2 miles after visiting Perry Oaks Sewage Farm.

STOKE NEWINGTON RESERVOIRS   OS 160

Less than 4 miles from St Pauls between Seven Sisters Road, A503 and Stamford Hill, A10. There are two small pools with artificial banks surrounded by small areas of grass. In a normal winter the reservoirs hold a number of diving duck and always a quite sizeable flock of smew. In hard weather these relatively small pools stay ice-free longer than the other waters of the London area and at such times several thousand birds have been counted.

WINTER: tufted duck, pochard, smew, great crested grebe.

Leave Seven Sisters Road on the first turning southwards immediately east of Manor House. Woodbury Grove leads in to Lordship Road. There is no access but both pools can be seen from the aqueduct bridge and between the concrete railings on the north side.

WALTHAMSTOW RESERVOIRS   OS 160 and 161

The reservoirs consist of twelve pools lying at the southern end of a 6 mile chain of reservoirs in the Lea Valley. The waters vary in depth from 10 feet to 34 feet and are all comparatively small. Wooded islands are present on six and they provide breeding sites for duck, grebe and the famous herons. Winter duck are present in fair numbers and this is one of the favourite resorts of smew in London.

WINTER: tufted duck, smew, great crested grebe.

SUMMER: heron, great crested grebe.

Leave central London on the A10 and turn right on to A503 past Tottenham. This leads over the Lea in Ferry Lane. Access is strictly by permit only from the Metropolitan Water Board. (see Barn Elms). The heronry can be seen from Coppermill Lane.

WALTON HEATH (Surrey)   OS 170

The Heath lies on the gentle northward slope of the North Downs between
the A217 and the B2032. Though a large part of it has been turned into
a golf course, there remain large areas of birch and bracken, with conifer
plantations, and thorn thickets. The area is a good breeding haunt of
warblers, and a variety of heathland species. It is a regular haunt of great
grey shrike in autumn and winter.

SUMMER: redpoll, willow tit, nightjar, warblers.

AUTUMN: great grey shrike.

Leave London on the A217 and fork right on to the B2032 at Banstead.
Park off the road after 1¼ miles and walk up alongside the golf course.

WIMBLEDON COMMON AND PUTNEY HEATH   OS 170

No more than 6 miles from Charing Cross, these two open spaces are
frequented by hordes of people on summer Sundays, are overrun by
hundreds of little boys who have never heard of the 1954 Bird Protection
Act, and yet harbour a rich and interesting collection of heath and woodland birds. Putney Heath is strictly speaking the smaller northern half,
but there is no boundary and the two areas can be considered as one.
The higher land to the north and east is heathland with damp and marshy
spots characterised by a strong growth of birch scrub and contains a
few old gravel diggings that hold waterfowl. As the land drops away
westward an area of oak wood dominates the valleys that run down to
a picturesque lake.

SUMMER: skylark, woodpeckers, cuckoo, willow warbler, whitethroat,
blackcap, spotted flycatcher, yellowhammer, tree pipit.

Stop at either Tibbett's Corner, The Windmill or the War Memorial.
Walk along one of the numerous bridle paths that run parallel to the
road forming the eastern boundary. Turn westward and explore the
woodland.

Isle of Man

ISLE OF MAN NATURAL HISTORY AND ANTIQUARIAN SOCIETY, FIELD SECTION. The Section is active in field work and special enquiries are conducted, for instance, on the status of the chough. It enjoys close contacts with the fine Natural History Department of the Manx Museum, and encourages holiday watchers to submit records.

READ: *The Naturalist in The Isle of Man*, Larch S. Garrad.

THE AYRES AND POINT OF AYRE   OS 87

This is an extensive area of sandhills that forms the northern end of the Island. The shore itself is vast and open and some waders often form large flocks. Divers and duck are frequently found on the sea. Passage periods are good but with regular working could be first class both on the sea and land.

WINTER: golden plover, curlew, goldeneye, merganser, snow bunting, raptors.

SUMMER: little, Arctic and common terns, wheatear.

AUTUMN: migrants on land and sea.

Leave Ramsey northwards on the A10 and turn right on to the A46 at Bride, or three unclassified roads past Bride to the sea. Access is generally unrestricted if the usual proprieties are observed.

Enquiries for accommodation to Ramsey Town Hall.

BALLAUGH MARSHES AND THE CURRAGH   OS 87

Situated between Ballaugh and Sulby villages on the main A3 between Ramsey and Peel. They form the only extensive area of marshland on the island and generally hold one of the best collections of birds. A wildfowl park has been established in part of the area.

SUMMER: duck, water rail, curlew, warblers, redpoll.

Leave Ramsey westwards on the A3. 1 mile past Sulby examine a coniferous plantation on the left and turn right just past the far end of this across the railway. Investigate from the roads, or ask helpful farmers for permission.

CALF OF MAN BIRD OBSERVATORY   OS 87

The Calf of Man is a small island at the southern tip of Man covering 616 acres, and belongs to the National Trust. Since 1952 the Calf has been administered by the Manx NT as a nature reserve and bird observatory. Among the breeding birds are large colonies of sea birds on the slate cliffs, and hooded crow and chough. There is evidence that the Manx shearwater has returned to breed.

On passage passerines are noted in good numbers and regularly include the odd rarity.

SPRING: whimbrel, turnstone, warblers, chats, Manx shearwater, gannet.

SUMMER: kittiwake, razorbill, guillemot, fulmar, puffin, hooded crow, chough.

AUTUMN: whimbrel, turnstone, warblers, chats, Manx shearwater, gannet, rarities.

Day visitors are free to land on the Calf and should make arrangements with the boatman at Port St Mary or Port Erin. The trip can be arranged with the Calf's regular boatman. Visitors to the observatory should obtain full details from the Secretary, The Manx Museum, Douglas. A resident warden is in charge of the old farmhouse which accommodates up to 10 visitors on hostel lines.

DERBYHAVEN, LANGNESS, CASTLETOWN BAY   OS 87

A narrow isthmus separates the two sandy bays and joins the rocky Langness area to the south-eastern corner of the island, near Castletown. Waders on passage can be numerous, especially in autumn. Derbyhaven is the best place on the island for divers, notably great northern, and there are always a few wildfowl about. Choughs regularly feed on the seaweed along the shoreline in winter.

WINTER: waders, great northern diver, chough.

SPRING: turnstone, terns.

AUTUMN: curlew, turnstone, knot, bar-tailed godwit, sanderling, curlew sandpiper, little stint, terns.

Leave Castletown on the A12 along Castletown Bay to Derbyhaven. Turn left for the Bay, and right for Langness. Paths and tracks lead north and south along the golf course.

Apply to the Castletown Commissioners for the *Tourist Guide*.

DOUGLAS BAY   OS 87

Douglas is a large sandy bay on the sheltered east coast surrounded by the largest Manx town. Summer sees the Bay covered with holiday makers but in winter it can be lonely. There is a large gull population and some waders. A few migrants always pass through and westerly gales bring sea birds in to shelter. The waders' roost is on rocks near Port Jack.

WINTER: turnstone, curlew, redshank, gulls, rock pipit.

SPRING AND AUTUMN: waders.

Access from Douglas promenade.

SPANISH HEAD AND CHASMS OS 87

Spanish Head is the extreme south-eastern point of the Isle of Man and lies just across Calf Sound from the Calf of Man. The area of 256 acres of clifftop moorland is the property of the Manx NT. The cliffs rise to 300 feet and are the breeding site of many species.

SUMMER: auks, fulmar, raven, chough, hooded crow.

Leave Port St Mary on the A31 to Cregneish which makes the ideal centre for a round walk of the clifftop footpath. A boat trip under the cliffs can be arranged from Port St Mary, which has a wintering flock of purple sandpipers.

Apply to the Town Commissioners, Port St Mary, for brochure.

Norfolk

The Naturalists' Trust was the first in Britain in 1926, owns a large number of outstanding reserves, and has set the pattern for the development of other Trusts.

READ: *Birds of Norfolk*, M. J. Seago.

BLAKENEY POINT AND HARBOUR AND MORSTON SALTINGS   OS 125; HT +0:12 King's Lynn

This large area lying immediately north of the coastal A149 consists of three distinct habitats. The Point, the Harbour north of the main channel, the beach as far as Cley, and the saltings immediately north of Blakeney village, amounting to some 1,335 acres, are the property of the National Trust, which maintains the dunes and shingle system of the Point as a bird sanctuary. Roughly 1 mile square, the point is extensively used by the public yet still holds 1,000 pairs of common terns and the largest colony of little terns left in the country. It is also ideally situated to receive passerine migrants and large falls occur most autumns, these naturally include a number of rarities.

Blakeney Harbour itself is the haunt of numerous waders, especially during autumn and winter. Brent geese reach a peak of up to 2,000 in January–February, the occasional rare grebe turns up, and the osprey is almost a regular autumn visitor.

The stretch of saltings between Morston and Blakeney holds a regular flock of up to 70 Lapland buntings.

WINTER: brent goose, wigeon, bar-tailed godwit, turnstone, knot, dunlin, Lapland bunting, twite.

SUMMER: common and little terns, ringed plover, oystercatcher, shelduck.

AUTUMN: godwits, turnstone, spotted redshank, passerines, migrants, rarities.

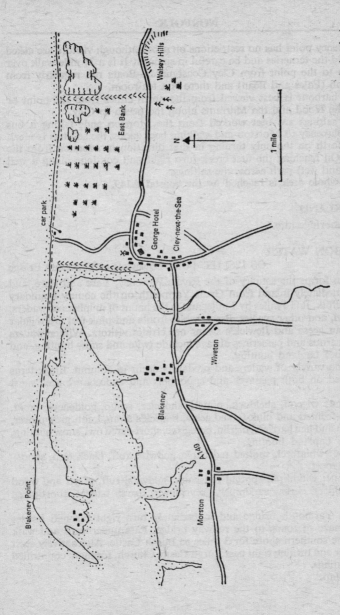

Cley and Blakeney; the East Bank is the most famous bird-walk in Britain and is excellent for waders. Blakeney Point can be reached on foot along the shore path and by boat from Morston-Blakeney

Blakeney point has no restrictions on access, though visitors are asked to avoid the terneries and be careful in summer. It is a $3\frac{1}{2}$ mile walk over shingle to the point from Cley Coastguards. Boats run regularly from Morston (Eales and Bean) and there is a tea-room.

The harbour is best viewed from the north either from the point or from the Hood and the Marrams along the beach to Cley.

The saltings are best worked from the Morston end; taking a bus from Blakeney to Morston and walking back along the saltings is ideal. Turn north on the only turning in that direction in Morston from the A149. On reaching the first creek turn right and continue along a well worn (and wet) path across the saltings.

The whole area is reached by the coastal A149.

BRECKLAND

See Cambridgeshire.

BREYDON WATER

OS 126; HT +0:01 Lowestoft at Yarmouth Bridge

Breydon forms the estuary of the Rivers Waveney, Yare and Bure, and lies immediately inland from Great Yarmouth on the county boundary with Suffolk. It is 3 miles by 1 mile, and is the haunt of numbers of waders, wildfowl, and other species. Brent, white-fronts and pink-feet are regular and bean geese and Bewick's swans are erratic visitors. Winter waders are numerous and passerines always include twite and snow bunting, and sometimes Lapland bunting.

A wide variety of waders and predators occur in autumn. Black terns are noted on both passages and spoonbills and avocets are seen most years.

WINTER: wigeon, shelduck, pintail, shoveler, scaup, goldeneye, brent, white-fronted and pink-footed geese, Bewick's swan, knot, grey plover, marsh and hen harriers, merlin, peregrine, short-eared owl, snow bunting, twite, Lapland bunting.

SPRING: whimbrel, spotted redshank, godwits, ruff, black tern, spoonbill, avocet.

AUTUMN: whimbrel, spotted redshank, godwits, ruff, green and wood sandpipers, curlew sandpiper, grey plover, marsh harrier, short-eared owl.

Cross Yarmouth bridge and immediately turn right through houses and a maze of roads to the railway bridge. Pass underneath and walk along the southern shore for 3 miles to Burgh Castle. Alternatively start the other end turning right past Burgh Castle Church, for more countrified surroundings.

See Map.

THE BROADS

The Broads are a series of freshwater lakes lying mainly in the valleys of the Norfolk rivers that eventually drain into Breydon Water and thus into the sea at Yarmouth. They are much reclaimed and overgrown with reeds, but still form a truly huge expanse of wetland. Though originally thought of as a vast silted up estuary, contemporary research has shown the Broads to be a series of pools created by man's peat digging activities. Most of them lie alongside rather than on the rivers, and several of them show parallel banks that have been left uncut, and which give rise to a series of islands in the open water.

Thousands of people hire motor boats and spend their holidays cruising the miles of connected waterways, yet the disturbance to the marshes is generally slight. Indeed the area remains very difficult to 'work' and in many cases access by water is far freer than by land. Out of season boats are cheap to hire, the birds are generally undisturbed and a splendid bird-watching holiday can be enjoyed in either spring or autumn. Esso publish a *Cruising Guide to the Norfolk Broads and Rivers* which clearly shows which broads are accessible by boat. They incidentally include Hickling and Horsey.

READ: *The Broads*, E. A. Ellis.

1. **Bure Marshes National Nature Reserve:** The reserve lies in the Bure Valley between Acle and Hoveton and covers over 1,000 acres of broad, reed marsh, fen and woodland. Declared in 1958 and owned partly by the Norfolk NT the reserve includes Ranworth and Cockshoot Broads, Woodbastwick Fen, and Hoveton Little Broad. Amongst an interesting collection of birds is a flock of feral greylags numbering 400, and feral flocks of Canada and Egyptian geese. Bearded tits are outstanding amongst an interesting collection of breeding species.

WINTER: feral greylag, Canada and Egyptian geese, gadwall, wigeon, pochard, cormorant.

SUMMER: common tern, bearded tit, sedge and reed warblers, teal, shoveler.

Access is by permits which are strictly limited: apply to the Nature Conservancy, 60 Bracondale, Norwich, NOR58B.

2. **Hickling Broad:** Hickling is one of the largest broads and lies north of Potter Heigham, 3 miles from the sea. It was declared a National Nature Reserve in 1958 but has been a reserve, largely owned by the Norfolk Naturalists' Trust, since 1945. The present reserve covers 1,204 acres of open water, reed marsh and fen and is an outstanding bird area at all seasons. Spring and autumn bring a host of passage waders, and

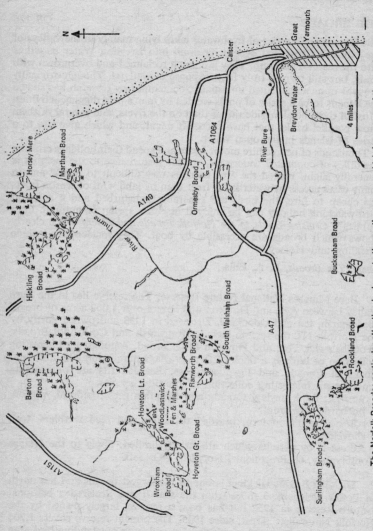

The Norfolk Broads: particular attention is drawn to the northern group which forms one of the most important wetland habitats in the country

black terns are regular. Breeding birds are quite outstanding though both harriers have deserted the area.

WINTER: wigeon, shoveler, pochard, goldeneye, gadwall, pintail, mute and Bewick's swans, marsh and hen harriers, short-eared owl.

SPRING: black and common terns, grey plover, black-tailed godwit, spotted redshank, green and wood sandpipers, ruff.

SUMMER: garganey, bittern, heron, bearded tit, common tern, sedge, reed and grasshopper warblers.

AUTUMN: marsh harrier, short-eared owl, black-tailed godwit, sandpipers, greenshank, spotted redshank, ruff, black tern, wildfowl

Though a reserve, sailing and use of the broad are unrestricted. Access can be obtained at the north-western corner southwards from Hickling village, and from the north side at Hill Common. Permits are required to visit the Sanctuary area and these are obtainable from The Norfolk NT, 4 The Close, Norwich, NOR16P.

3. **Horsey Mere:** Horsey is the property of the National Trust and one of the most famous of the East Anglian bird resorts. The Mere covers 120 acres and is surrounded by extensive reed beds. Its position, 1½ miles from the sea, has added to its attractions. Winter brings large numbers of wildfowl, including occasional herds of Bewick's swans, and hen and marsh harriers are noted. Waders pass through but in neither the number nor variety as on the Hickling wader grounds. Bearded tit, water rail, bittern and short-eared owl breed. Marsh and Montagu's harriers are regularly noted but do not now breed. Autumn brings a return passage of waders with terns, and a variety of passerines, hawks, etc.

WINTER: wigeon, pochard, goldeneye, Bewick's swan, hen and marsh harriers, hooded crow, great grey shrike.

SPRING: ruff.

SUMMER: bearded tit, water rail, bittern, sedge, reed and grasshopper warblers, short-eared owl, stonechat.

AUTUMN: waders, terns, passerines, harriers.

Leave the A149 1 mile north of Rollesby eastwards on the B1152 to Martham. Continue via B1159 to Horsey. Some of the area can be seen from the windmill on the left half a mile before the village.

4. **Rockland Broad:** Rockland lies in the Yare Valley, 8 miles east of Norwich. Its 48 acres are the largest area of open water left in the valley, and though greatly disturbed it does have a definite attraction. Wildfowl are present throughout the winter but February, especially if severe, brings herds of both wild swans and often quite large numbers of smew, goosander and scaup. Spring passage occasionally brings numbers of black terns.

WINTER: wigeon, pochard, tufted duck, smew, goosander, scaup, whooper and Bewick's swans.

SPRING: black tern.

Leave Norwich south-eastwards on the A146 and after crossing the Yare fork left on to unclassified roads through Bramerton to Rockland St Mary. The path round the south side of the Broad begins at the New Inn at the far end of the village.

BURNHAM OVERY   OS 125; HT +0:20 King's Lynn

Though forming only a small part of the huge area of north Norfolk salt marsh and sand banks, the Overy has a charm and attraction of its own. The area covered lies between the two walls that enclose what is in fact the estuary of the River Burn. Large areas of saltings are intersected by numerous creeks and a substantial area of mud is exposed on the eastern side out of Overy Staithe. The area is attractive to waders and hen harrier and merlin in winter.

WINTER: bar-tailed godwit, knot, oystercatcher, wigeon, merlin, hen harrier.

SUMMER: oystercatcher, shelduck.

PASSAGE: waders.

On the eastern side turn north off the A149 opposite 'The Hero' Overy Staithe to the quay. At the right hand end a wall leads northwards past the largest areas of exposed mud towards the sandhills of Gun Hill. Continue to the sea and sand banks. At high tide watch for waders flighting to Scolt Head Island.

To reach the western side watch out for an old windmill on the southern side of the A149 half a mile west of Overy Staithe, and for the delightful old maltings and water mill on the River Burn if coming from Burnham Norton. Opposite both mills, paths run down to the sea wall which then leads out towards Scolt Head.

CLEY AND SALTHOUSE MARSHES   OS 125

There can hardly be a serious bird-watcher in the country who has not made the pilgrimage to Cley. It has been the Mecca of ornithologists for the last 140 years during which over 275 distinct species have been recorded within the parish boundaries, including a most remarkable list of rarities. Cley and Salthouse lie at the eastern end of the long stretch of marshes and tidal saltings that guard the north Norfolk coast, and provide the most extensive area of fresh marsh on the whole coastline. Yet this alone does not account for the remarkable attraction that the area has for birds. It is perhaps its geographical position, at the point where the Norfolk coast begins to run directly east to west, that is the dominant factor. Whatever the causes, the East Bank at Cley is the best place in England to see passage waders – and to meet well-known bird-watchers.

The main bird-watching areas lie between the villages of Cley and Salthouse and between the sea and the A149. The large shingle beach protects a series of semi-saline lagoons, the best of which are those known as Arnold's Marsh, lying immediately east of the East Bank. This area of 29 acres is owned by the National Trust and is administered by the Norfolk NT which owns the 435 acres forming Cley Marshes proper on the other side of the East Bank. Gradually the open lagoons give way to a series of reed fringed pools with large reed beds and fields of rough grazing. The eastern end of Blakeney Harbour lies behind the beach to the west of Cley but I have included the area up to the western end of the Marrams.

Immediately behind the beach, west of the Cley Coastguard Station, are several areas of sueda bushes providing immediate cover to incoming migrants. The area of elder, brambles and osiers at Walsey Hills on the Salthouse boundary used to be used by Cley Bird Observatory as a trapping station and the disused Heligoland traps can still be seen.

Cley's specialities are unusual birds, migrants and vagrants of all shapes and sizes as well as an interesting collection of breeding marsh birds. Little gulls are daily in autumn, and the beach holds shore larks, and huge wintering flocks of snow buntings from October onwards. The lagoons are the haunt of waders throughout the year. Black-tailed godwits and ruffs usually manage to stay late and display in May.

The reeds and open pools provide Cley's main attractions during the breeding season with bearded tits quite numerous. On passage, marsh and Montagu's harriers quarter the reed beds and spoonbills are often seen in autumn.

WINTER: wigeon, shoveler, brent goose, snow bunting, shore lark, waders.

SPRING: ruff, black tern, fulmar, waders.

SUMMER: bearded tit, bittern, sedge and reed warblers, water rail, garganey.

AUTUMN: curlew, wood and green sandpipers, little stint, marsh and Montagu's harriers, snow bunting, shore lark, little gull, three skuas, eider, terns, rarities, bluethroat, barred warbler, Mediterranean gull, waxwing.

The A149 runs through Cley and Salthouse.

The Norfolk NT Sanctuary is equipped with several hides providing first class views over the whole reserve. Permits are available every day except Mondays from The Secretary, Norfolk NT, 4 The Close, Norwich, NOR16P. Unsold permits of a day's quota may be obtained from the Warden at Cley after 10 am on the day concerned.

See Map, page 153.

READ: *Birds of Cley*, R. A. Richardson.

HEACHAM
OS 124; HT —0:14 King's Lynn

Heacham is on the east coast of the Wash between Hunstanton and Snettisham and, like those places, has no saltings. At low tide, however, large areas of sand and mud are exposed and there are mussel beds offshore that are of great attraction to sea duck. The vast flocks of wildfowl in the new year, with maxima in February–March, can be a mile or two north or south of Heacham. Maxima include 500 scaup and, quite outstanding for southern England, 200 velvet scoter and 40 long-tailed duck. High tide produces a huge wader roosting flight with knot and bar-tailed godwit by the thousand. A small flock of a dozen or so purple sandpipers is regular between here and Hunstanton.

WINTER: scoter, scaup, goldeneye, merganser, eider, velvet scoter, long-tailed duck, knot, bar-tailed godwit, turnstone.

AUTUMN: waders.

Leave the A149 at Heacham westwards through the village to the beach on either of two routes. See Map, page 139.

HOLKHAM HALL LAKE
OS 125

Holkham is the seat of the descendants of Thomas William Coke, the pioneer of the early nineteenth century agrarian revolution. A huge monument to his achievements stands in the grounds of the Hall and can be seen towering above the trees from Holkham Gap. The lake is the main attraction to bird-watchers. Lying just over a mile from the sea and largely secluded and undisturbed it provides an excellent roost for the wildfowl of a large stretch of the coast. The lake is also famous for the flock of over 2,000 Canada geese.

WINTER: mallard, wigeon, Canada and Egyptian geese.

SUMMER: woodland species, geese.

Access to the Hall is along a gravel drive from the centre of Holkham southwards off the A149 and directly opposite the road running northwards to Holkham Gap. Watch out for the Pottery signs. Access is by permit obtainable in advance from the Estate Office, Holkham, Nr. Wells. The Hall is open to the public at certain times during the summer.

HOLME AND THORNHAM HARBOUR
OS 124; HT —0:15 King's Lynn

Holme is strategically sited on the north Norfolk Coast just as it turns southwards into the Wash. It is ideally situated to receive migrants, a fact which is enhanced by a small plantation of pines and scrub on the immediate landward side of the coastal dunes. This is the only cover for a mile or more. Red-breasted flycatchers are almost annual visitors, and there was once a yellow-browed warbler and a Pallas's warbler in the same tree within 5 days of one another. The usual small passerine migrants are often plentiful. The Broad Water behind the dunes and pines has an extensive reed bed that regularly fills up with bearded tits in autumn, and this species has recently started to breed here. The muddy edges prove an attraction to numerous waders, as does the shore itself. At high tide waders pass eastwards in huge numbers to roost on Thornham Island which can be seen from the eastern end of the high dune system. These movements continue throughout the winter when knot are estimated to number over 25,000.

WINTER: knot, bar-tailed godwit, sanderling, brent goose, great grey shrike, hen harrier, short-eared owl, Lapland and snow buntings, shore lark.

SPRING: Bewick's swan, bar-tailed godwit, terns, passerines.

SUMMER: little tern, ringed plover, oystercatcher, grasshopper warbler, red-backed shrike, bearded tit.

AUTUMN: bar-tailed godwit, grey plover, whimbrel, knot, little stint, wood and green sandpipers, spotted redshank, passerines, chats, fly-catchers, bearded tit, rarities.

Leave the A149 northwards at Thornham on to a track out to the old jetty. A sea wall on the western side leads out to Thornham Harbour. For Holme Nature Reserve leave the A149 at the Holme Beach sign and follow lanes to the white house at the centre of the reserve. Limited overnight accommodation is available.

For the Bird Observatory write to The Hon. Warden, Holme Bird Observatory, Holme-next-Sea, Norfolk.

HUNSTANTON   OS 124; HT —0:14 King's Lynn

This town, on the north-eastern corner of the Wash, is a Victorian seaside resort, and provides excellent winter bird-watching from the deserted promenade and cliff tops. Hunstanton forms the northern limit for most of the duck found off Heacham, though the long-tailed duck can often be found in the area. It does, however, attract several marine species that are rarer to the south, notably the three divers and more unusual grebes, especially black-necked. In autumn it is one of the main sea-watching points in the county.

There is a huge movement of waders at high tide to the roost near Holme at Thornham Island, and to Scolt Head.

WINTER: long-tailed duck, merganser, goldeneye, divers, black-necked grebe, knot, bar-tailed godwit, turnstone, purple sandpiper.

AUTUMN: knot, bar-tailed godwit, shearwaters, skuas, fulmar, gannet, kittiwake.

The A149 runs along the eastern side of the town. Turn left at centre to the station and park near the promenade. Walk northwards below the cliffs. At the end of the concrete promenade climb the steps and continue northwards at cliff top level towards Holme. See Map.

OUSE MOUTH: WOLFERTON–WOOTTON

OS 124; HT at King's Lynn

This area provides the main saltmarsh area on the east coast of the Wash and lies between the mouth of the River Ouse and Estuary Farm some 3 miles to the north. It is notoriously difficult to work with awkward access and the usual Wash necessity of a high tide, and has been to some extent neglected. The numbers of waders are not outstanding but wildfowl, especially dabbling duck, are excellent. There are sometimes pink-feet on the marshes near Estuary Farm.

WINTER: wigeon, pintail, teal, scaup, goldeneye, pink-footed goose, short-eared owl.

Find the way through a veritable maze of turnings, and leave King's Lynn docks on the track running down the eastern wall of the River Ouse and continue northwards for 1½ miles to the old lighthouse. Park and follow walls eastwards, then northwards out to Vinegar Middle where a new sea wall has been built enclosing an area of former saltings. This wall continues northwards and rejoins the old wall west of Estuary Farm. See Map, page 139.

SCOLT HEAD ISLAND

OS 125; HT —0:15 King's Lynn

The island lies offshore between Brancaster and Burnham Overy, stretches 3½ miles from east to west, and covers 1,821 acres. It has been a National Nature Reserve since 1954. The birds of the area are varied and provide excitement at all seasons. Outstanding are the breeding colonies of terns, which include 1,400 pairs of Sandwich and 600 of common.

Winter brings good numbers of wildfowl with the flock of up to 850 brent geese that feed around Cockle Bight being the main attraction, along with huge numbers of waders.

Passage brings a large variety of waders, terns including roseate, kittiwakes especially in July and a fair number of passerines.

WINTER: brent goose, wigeon, goldeneye, merganser, eider, knot, turnstone, bar-tailed godwit, grey plover, hen harrier, merlin, short-eared owl, twite.

SUMMER: common, Sandwich and little terns, short-eared owl, oystercatcher, shelduck.

AUTUMN: bar-tailed godwit, whimbrel, spotted redshank, turnstone, grey plover, short-eared owl, peregrine, roseate, and other terns, kittiwake.

Access is by boat, or by foot with care at low tide from Brancaster Staithe which is on the main A149; watch out for signpost 'To Scolt Head'. There are no restrictions on landing and one is free to roam everywhere except over the terneries during the breeding season.

SNETTISHAM   OS 124; HT —0:14 King's Lynn

On the east coast of the Wash at the northern end of the vast area of saltings that is such a feature of other parts of this area. At Snettisham one can sit on the sandy, pebbly beach and look directly on to the muddy feeding grounds of waders. The area has been considerably spoiled by a bungalow and beach-hut development but in winter, when the birdwatching is best, there are no holiday makers. Snettisham is undoubtedly outstanding from a wader point of view, and the main attraction comes just before high tide when a huge movement of these birds passes down the coast at Snettisham Scalp. Maxima are 20,000 knot, 4,000 dunlin, 2,000 bar-tailed godwit. The 1,000 sanderling in autumn are quite unique in the Wash area.

The old gravel pits to the south are frequented by wildfowl. Snow buntings are often quite numerous, and Lapland buntings and shore larks are reasonably regular. The bushes at the southern end of the pits should be inspected for migrants. This area is now a reserve.

WINTER: goldeneye, merganser, knot, bar-tailed godwit, snow and Lapland buntings, shore lark.

AUTUMN: sanderling, skuas.

There are two main points of access, though they are only walking distance apart:

1. Leave the A149 westwards in Snettisham to the beach. Park amongst the bungalows and snack bars and walk southwards down the beach.

2. Leave the A149 in Dersingham signposted westwards to the station. Continue on a good concrete block track to the sea wall. Walk southwards round the southern end of the old gravel pits.

TERRINGTON MARSH   OS 124; HT at King's Lynn

The marsh lies on the south side of the Wash between the outfalls of the rivers Nene and Ouse. There is a large area of low lying reclaimed fields protected by a sea wall and a large expanse of saltings, which provide a secure roost for a mass of waders. On the highest tides they are forced on to the fields and have been caught in their hundreds in autumn by the Wash Wader Ringing Group with rocket-propelled nets. Maxima usually occur in autumn though high numbers are present throughout the winter.

High tide is essential.

WINTER: knot, dunlin, grey plover, turnstone, twite, hen harrier.
AUTUMN: grey plover, turnstone, greenshank, godwits, sandpipers, whimbrel, little stint, black tern, skuas, marsh harrier.

Leave the A17 3 miles west of the bridge over the Ouse at King's Lynn northward to Little London, where, after turning left, take a right hand turn past The Dun Cow signposted Terrington Marsh. After 1 mile turn right and continue to Ongar Hill. Park at the end and climb over stile on to sea wall. Turn left and then right out to Admiralty Point.

See Map, page 139.

WELLS-NEXT-THE-SEA   OS 125; HT —0:16 King's Lynn

Wells was for long noted as 'the' haunt of geese on the Norfolk coast, up to 8,000 pink-feet having wintered in the area for at least a hundred years prior to 1938. This habit was destroyed by various war-time measures, including artillery practice and the ploughing up of the grass-land leys which provided feeding grounds. Since then Wells has largely been noted for its waders and the flock of up to 1,000 brent that winter on the tidal flats.

A belt of pines is now part of a National Nature Reserve of free access. Across the caravan site is a lake with an interesting reed bed. There is a path between the pines and lake which is excellent for migrants.

At Holkham Gap the pine plantations stretch away along the dunes to east and west. The right hand group is freely accessible, easy to work, and is backed by birch, elder and bramble scrub that is attractive to small passerine migrants.

WINTER: brent goose, turnstone, bar-tailed godwit, oystercatcher.
AUTUMN: migrants, goldcrest, rarities.

Wells is on the coastal A149. From the main road follow signpost 'Wells Quay and Town Centre', turn left at the quay and continue north-wards with the high sea wall on right.

Northamptonshire

BILLING GRAVEL PITS AND AQUADROME OS 133

Situated in the Nene Valley 3 miles east of Northampton. There are two groups of pits separated by the road from Great Billing to Brafield. The old pits in the west have been landscaped and turned into an Aquadrome with restaurant, café, garage, etc., and the main attraction here is the wildfowl collection. To the east, the pits are still being excavated and duck and waders occur in the appropriate seasons.

RESIDENT: wildfowl collection, duck, geese.
WINTER: diving duck.
SUMMER: sedge warbler, tufted duck, redshank, great crested grebe.
AUTUMN: wildfowl, waders.

Leave Northampton eastwards on the A45 and turn right in 3 miles to Little Billing. Turn left to the Aquadrome. There is an admission charge to the gardens and wildfowl collection. Continue to a T-junction and turn right to Billing Gravel Pits by the river. Permission to walk round can be obtained from the Site Office.

CASTOR HANGLANDS OS 134

Situated in the Soke of Peterborough, 5 miles north-west of the town, this is a National Nature Reserve covering 221 acres. The area, which lies on the edge of the fens, consists of grass heath with scrub and oakwood. The similar Ailsworth Heath lies alongside and maps at the reserve entrance show visitors where they can and cannot go without a permit. There is a wide range of breeding species.

WINTER: redpoll, siskin, sparrowhawk.

SUMMER: nightingale, grasshopper warbler, woodcock, marsh and willow tit, long-eared owl.

Leave the A47 at Ailsworth northwards onto an unclassified road. After 2-3 miles there are conifers on the left in new plantations. Past here a path leads westwards to the reserve notice board.

ECTON SEWAGE FARM   OS 133

The Sewage Farm lies immediately north-east of Billing Gravel Pits, 5 miles east of Northampton. Though it has been partly modernised enough of the old open irrigation farm remains to make it attractive to a variety of species. Passage brings numbers of waders.

WINTER: wigeon, teal, snipe, finches, tree sparrow.

SUMMER: redshank, tufted duck, sedge warbler, corn bunting.

AUTUMN: snipe, curlew, redshank, ruff, finches.

Leave Northampton eastwards on the A45 and turn right after 4 miles to Great Billing. Turn left past the village and immediately fork right into the Farm. Permission to drive along this track can usually be obtained from the Site Office. Permission to explore from the Borough Engineer, Engineer's Office, Town Hall, Northampton.

HARLESTONE HEATH   OS 133

The Heath lies 4 miles north-west of Northampton on the A428. Though consisting of little more than 1 square mile of mixed woodland the area is close to Northampton and holds a variety of species. This includes crossbills in invasion years.

WINTER: siskin, redpoll.

SUMMER: warblers, woodland birds.

Leave Northampton north-westwards on the A428 and park at Harlestone Heath after 4 miles. There are many paths and rides to be explored from the central entrance on the eastern side.

HOLLOWELL RESERVOIR   OS 133

The Reservoir lies alongside the A50 10 miles north of Northampton and covers 50-60 acres. Though less than 5 miles from Pitsford, this reservoir is important in its own right and is ranked fifth in England and Wales. The commoner duck have maxima of several hundred, while shoveler and goldeneye reach good figures.

WINTER: wigeon, pochard, shoveler, goldeneye, pintail, goosander, smew.

SUMMER: great crested and little grebes, sedge warbler, redshank.

Leave Northampton northwards on the A50 and after 9 miles turn left to Hollowell. Fork right in the village and continue towards Guisborough, looking right over the reservoir at a distance. Day permits are available with 24 hours notice from The Engineer and Manager, Mid-Northants Water Board, Cliftonville, Northampton.

PEAKIRK WATERFOWL GARDENS AND
BOROUGH FEN DECOY   OS 123

Placed on the western boundary of the fenland about 6 miles north of Peterborough, just east of the main A15. The area is owned by the Wildfowl Trust and a series of shallow pools have been created which house an impressive collection of wildfowl. Only Peter Scott's *Wildfowl of the World* will enable you to identify all you see, which includes whooper swans, red-breasted geese, Barrow's goldeneye, etc. It is an excellent place to mug up your identification of rare vagrants from foreign parts, or merely to enjoy a good look at what elsewhere are often only specks on the reservoir.

Wild birds include a large colony of collared doves that subsist largely on the grain provided for the wildfowl; they breed from March to November. Wild duck, particularly shoveler, visit the grounds.

The decoy at Borough Fen, 2 miles away, is one of the oldest in the country and has been used for ringing duck since 1949. The pool covers 2½ acres and is set in a secluded wood of 14 acres. It has 8 pipes and often over a thousand ducks come in to roost. It is usually open to visitors during one weekend in May.

RESIDENT: wildfowl, duck, geese.

Leave the A15 5 miles north of Peterborough at Glinton eastwards to Peakirk. Watch out for a sign on the left in the village to 'Peakirk Waterfowl Gardens' along Chestnut Close. Admission is daily, times varying according to the season. Members of the Wildfowl Trust enter free and may take a guest. The Gardens are open daily at 9.30 (12.00 am Sunday, except for members) and close at 6.30 pm in summer and half an hour before sunset in winter.

PITSFORD RESERVOIR   OS 133

The Reservoir covers 800 acres, was flooded in 1955, and lies 8 miles north of Northampton. Apart from the dam and central causeway the banks are natural and gently shelving. Wildfowl are very numerous making this the fourth best reservoir in the country. Pochard have found conditions ideal and have numbered up to 2,000 and other common species are present in good numbers. Bewick's swans are regular and a few geese are recorded annually.

Wader passage is good and autumn also brings terns, including black terns.

WINTER: pochard, wigeon, shoveler, pintail, goldeneye, Bewick's swan, geese.

SPRING: waders.

AUTUMN: little ringed plover, grey plover, green and wood sandpipers, knot, curlew sandpiper, ruff, black and commic terns.

Leave Northampton northwards on the A50 and keep right after 2 miles on the A508. Turn right at Brixworth and obtain distant views over the reservoir from the road. Later at the causeway look north and south over about half the total water. Permits are required for access. For details write to the Northants NH and Field Club.

RAVENSTHORPE RESERVOIR   OS 133

Lies alongside Hollowell Reservoir, 9 miles north of Northampton. Though within a mile of the fifth, and 6 miles from the fourth, best reservoirs in the country, Ravensthorpe should not be overlooked. Dabbling duck are numerous and diving duck are present throughout the year. Bewick's swans, pintail and goldeneye are recorded annually and the odd tern and wader appears in autumn.

WINTER: wigeon, tufted duck, pochard, pintail, goldeneye, Bewick's swan.

SUMMER: great crested grebe, tufted duck, shoveler.

AUTUMN: terns, waders.

Leave Hollowell (inevitably visited first) opposite the main entrance to the Reservoir and continue to the causeway across Ravensthorpe. Permits can be obtained under the same conditions as at Hollowell.

SALCEY FOREST   OS 146

The Forest lies on the Buckinghamshire border between the A50 and the M1 about 7 miles south of Northampton. It is a deciduous forest approximately 2 miles square and is of general public access from forest rides with a good variety of breeding species.

SUMMER: woodcock, nightjar, nightingale, lesser spotted woodpecker, grasshopper warbler, woodland species.

Leave Northampton southwards on the A50. Two miles past Horton turn right towards Hartwell into the Forest. Hartwell Clear Copse should be visited.

Northumberland & Durham

NORTHUMBERLAND AND DURHAM NATURAL HISTORY SOCIETY.
Hancock Museum, Newcastle upon Tyne, 2.
The Society publishes a lavish report on the birds of the two counties and is active in ringing, especially terns, on the Farne Islands.

TYNESIDE BIRD CLUB.
The Club is a very active group, and with the fashion for long sea-watches has gathered a great deal of knowledge of movements of these species in the north-east. Their duplicated report is written in diary form and includes splendid papers on sea bird identification.

TEESMOUTH BIRD CLUB.
The Club is an active conservation body and has set the pattern for dealing with illegal shooting in a semi-urban environment.

NORTHUMBERLAND AND DURHAM NATURALISTS' TRUST.
Hancock Museum, Newcastle upon Tyne 2.

BAMBURGH–SEAHOUSES (N'land)   OS 71; HT —0:51 River Tyne

This is a stretch of sandy coastline 3 miles long, interrupted here and there by rocky stretches, notably at Stag Rocks, Monk's House and Seahouses. The Farne Islands lie less than 2 miles offshore and dominate the sea view. The entire stretch is very good in winter and Slavonian and red-necked grebes, all three divers, and sea duck are all comparatively common, especially off Stag Rocks.

A variety of waders occurs on autumn passage when sea birds are seen offshore. Arctic skuas are seen almost daily in summer and in autumn are sometimes very numerous, and great skuas are quite frequent. Terns include all five British breeding species.

Passerine migration is very good in autumn and was extensively studied at Monk's House Observatory. The commoner warblers, chats and flycatchers annually include a mixture of less usual species.

WINTER: divers, Slavonian and red-necked grebes, long-tailed duck, scoter, velvet scoter, eider, purple sandpiper, sanderling, turnstone, knot.

SUMMER: terns, Arctic skua.

AUTUMN: sanderling, turnstone, little stint, Arctic and great skuas, gannet, terns, roseate tern, warblers, chats, flycatchers.

The whole area of foreshore from the coastal B1340 is of free public access the southern half belonging to the National Trust. The entire area can and does produce birds but Stag Rocks, called Islestone on OS is best for sea birds, especially in winter. Monk's House should be visited.

Bamburgh lies at the eastern end of the B1342 and B1341 which leave the A1 south of Belford.

READ: *The House on the Shore*, Eric Ennion.

CRESSWELL PONDS (N'land)   OS 71 and 78

The ponds are on the coast 4 miles north of Ashington and 1 mile north of Cresswell. They are of recent origin due to mining subsidence and their proximity to the sea makes them attractive to a large variety of waders and other migrants. Over 180 species have been noted in 10 years including a fair number of rarities. The area around the ponds is mainly water meadows. There is also a considerable growth of hedge that is attractive to passerine migrants.

The foreshore is frequented by many waders, and terns are often numerous offshore in summer, as are sea duck in winter. Passerines including the commoner chats, flycatchers and warblers are found in the small mixed woodland south-west of the main pond.

WINTER: turnstone, sanderling, purple sandpiper, scaup, scoter, long-tailed duck, eider, merganser, snow bunting.

SPRING: green sandpiper.

SUMMER: commic and roseate terns.

AUTUMN: ruff, spotted redshank, whimbrel, wood sandpiper, curlew sandpiper, little stint, terns, black tern, skuas, great skua, chats, flycatchers, warblers.

Leave Ashington westwards on the A197 and on the outskirts turn north on to the A1068 to Ellington. Turn right and left to Cresswell village and turn left again along the coast road from which good views can be obtained of the shore, the sea and the ponds. Three footpaths lead inland, but see map.

The area is heavily shot over, largely by unauthorised gunners. All the ponds are on private land.

DUNSTANBURGH–CULLERNOSE POINT (N'land)   OS 71

This is a stretch of cliffs with a rocky foreshore, 3 miles long, lying some 7 miles north-east of Alnwick. Dunstanburgh Castle dates from the fourteenth century and is an excellent place for sea watching in autumn when skuas, terns and gannets are noted. In summer the cliffs are the haunt of breeding sea birds and a colony of cliff-breeding house martins.

SUMMER: kittiwake, fulmar, guillemot, house martin.

AUTUMN: skuas, terns, gannet.

Leave Alnwick north-eastwards on the B1340 and after 3 miles turn right at Hocketwell. Immediately turn left on to unclassified roads to Craster. Explore along coastal footpaths to Cullernose to the south and Dunstanburgh to the north.

FARNE ISLANDS (N'land)   OS 71

The Farnes consist of some 30 islands lying 2–5 miles offshore near Bamburgh. The majority of the islands belong to the National Trust and are of straightforward access. They have long been a bird-watchers' Mecca and annually attract large numbers of observers to see the breeding seabirds. Four species of tern breed annually, including the rare roseate.

Passage periods bring a variety of waders, and sea watching is good

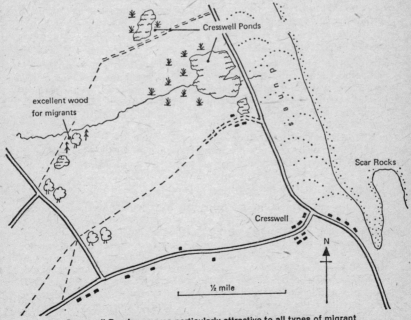

Cresswell Ponds: an area particularly attractive to all types of migrant

with divers, shearwaters and skuas, though as an observatory the islands have so far not enjoyed the full daily coverage that is needed in autumn. Nevertheless, chats, warblers and flycatchers are often quite numerous and rarities are occasionally seen.

Amongst the oddities are the small party of greylag geese that spend late summer on the outer isles.

SPRING: turnstone, whimbrel, divers, skuas, scoter.

SUMMER: common, Arctic, Sandwich and roseate terns, cormorant, shag, eider, guillemot, razorbill, puffin, oystercatcher, ringed plover, fulmar, kittiwake.

AUTUMN: terns, eider, scoter, whimbrel, turnstone, knot, purple sandpiper, divers, Manx shearwater, Arctic and great skuas, chats, warblers, flycatchers, rarities.

The islands are reached by motor boat from Seahouses and a landing fee is charged for non-members of the National Trust. The Brownsman is closed to visitors during the breeding season, though all the species there can be seen on The Inner Farne which is the best island.

A great deal of ringing is undertaken by the Northumberland and Durham Natural History Society and a report on the Islands is included in that Society's annual report.

GOSFORTH PARK LAKE (N'land)   OS 78

The lake lies immediately north of Newcastle, within a mile of the A1 and some 7 miles from the sea. In spite of its small size, it is one of the best inland waters for duck in the county and is preserved as a sanctuary by the Northumberland and Durham Natural History Society.

WINTER: teal, wigeon, tufted duck, shoveler, pochard, goldeneye, woodland species.

AUTUMN: greenshank, sandpipers.

Access is available only to members of the Northumberland and Durham Natural History Society; enquiries to the Secretary.

GRINDON LOUGH (N'land)   OS 77

The Lough lies 700 feet up in the Roman Wall country west of Hexham and on the direct route near the Tyne valley between the Solway and the east coast. It is the best of the Northumberland loughs in the area which includes Greenlee, Broomlee and Crag Loughs. Like most upland waters, Grindon is largely ignored by wildfowl with the exception of a herd of whooper swans that winter there. On passage, however, the Lough sometimes holds large numbers of duck for short periods and goosander and goldeneye have been quite numerous. An unusual development has been the increasing habit of a flock of bean geese to spend February in the neighbourhood.

WINTER: whooper swan, goosander, goldeneye.
SPRING: bean goose, duck, curlew.
SUMMER: black-headed gull.
The Lough is private but can be viewed from the road to the south.
Leave Hexham westwards on the A69 to Haydon Bridge. Turn right on
the B6319 and immediately under the railway bridge turn left. After
2 miles turn left at a cross-roads and view the Lough on the right side
after 1 mile.

HARTLEPOOL (Durham)   OS 85; HT —0:21 Middlesbrough

Birds congregate in Hartlepool Bay and in rough weather some take
shelter in the docks. Scoter are present in the Bay during the winter and
can be seen off Seaton Carew with a variety of other sea ducks. Divers,
especially red-throated, grebes, gulls, auks and a variety of waders are
all fairly regular throughout the winter. In autumn shearwaters and
three species of skua pass offshore.
   WINTER: divers, scoter, velvet scoter, eider, long-tailed duck, scaup,
   waders.
   SPRING: sea birds, waders.
   AUTUMN: divers, Manx shearwater, fulmar, gannet, Arctic, great and
   pomarine skuas, terns, auks.
The docks can be seen from various roads along which there is straightforward access. The best place to sea-watch is near the lighthouse, and
Seaton Carew lies 2 miles south along the coast road, the A178.

HAUXLEY (N'land)   OS 71

Hauxley lies on a peninsula 2 miles south of Amble. Coquet Island lies
offshore and the sandy foreshore is interrupted by quite extensive areas
of rock. The area, which is strictly private away from the foreshore and
rights of way, is covered by the Hauxley Ringing Station where about
180 species are recorded annually. Though the area draws its share of
rarities, the shore is the main attraction to the casual watcher. Waders are
quite numerous on passage and the strategic position jutting out into the
North Sea makes the area an excellent one for sea-watching from July till
October.
   SPRING: divers, terns, turnstone, chats.
   AUTUMN: divers, terns, Manx and other shearwaters, fulmar, gannet,
   auks, skuas, waders, chats.
Leave Amble southwards on the landward unclassified road towards
Radcliffe. Turn left after 1 mile to Hauxley and continue to Low Hauxley.
The continuation of this road southwards to Bondicarr is a public foot-
path.

HOLYWELL PONDS (N'land) OS 78

These ponds form the inland point of a notable triangle of bird-watching places all within a radius of 2 miles, the others being Seaton Sluice and St Mary's Island. The ponds lie on farmland and are due to mining subsidence. They are the haunt of a variety of wildfowl, including many duck and whooper swans. Passage periods bring the usual 'fresh' waders.

WINTER: wigeon, pochard, tufted duck, pintail, shoveler, goldeneye, whooper swan.

SPRING AND AUTUMN: wood and green sandpipers, greenshank, jack snipe.

The area which includes a number of small ponds is a reserve of the Northumberland and Durham Naturalists' Trust. The largest water can, however, be seen from the public footpaths that run along the southern side from the eastern end of Holywell village.

HURWORTH BURN (Durham) OS 85

This is a small reservoir, less than half a mile long, 6 miles west of Hartlepool. It has a small duck population of the commoner species and there is usually a passage of waders, terns, and notably, little gulls, in autumn.

WINTER: wigeon, tufted duck, shoveler, whooper swan.

AUTUMN: waders, terns, little gull.

Leave Hartlepool westwards on the A179 and continue on the B1280 when it joins the A19. After 1 mile turn left, fork right and turn right to the reservoir. A public footpath runs along the western side and must be strictly kept to.

LINDISFARNE (N'land) OS 64 and 71; HT —0:46 River Tyne

Lindisfarne lies on the coast equidistant from Berwick and Alnwick and is a National Nature Reserve that will, when fully declared, exceed 6,000 acres. It will then cover the entire inter-tidal area between Budle Bay in the south and Cherwick Sands in the north, plus a separate area near Cheswick Black Rocks, as well as the large area of dunes on Holy Island and the mainland at Ross Links. The area includes a whole series of exceptionally fine bird habitats with Goswick Sands, Fenham Flats, Skate Road, Ross Links, Holy Island Lough and Budle Bay being the most outstanding.

The Reserve is being managed in the same way as the successful Caerlaverock Reserve in Dumfries with orderly shooting on a controlled basis. This will thus ease the position of Budle Bay which has been made untenable in the past by constant disturbance. Amongst the wildfowl the brent geese, 500–2,000, are the major interest. The majority of these

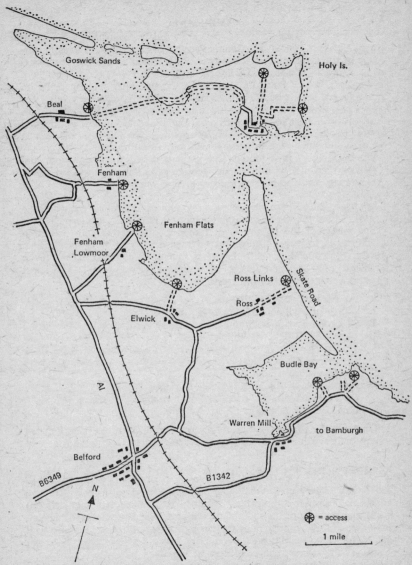

Goswick Sands

Holy Is.

Beal

Fenham

Fenham Flats

Fenham
Lowmoor

Skate Road

Ross Links

Ross

Elwick

Budle Bay

Warren Mill

to Bamburgh

Belford

B6349

N

B1342

⊛ = access

1 mile

**Lindisfarne National Nature Reserve: showing the main access points and outstanding
bird areas**

are of the light-bellied or Atlantic race and large numbers usually only occur in the latter part of the winter. Pink-footed and greylag geese are also frequently present and whooper swans reach 450, the biggest herd in England. A few Bewick's also occur. On the open sea, especially off Skate Road, sea duck are numerous. This area is also very good for grebes and divers and concentrations of a variety of species are regular.

Waders too are numerous with a variety of species present in flocks of several hundreds in autumn. Almost anything can and does turn up in the area, though barnacle geese in autumn are annual.

WINTER: brent, pink-footed and greylag geese, whooper, mute and Bewick's swans, wigeon, eider, scoter, goldeneye, long-tailed duck, Slavonian and red-necked grebes, divers, waders.

SPRING: waders.

AUTUMN: duck, barnacle goose, grey plover, bar-tailed godwit, little stint, whimbrel, wood sandpiper, spotted redshank, sanderling.

The whole of the reserve is of free public access though collecting specimens is by permit only and no mist-netting of birds is allowed. Access to farmland on Holy Island is not allowed, and to that on the mainland only by permission of individual landowners. The most important access points from north to south are:

1. At Fenham near Mill Burn.
2. North of Fenham le-Moor at Lowmoor Point.
3. The road east of Beal and the causeway across to Holy Island.
4. North of Elwick to Whitelee Letch.
5. East of Ross a footpath leads across Ross Links to Ross Back Sands and Skate Road.
6. North-east of Budle.
7. North-west of Budle at Heather Cottages.
8. On Holy Island, the road leading north to The Links.
9. East of Holy Island to Sheldrake Pool.

The main A1 passes within a mile or two of all of these sites, some 14 miles north of Alnwick, and there is a tidal road to Holy Island.

MARSDEN ROCKS (Durham) OS 78

The Rocks lie between South Shields and Sunderland on a rather attractive cliff-backed stretch of coastline. Marsden Rock itself is a high, rugged stack separated from the mainland cliffs but joined by the sandy beach. Its ledges and flat top harbour nesting sea birds and the area is also well placed for sea-watching on a productive coast.

SUMMER: kittiwake, shag, cormorant, fulmar.

Leave South Shields southward on the coastal A183. At Marsden Bay a footpath leads along the cliff top to the Rocks.

NEWTON POOL (N'land)   OS 71

Though little more than a quarter of a mile long, the Pool is an attractive haunt of both wildfowl and waders, due to its position within 200 yards of the sea. In spring and autumn fresh waders are present and though more erratic, duck usually include good numbers of sea duck.

WINTER: sea duck, goldeneye, waders.

SPRING AND AUTUMN: greenshank, sandpipers, etc.

Leave Alnwick northwards on the A1 to Charlton Mires. Turn right on the B6347 and follow its zigzag course for 4 miles to Christon Bank and its junction with the B1340. Turn left and in 1½ miles turn right to High Newton-by-the-Sea. Continue to Low Newton-by-the-Sea. A footpath leads along the seaward side of Newton Pool from which views over this private water may be obtained.

ST MARY'S ISLAND (N'land)   OS 78

Two miles north of Whitley Bay, and about half a mile from the coastal A193, a lighthouse is situated on a small island attached to the mainland by a causeway some 100 yards long which is covered at high tide. Large flocks of waders are present in winter when sea duck, divers and auks are frequently noted. During passage periods, particularly autumn, the area is one of the best in the county for sea watching.

WINTER: sea duck, divers, auks, knot, turnstone, purple sandpiper, sanderling.

SPRING: sea birds, terns, waders.

AUTUMN: terns, gannet, divers, skuas, shearwaters, waders, chats.

Leave Whitley Bay northwards on the A193 and where it turns sharply left after 1½ miles, continue half right on to a track leading out to St Mary's Island. Cars are charged on entering for use of car park, no charge to pedestrians. The causeway to the Island is open to all – but do not get cut off by the tide.

SEATON SLUICE (N'land)   OS 78

The sluices form the outlet of Seaton Burn exactly half way between Blyth and Whitley Bay. The rocky coastline which stretches southwards includes a small island, with a coastguard look out, connected to the mainland by a foot bridge. To the north the coastline is backed by extensive dunes which are of free access. Winter brings large numbers of sea duck as well as flocks of the commoner waders. Sea watching is generally good, though possibly better at St Mary's Island, 1½ miles south.

WINTER: wigeon, scoter, eider, knot, oystercatcher, purple sandpiper, turnstone, sanderling.

SPRING: waders, migrants.
SUMMER: terns.
AUTUMN: waders, terns, skuas, gannet, shearwaters, chats, warblers.
Leave Whitley Bay northwards on the coastal A193 and arrive in
Seaton Sluice in 3 miles. There are several car parks behind the dunes
for which there is a charge. The whole area is generally of free public
access, but try the walk down the coast to St Mary's Island.

SWALLOW PONDS (N'land)   OS 78

These ponds, which lie immediately north of Wallsend in the Tyneside
conurbation, were formed by mining subsidence. In spite of the depressing
surroundings which include pit heaps and a rubbish tip, the area is
attractive to birds, including both wild swans in winter and a variety of
fresh waders on passage. Recently attempts have been made to 'smarten
up' the ponds, but this involves reducing their attraction to birds.
WINTER: whooper and Bewick's swans, tufted duck.
SPRING AND AUTUMN: waders.
Leave Newcastle northwards on the A1 and after 2½ miles turn right at
Gosforth on to the A191. Continue for 3 miles until this road merges
with the A186 and then stop in half a mile where a track leads off to the
right. Swallow Pond is on the right down this public right of way but is
private and must be viewed from the footpath.

TEESMOUTH (Durham)   OS 85 and 86; HT at Middlesbrough

The estuary of the River Tees is virtually surrounded by industrial
development, and abuts on to the Middlesbrough-Stockton conurbation.
In spite of this the numbers of birds has increased in recent years and the
area is one of the most important for waders in the north-east Wildfowl
are quite numerous on Seal Sands and many resort to the fleets and
dykes of the adjacent marshes. Waders use the same areas and a wide
variety of species is found in winter and on passage. Cowpen Marsh is
a bird reserve and a particularly rich wetland habitat.
Terns of five species frequently gather in the estuary in August and
skuas are sometimes quite numerous. The latter are also noted offshore
from South Gare at the estuary mouth, together with sea duck, divers,
gannets and other sea birds.
WINTER: wigeon, shelduck, scoter, whooper and Bewick's swans, knot,
bar-tailed godwit, golden and grey plovers, sanderling.
SPRING: waders, duck.
SUMMER: waders, duck.
AUTUMN: godwits, whimbrel, ruff, spotted redshank, greenshank, sandpipers, grey plover, little stint, commic, roseate and black terns, skuas,
scoter, velvet scoter, gannet, fulmar, kittiwake, eider.

Access details are changing very rapidly and anyone interested in watching in the area should contact the RSPB Warden at Cowpen Marsh, Mr Norman Sills, 315 Wolviston Back Lane, Billingham, Teesside.

1. NORTH GARE BREAKWATER: can be reached by walking along the beach from Seaton Carew or by walking across the North Gare sands from a private road owned by the Tees Conservancy Commissioners.

2. SEAL SANDS: can be viewed from a public hide at Long Drag.

3. SOUTH GARE BREAKWATER: access is by a private road owned by Dorman Long (Steel) Ltd and the Tees Conservancy Commission, and public access may be limited in future. The area can also be reached on foot from Redcar along Coatham Sands.

4. COWPEN MARSH: contact RSPB.

READ: *Birds of Teesmouth*, P. J. Stead.

TYNEMOUTH AND NORTH SHIELDS (N'land)
OS 78; HT at River Tyne

The two towns lie at the mouth of the River Tyne on the northern shore 8 miles east of Newcastle. Though this is predominantly an urban area it provides bird-watching at all seasons. In summer many ornithologists leaving for holidays in Norway have been surprised to find kittiwakes breeding on quayside warehouses as they left the Tyne. During passage periods Tynemouth is better with Priors Park and Tynemouth Park good for passerine migrants. The latter once produced an ortolan bunting and a yellow-browed warbler within a week. The Haven also holds migrants, while offshore there is a regular passage of sea birds.

SUMMER: kittiwake.

AUTUMN: duck, waders, terns, gannet, skuas, warblers, chats, flycatchers.
Tynemouth Park and the Haven, and North Shields Fish Quay are all of straightforward access and easy to find. Prior's Park is private.

TWEED ESTUARY (N'land)
OS 64; HT —0:58 River Tyne

The Tweed enters the sea 3 miles south of the Scottish border between Berwick and Tweedmouth. Being both small and completely enclosed by urban development the area is not outstanding but does offer a variety of species, often at quite close range. The tidal area stretches inland 2 miles to Yarrow Slake though the best part is on the northern shore near the mouth. Waders congregate on the sandy beach just north of the pier at high tide.

WINTER, goldeneye, grebes, divers, waders.
SPRING: waders.

SUMMER: terns, mute swan.

AUTUMN: waders, sea birds.

The water front at Berwick east of the bridges is of straightforward access leading out to the pier which is good for waders and sea bird passage.

WHITTLEDENE RESERVOIRS (N'land)   OS 77 and 78

The reservoirs were formed by damming the Whittle Burn, a tributary of the Tyne, 12 miles west of Newcastle. Four quite small reservoirs with stone banks have been created and these have proved attractive to a number of species of wildfowl. They are the stronghold of the tufted duck in Northumberland and Durham with up to 350 present on occasion.

WINTER: tufted duck, pochard, goosander, smew.

The main pool can be seen from the Newcastle–Carlisle road along Hadrian's Wall, the B6318, half a mile west of Harlow Hill and some 4 miles west of Heddon-on-the Wall. The B6309 runs southwards at the western edge between two smaller pools. Permits are available to a limited number of individuals for this Reservoir, from the Secretary of the Tyneside Bird Club. It would be appreciated if casual watchers would not apply – most of the water can be seen from the roads anyway.

Nottinghamshire

READ: *The Birds of Nottinghamshire*, Trent Valley Bird-Watchers.

ATTENBOROUGH GRAVEL PITS OS 112, 121

The pits lie in the Trent Valley just upstream from Nottingham and have been made a nature reserve. There are some areas of reed, and fairly thick vegetation of alder and willow flanks the River Trent. Wildfowl are quite plentiful and odd visitors include sawbills on the Trent. On passage common terns (which breed in the vicinity) and black terns are frequently noted, with small numbers of waders.

WINTER: wigeon, tufted duck, pochard, sawbills.
SPRING: waders, common and black terns.
SUMMER: sedge and reed warblers, wagtails, pochard, shoveler.
AUTUMN: common and black terns, sandpipers, greenshank.

Access is unrestricted. There are three possible entrances, all originating from the A453 west of Nottingham:

1. From Beeston Rylands to the Lock and then along the Trent.

2. From Chilwell Golf Course approach, take the Crescent at the end and follow the path eastwards to the river.

3. From Attenborough Station, and south-east to the river.

BESTHORPE FLEET AND GRAVEL PITS OS 113

Situated 6 miles north of Newark between the A1 and the B1186. The Fleet is an old, shallow water with emergent vegetation, lying between Besthorpe and Girton. Recent gravel excavations have created a series of pools to the west covering over 100 acres. Sometimes the Trent floods and this usually brings exceptional numbers of the commoner wildfowl which are frequently joined by goosander, smew and, occasionally, Bewick's swan. Good numbers of waders appear on passage.

WINTER: wigeon, pochard, shoveler, goldeneye, goosander.

SPRING: waders.

AUTUMN: golden plover, curlew, greenshank, dunlin, ruff.

Leave Newark northwards on the A46 and turn left on the outskirts on to the B1186. At Besthorpe take the path by the Church around the southern end of the Fleet and up the west bank. Turn left to the gravel pits and walk along their edge northwards. Continue, cross a stream, and walk up the right hand bank of the Trent to a further pit half a mile north.

CLUMBER PARK   OS 103 and 112

The Park lies 2½ miles south-east of Worksop and is the only one of the three large Dukeries lakes open to the public. The main attraction is the winter wildfowl and there is a great deal of movement between this lake and those at Welbeck and Thoresby. The Park also holds a variety of woodland species.

WINTER: shoveler, pochard, goldeneye, goosander, Canada goose, siskin, redpoll.

SUMMER: redstart, nightingale, warblers, goldcrest.

Leave Worksop westwards on the A57 and enter the Park at Manton Lodge on the right after 3 miles. Other points of access are A614, Apley Head Lodge, Normanton Gate and Drayton Gate; A6009 Carburton cross roads; A6009 Clumber Lane End.

The area is a favourite one for fishermen in winter and weekday visits are advised if possible as the birds are then generally less disturbed. The Park is owned by the National Trust.

GUNTHORPE GRAVEL PITS   OS 112

The pits lie 6 miles north-east of Nottingham alongside the River Trent. The wildfowl in winter are sometimes interesting though waders are largely confined to autumn, and then only the commoner species occur.

WINTER: tufted duck, teal, pochard, pintail, shoveler.

AUTUMN: green and common sandpipers, greenshank, dunlin.

Leave Nottingham on the A612 north-eastwards to Lowdham. Turn right to Gunthorpe. At the bridge park on the right and walk upstream beside the Trent. Cross a bridge where a tributary joins the Trent and bear right. This gives good views of two of the pits.

HOVERINGHAM GRAVEL PITS   OS 112

Situated 10 miles north-east of Nottingham to the north of the River Trent. A number of pits have been and are being excavated and a large area of open water has been created. Diving duck are as numerous as anywhere in the Trent Valley. Waders on passage include a scattering of the commoner species, and commic terns are regularly noted.

WINTER: pochard, tufted duck, goosander, goldeneye.

AUTUMN: waders, commic terns.

Leave Nottingham eastwards on the A612 to Lowdham. Turn right and then left to Caythorpe an attractive road beside the Trent. After a sharp corner leaving the river, turn right through Hoveringham. As the road bends outside the village watch out for a tiny stream and bridle path sign on right. Close gate and walk along southern side of the best pits.

Shropshire

ALLSCOT SUGAR FACTORY   OS 118

The factory is 2 miles north-west of Wellington and consists of a number of settling beds that, as in several parts of East Anglia, attract a variety of marsh species. It is one of the principal habitats of waders in the county.

SPRING: waders.

AUTUMN: little ringed plover, green and wood sandpipers, spotted redshank, ruff.

Leave Wellington northwards on the A442 and turn left in 1½ miles on to the B4394. The entrance to the factory is 2 miles. Access is by permit.

LONG MYND   OS 129

This is an extensive area of moorland in the south-west of the county near the Welsh border. Its upland qualities give it a bird population with closer affinities to that country than to neighbouring England. The wooded valleys and streams hold the usual species.

SUMMER: red grouse, ring ouzel, whinchat, grey wagtail, dipper, pied flycatcher, wood warbler, redstart.

Leave Shrewsbury southwards on the A49 and turn right on to the B4370 to Church Stretton. Carding Mill Valley is worth exploring and the whole area is of generally unrestricted access.

NORTH SHROPSHIRE MERES   OS 118

These are a group of natural meres lying south and east of Ellesmere to the north-west of Shrewsbury. The largest is the lake at Ellesmere itself covering 114 acres and extensively used for boating. The resort aspect is intensified near the church on the A528 where seats overlook the water and Canada geese browse the roadside verge. Other waters include Cole Mere, White Mere, Blake Mere, Crose Mere and Newton Mere. They are extensively used by wildfowl, and a variety of aquatic species, including black-necked grebe and roosting gulls; great crested grebes breed on Ellesmere and Newton Meres.

WINTER: wigeon, shoveler, pochard, goldeneye, goosander, Canada goose, cormorant, gulls.

SUMMER: great crested grebe, reed and sedge warblers.

AUTUMN: waders, black tern, commic tern, black-necked grebe.

1. ELLESMERE: adjacent to the A528 on the east side.

2. WHITE MERE: 1½ miles south of the A528.

3. COLE MERE: leave the A528 eastwards at the north end of White Mere and in 1 mile turn left in the village to a track along the south side of the mere.

4. BLAKE MERE: stop on the A528 at its junction with the A495 and walk along the canal towpath eastwards.

5. NEWTON MERE: leave the A528 on to the A495 and take the first right after 1 mile. This leads to the south side of the mere.

VENUS POOL   OS 118

This water lies 5 miles south-east of Shrewsbury, south of the A458 between Cross Houses and Cound. It is an important site for wildfowl, and waders are frequently noted on passage, with green sandpipers sometimes quite numerous.

WINTER: teal, wigeon, shoveler, tufted duck, pochard, shelduck, Canada goose.

SUMMER: tufted duck, mute swan, great crested grebe.

AUTUMN: ringed plover, green sandpiper, ruff.

Leave Shrewsbury southwards on the A458, half a mile past Cross Houses turn left towards Upper Cound, cross the railway and the Pool is on the left. Access is strictly by permit.

Somerset

AXE ESTUARY AND BREAN DOWN   OS 165; HT —0:05 Cardiff

The estuary forms the southern arm of Weston Bay and lies within 1 mile of Weston-super-Mare. The Axe Estuary attracts small numbers of waders, duck and gulls and is locally considered worth a look after Brean Down. This 300 foot limestone outcrop juts out 1 mile into the Bristol Channel and is cliff bound on the southern side. It is National Trust property and is maintained by Axbridge RDC. It is an ideal migration watch point and grounded passerines are sometimes numerous. Visible migration is heavy in October, and in winter odd sea duck occur offshore – rare for Somerset.

    WINTER: sea duck, duck, knot, redshank, ringed plover.
    SPRING: waders, migrants, chats, grasshopper warbler.
    SUMMER: stonechat, raven, kestrel.
    AUTUMN: warblers, chats, goldcrest, visible migrants, knot, ringed plover.

    Leave Weston southwards on the A370 and turn right to Lympsham after 4½ miles. Half a mile after the village turn left and later right to Brean. Turn north to Brean Down. A path leads up to the top from the café and access is unrestricted. A path past Brean Down Farm leads out to the sea wall along the southern side of the Axe. There is a foot-ferry from Uphill for access to the area from Weston.

BARROW GURNEY RESERVOIRS OS 165

The reservoirs lie on either side of the A38 4 miles south-west of Bristol. The three small pools cover a total of 125 acres, are concrete banked and attract moderate numbers of wildfowl. Other species including waders and divers are irregular in small numbers.

WINTER: teal, tufted duck, pochard, wigeon, shoveler, waders, divers. Access is by permit only, details as at Chew.

BLAGDON RESERVOIR OS 165

Blagdon is some 10 miles south-west of Bristol on the northern side of the Mendip Hills. The water is 1½ miles by half a mile, and covers 430 acres. Though rather overshadowed by the Chew Valley Reservoir, 2 miles to the east, Blagdon is considerably older (1904), has its own attractions, and is still ranked as the seventh best reservoir for wildfowl. These include maxima of over a thousand each of wigeon, teal and pochard.

Waders are not as plentiful as at Chew, but autumn brings spotted redshank and sandpipers as well as black terns.

WINTER: wigeon, teal, shoveler, pochard, tufted duck, pintail, goldeneye, redpoll, siskin.

SPRING: waders, yellow wagtail.

AUTUMN: spotted redshank, greenshank, black tern.

Leave Bristol southwards on the A38 and turn left at Cowslip Green 1 mile past Redhill. After threequarters of a mile turn left and, after a similar distance, right to the dam from which views can be obtained. Entry is by permit only, details as at Chew.

BRIDGWATER BAY NATIONAL NATURE RESERVE
OS 165; HT at Cardiff

The Reserve consists of the Parrett Estuary, the Huntspill River and Stert Island, but for the purpose of this note areas outside the Reserve proper are included. The Reserve covers 6,076 acres, all of which is of free access except Stert Island. Habitats include mud flats, shingle banks, salting and farmland, and the variety of birds is wide. Wildfowl are numerous and the area is a regular haunt of 1,500 white-fronts. It is unique as the British moulting ground for up to 3,000 shelduck in autumn, and 500 are present in winter.

Waders are numerous, especially in autumn, and large numbers flight up river at high tide. Avocets are at Stert Point from September to March. Merlins and short-eared owls are regularly present in winter.

WINTER: white-fronted goose, wigeon, pintail, shoveler, knot, turnstone, merlin, short-eared owl, avocet.

SPRING: whimbrel.
SUMMER: redshank, ringed plover, shelduck.
AUTUMN: shelduck, grey plover, whimbrel, godwits, knot, spotted redshank.
The area can be worked from two sides:

1. Leave Bridgwater westwards on the A39 and turn right at Cannington on to unclassified roads past Combwich to Steart. Walk northwards from here out towards Stert Point.

2. Leave Bridgwater northwards on the A38 to West Huntspill and follow the footpath along the Huntspill River out to the Island. Walk northwards for views over the flats and Stert Island.
High tide visits advised.

CHEDDAR RESERVOIR
OS 165

Immediately south of the Mendip Hills 1 mile west of Cheddar, the reservoir is circular, just under threequarters of a mile across, covers 234 acres, and was flooded in 1938. The banks are raised and are wholly concrete and thus unattractive to waders and dabbling duck. Diving duck are, however, very numerous with pochard (2,000) quite outstanding. Other species include scaup and occasional red crested pochard. During sea bird 'wrecks' Cheddar seems always to attract some of the more interesting species and in exceptional freeze-ups remains free longer than other waters.

WINTER: pochard, tufted duck, goldeneye, wigeon, pintail, goosander, scaup, divers, rock/water pipit.
AUTUMN: red crested pochard, commic terns.
The entrance is on the northern side and access is by permit only, details as at Chew. A key for permit holders is obtainable from the pumping station manager. The reservoir is just visible from the road at the junction with the Axminster slip road, but a telescope is essential.

CHEW VALLEY RESERVOIR
OS 165

The reservoir lies some 8 miles south of Bristol and is 2 miles by over 1 mile. It was formed by damming the Chew River just east of Chew Stoke in 1953, and now covers 1,210 acres. The banks are mostly natural and there is a sizeable island in the north-eastern corner. The lake is the second most important reservoir for wildfowl in Britain. Surface feeders notably pintail and shoveler are dominant though both pochard and tufted duck have exceeded a thousand. Among the more exciting wildfowl, gadwall (100) in autumn, garganey in spring and summer, and smew are regular, and white-fronts are frequently present in small parties.

In spring and autumn Chew is outstanding for waders. Divers turn up occasionally in winter as do black-necked and Slavonian grebes, and great crested grebes usually breed in some numbers. Other species include the occasional little gull and a quite heavy double passage of black terns. In winter the lake is a sizeable gull roost and it is also the foremost trout lake in England.

WINTER: gadwall, wigeon, shoveler, pintail, pochard, goldeneye, smew, white-fronted goose, Bewick's swan, divers, waders, rock/water pipit.

SPRING: gadwall, garganey, waders, black tern, yellow wagtail.

SUMMER: gadwall, great crested grebe.

AUTUMN: gadwall, grey plover, jack snipe, godwits, green and wood sandpipers, spotted redshank, curlew sandpiper, little stint, ruff, black tern.

Leave Bristol southwards on the A38 and turn left after 5 miles on the B3130 to Chew Magna. Turn right before the village on the B3114 to Chew Stoke. Various cul-de-sacs lead to the reservoir surrounds but it can also be viewed from the public highway at Villice Bay, Heron Green, Herriott's Bridge and the dam. For regular visitors entry may be obtained by permit and on payment of an annual fee. This permit entitles the holder to visit all of the important Somerset reservoirs and is available from The Recreations Manager, Bristol Waterworks Co, Woodford Lodge, Chew Stoke, Bristol. Day permits are available on application (SAE), for a small sum.

DURLEIGH RESERVOIR
OS 165

This is a shallow, natural banked reservoir, covering 85 acres, and lies 2 miles west of Bridgwater. Its attraction to dabbling ducks in particular is responsible for its status as a strictly preserved nature reserve. A number of duck species reach maxima of several hundred and in autumn the passage of waders is good, and there is an annual gathering of up to 100 mute swans in July–August.

WINTER: pintail, shoveler, pochard, goldeneye, Bewick's swan.

AUTUMN: mute swan, waders.

Leave Bridgwater on the unclassified Four Forks road and view 300 yards past the Durleigh village road. Return to Durleigh and turn right out of the village to view from the southern bank. Do not miss the area of reeds and shrubs at the western end.

EXMOOR
OS 163, 164

Exmoor lies within a rectangle with Lynmouth, South Molton, Dulverton and Minehead at its corners and consists of grass and heather moors with sheltered combes and deep-wooded valleys. Most of the moor is not commonland though Withypool Common (1,866 acres) and Porlock

Common (482 acres) are exceptions. The wooded valleys with their fast flowing streams are most attractive while higher up red grouse are found with black grouse in a few areas. Merlins usually try to breed.

SUMMER: buzzard, merlin, ring ouzel, dipper, grey wagtail, red and black grouse, pied flycatcher, wood and grasshopper warblers, nightjar.

Exmoor is not the place for a day out, and any bird-watching holiday should include exploration with the aid of OS maps. The area between Porlock and Dulverton is as good as any. Access to large areas is unrestricted, and many of the woodlands are open. Disturbance of the more unusual species should be avoided, and watchers particularly anxious to see black grouse and merlin are advised to look elsewhere. There are very few on Exmoor.

LEIGH WOODS   OS 155

Situated immediately west of Bristol on the Somerset side of the Clifton Suspension Bridge over the Avon, the woods belong to the National Trust and extend to 159½ acres of mixed oak, birch, ash and sycamore. The typical mixed broad-leaved woodland bird population is found in summer including wood and grasshopper warblers and hawfinch.

SUMMER: woodpeckers, redstart, nightingale, wood and grasshopper warblers, tree pipit, hawfinch.

Leave Bristol across the Clifton Suspension Bridge (toll) and turn right on to North Road, Leighwoods. The main entrance is on the right and there are no restrictions on access.

MINEHEAD–DUNSTER BEACHES   OS 164

The beaches are immediately east of Minehead Golf Club and consist of sand, mud and shingle stretching almost a mile out into the Bristol Channel. They are backed by pebble and sand dunes, and by the Golf Course as far east as the mouth of the River Avill. Between this and the A39 is an area of open grassland. East of the Avill is a chalet estate and beyond that fields to the Blue Anchor. In winter duck and a small flock of white-fronts haunt the fields while the shore holds good numbers of waders including the occasional purple sandpiper.

WINTER: white-fronted goose, wigeon, shoveler, turnstone, sanderling, purple sandpiper, golden plover.

AUTUMN: waders, terns.

Leave Minehead eastwards along The Strand to the Golf Course. A footpath from here runs to the mouth of the Avill, and the shore and beach are open. A metalled road from Marsh Street, Dunster runs out to the shore east of the estate and there is a charge for use of the car park in summer. The white-fronts are easily visible from the beach path and must not be disturbed. High tide visits are advised.

PORLOCK MARSH
OS 164

The marsh is immediately behind the beach in Porlock Bay 6 miles west of Minehead. The area is mainly grazing land with pebble banks, gorse, a reed bed and some shallow pools. Duck are present in winter with small numbers of the commoner waders. On passage fresh waders are frequently present and more irregular visitors include bittern and the occasional rarity.

WINTER: wigeon, teal, shoveler, waders.

SPRING AND AUTUMN: whimbrel, sandpipers, greenshank, little stint, ruff.

Leave Porlock and the A39 by Sparkhayes Lane 100 yards north-east of the Church and continue on foot to the shore. Access, which is restricted to the beach and the footpath behind it, can also be obtained directly along the coast from Porlock Weir and Bossington Beach.

SHAPWICK HEATH
OS 165

Shapwick Heath is an area of ancient peat works, still partly exploited, which was made a National Nature Reserve in 1961 and covers 546 acres. There is a large flora and fauna due to the diverse habitats provided by the peat cutting and varying degrees of acidity. The areas of damp heathland with sedges and bush cover are important to a variety of breeding birds. The heath is of outstanding botanical importance.

SUMMER: nightjar, grasshopper warbler, willow tit, nightingale, curlew, water rail.

Access to the Reserve is granted (if justified) by the Nature Conservancy Furze Brook Research Station, Nr Wareham, Dorset. A variety of species, including nightjar, can be seen from footpaths and from the road along the western boundary. Leave Glastonbury westwards on the A39 and turn right half a mile past Ashcott to Shapwick. The Heath is 1½ miles past the church on the right.

A similar area, 2½ miles west of Chilton Moor has been converted to farmland but still attracts a number of birds.

STEEP HOLM
OS 165

This is a limestone plateau half a mile long lying some 5 miles west of Weston-super-Mare, and covers about 47 acres. The island has a breeding colony of 5–6,000 pairs of herring and lesser black-backed gulls with c. 75 pairs of greater black-backed gulls and 20–30 pairs of cormorants on the cliffs. In all twelve species breed. Ornithological work is directed by the Steep Holm Gull Research Station, and the main activity is ringing gull chicks.

SUMMER: herring, lesser black-backed, and greater black-backed gulls, cormorant.

Access to the island is controlled by the Steep Holm Trust and is limited to small parties at weekends in charge of leaders supplied by the Trust. Details from The Secretary, 11 Kendon Drive, Westbury-on-Trym, Bristol. The Gull Research Station is manned at irregular intervals and details are available to serious enthusiasts from The Secretary, 64 Standish Avenue, Patchway, Bristol.

Overnight accommodation is limited to camp beds and a cooker.

SUTTON BINGHAM RESERVOIR   OS 177

The reservoir lies on the Dorset border 3 miles south of Yeovil. It is T shaped, covers 145 acres, and was flooded in 1956. Its mainly natural, gently sloping banks make it attractive to good numbers of dabbling duck and the size of pintail flocks seem to be increasing. There is usually a trickle of waders on passage, and black terns are regular in autumn.

WINTER: wigeon, shoveler, pintail, gadwall, goldeneye, goosander, Bewick's swan.
SPRING: waders.
AUTUMN: waders, black tern.

Leave Yeovil westwards on the A30 and turn left outside the town on to the A37. After 1½ miles turn right on to an unclassified road leading to Sutton Bingham. This road provides excellent views over the reservoir, particularly from the causeway before the village. There are numerous vantage points to the south.

WET MOOR   OS 177

Wet Moor lies on the south side of the River Yeo, 7 miles north-west of Yeovil. Of all the Somerset Levels, this is the most reliable for winter flooding usually being 4 feet deep from mid-January to mid-February. During this period it is frequented by large numbers of dabbling duck as well as Bewick's swans. There are waders on passage in spring and autumn.

WINTER (Jan–Feb): wigeon, pintail, shoveler, tufted duck, pochard, Bewick's swan, golden plover.
SPRING: black-tailed godwit.
SUMMER: redshank, curlew, corn bunting.
AUTUMN: greenshank, snipe, ruff.

Leave Langport eastwards on the A372 and turn south on the B3165 at Long Sutton. Stop at the bridge over the Yeo just before Long Load, where footpaths lead westwards along both banks. Several minor roads lead into the Moor from the Long Load–Muchelney Road.

Suffolk

ALDE-ORE ESTUARY   OS 150; HT +3:14 Harwich at Snape Bridge

The main tidal reaches lie inland and the river enters the sea through a comparatively narrow channel which lies 9 miles south at Shingle Street. The attractions to the bird-watcher are the waders and duck, especially in winter and on passage. Avocets sometimes fly over from Havergate during the summer.

WINTER: wigeon, pintail, shelduck, turnstone, grey plover.

SUMMER: avocet.

PASSAGE: waders.

Leave the A12 3 miles south of Saxmundham, turning eastwards on to the A1094. Turn right (south) on the B1069 after 2 miles, just past Snape. After a further 1½ miles note the beautiful malt houses on the left and turn left following the signpost to Orford; then take the first on the left, signposted Iken. After 200 yards a car park sign on the left leads into a large field overlooking the estuary. Walk directly towards the estuary and take a narrow path off to the left opposite a small row of cottages.

BENACRE, COVEHITHE AND EASTON BROADS   OS 137

These coastal broads are similar and attract similar species of birds. Each is separated from the sea by only a narrow shingle beach and has a fairly large area of open water surrounded by a dense growth of reeds. Rough grazing meadows stretch inland from the broads. There are coverts of both deciduous and coniferous trees which, though strictly private, can provide interesting bird-watching from public footpaths.

Winter watching includes a good collection of duck and divers are sometimes present. Marsh harriers often fly up from Minsmere.

WINTER: teal, wigeon, goldeneye, smew.
SUMMER: sedge and reed warblers.
AUTUMN: terns, gulls, waders, marsh harrier.

Leave the A12 at Wrentham and turn eastwards to Covehithe, walk north to Benacre and south to Easton taking in the smaller Covehithe Broad on the way. Easton can also be approached northwards along the beach from Southwold via Easton Bavents, where quite recently built houses are tumbling into the sea. Sea watches from Covehithe cliffs are good.

BENACRE PITS AND NESS   OS 137

Benacre Ness lies 8 miles south of Lowestoft on the coast and 3 miles east of the A12. The Ness is an area of shingle built up by the sea that has been commercially exploited in the past and four large pits have been created parallel to the beach and separated from the sea by a hundred yards of shingle. There are patches of gorse and elder, and a long dense thorn hedge runs the length of the landward side of the northern pits. The locality is much frequented by sea fishermen especially in winter.

There are few birds of interest in the breeding season but during passage periods and in winter Benacre is a place not to be missed. The main attractions are the sea birds with divers, scoter and sawbills dominant. In autumn passerines are often present in good numbers along the thorn hedge.

WINTER: red-throated diver, sea duck, sawbills, snow bunting.
PASSAGE: terns, waders, chats, warblers.

Leave the A12 at Wrentham and turn eastwards to Covehithe. Access is on foot along the beach northwards from Covehithe, taking in Benacre Broad en route. For the fit and car-less a walk along the beach from Kessingland (A12; buses from Lowestoft) to Southwold, taking in Benacre Pits and Broad, Covehithe and Easton Broads would make a fine day.

BLYTH ESTUARY   OS 137; HT +0:35 Lowestoft at Southwold

The estuary is directly east of the A12 at Blythburgh, which is 10 miles north of Saxmundham. The River Blyth formerly ran between high banks with water meadows on either side but floods in 1921 and 1926 broke the walls and a large area became tidal. Recent attempts to reclaim the north-western section have been unsuccessful but have allowed some emergent vegetation to flourish, improving its attraction for certain species. Parts of the old embankments still exist and excellent views of the estuary can be obtained from these. They serve as roosts for waders and gulls.

The main attraction is the number of waders and black-tailed godwits are particularly numerous in spring, often reaching 300. Autumn passage is good and several hundred duck are present in winter. Gadwall and spotted redshank in winter are specialities. There is considerable movement to Walberswick marshes at high tide. Both areas are part of the Walberswick National Nature Reserve.

WINTER: spotted redshank, wigeon, shelduck.
SPRING: black-tailed godwit, bar-tailed godwit, grey plover, whimbrel.
SUMMER: redshank, common tern, shelduck.
AUTUMN: spotted redshank, little stint, knot, grey plover, whimbrel.

Good views can be obtained from the roadside embankment a quarter of a mile north of Blythburgh on the A12. Further views can be obtained by walking eastwards along a footpath starting at a row of cottages near the inn. This is an old railway track and surrounding land is private. Southwold is an ideal centre and the quay at Reydon allows access to another excellent area.

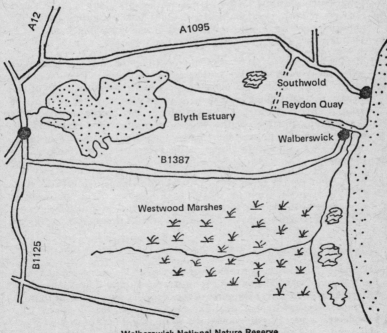

Walberswick National Nature Reserve

BRECKLAND

See Cambridgeshire.

DEBEN ESTUARY OS 150; HT +0:43 Harwich

The estuary stretches from the coast 2 miles north of Felixstowe some 8 miles inland to Woodbridge. It is a narrow estuary especially in the lower reaches, and though it is a major wildfowl resort birds tend to be spread out along the entire length and are, therefore, less immediately impressive than the concentrations on, for instance, the Stour to the south. For this reason the Deben has been rather neglected.

WINTER: teal, wigeon, shelduck, turnstone.
SPRING: turnstone, black-tailed godwit.
AUTUMN: waders.

1. Leave the A12 at the Woodbridge by-pass and follow signposts towards the town. At Melton, 1 mile to the north, turn eastwards over the river and take the right hand fork on to B1083. Continue for 4 miles and turn right by Shottisham Hall half a mile past Shottisham. After 1½ miles turn right for Ramsholt Quay.

2. Leave the A12 at Martlesham opposite the Red Lion, 2 miles south of Woodbridge turn eastwards into a maze of tiny lanes and follow signposts to Waldringfield. A footpath along the edge of the estuary to the north gives extensive views over the best part of the saltings after 600 yards. This right of way has been camouflaged by the yachting interests of the village. A notice with 'PRIVATE' in capital letters deters most but small letters, insignificant at a distance, explain that visitors must keep to the footpath and not stray on to the quay.

3. Kirton, which is signposted Newbourn/Hemley from Waldringfield, and Kirton from the A1093 to Felixstowe. A signpost points eastwards in the village to Park Lane. Follow this until the metalled surface ends. Turn right along the footpath to the shore.

HAVERGATE ISLAND OS 150

Havergate is situated in the estuary of the Ore and is only separated from the sea by the shingle spit of Orfordness. Two miles downstream from Orford, the island covers 280 acres of former water meadows that through wartime neglect and subsequent management have been converted into a wonderful wader marsh. Almost the entire island lies below high water mark and newly constructed sluices enable the water level to be carefully controlled to attract the maximum number of species. The RSPB was quick to acquire the island when avocets were found breeding in 1947 and it has since become synonymous with the avocet so that its other attractions tend to be unnoticed. Winter brings a very large wildfowl population amongst which pintail and Bewick's swans are notable.

WINTER: pintail, shoveler, wigeon, Bewick's swan, knot, grey plover, short-eared owl, merlin, hen harrier.

SPRING: godwits, whimbrel, turnstone.

SUMMER: avocet, common and Sandwich terns, short-eared owls.

AUTUMN: godwits, ruff, greenshank, green, wood and curlew sandpipers, little stint.

Access to the island is by boat from Orford Quay, escorted by the Warden. Permits must be booked in advance from the RSPB and are limited to twelve on any one day. The reserve is not open every day and intending visitors should consult the Society well in advance.

LOWESTOFT HARBOUR AND NESS OS 137

The harbour is a formal concrete and wood structure and is the centre of Lowestoft's commercial life, thronged with fishing boats throughout the year. It is little more than 400 yards long and lies to the north of the swing bridge that links the two halves of the town.

The Ness is the easternmost point of England and lies a quarter of a mile north of the harbour. It is a somewhat uninspiring spot consisting of a concrete promenade and numerous wooden groynes.

Both localities are for winter bird-watching only. The harbour frequently holds sea duck and the sea outside is one of the main resorts of pochard in Suffolk. Purple sandpipers, rare on this coast, winter. The Ness is thronged by gulls and the occasional rarity can be spotted. Summer visitors should see the kittiwake colony on South Pier.

WINTER: eider, pochard, grebes, gulls, purple sandpiper.

SUMMER: kittiwake.

The harbour is easily found and is best worked from the northern end and southward along the sea wall to the harbour mouth. Returning northwards continue straight on to the Ness.

MINSMERE OS 137

Minsmere is situated on the coast about 2 miles south of Dunwich. It is one of the most important reserves of the RSPB and covers 1,500 acres of marsh, lagoon, reed, heath and woodland. From the point of view of the number of species seen it is probably the best place in Britain for a day's bird-watching. In many ways it is similar to the Walberswick area to the north but has been considerably improved to attract and leave undisturbed a great variety of unusual birds. The coastal dune system protects large lagoons with islands known as 'The Scrape' that harbour breeding avocets and terns and swarm with waders in spring and autumn. Westwards there is an extensive reed bed with large patches of open water, providing a habitat for duck and the regular spoonbill. The woodland is a delightful area and contains most of the song birds one could expect to see in southern England, while the heath is excellent and stone curlew breed on the specially prepared fields. There are several well sited hides giving undisturbed views over the most interesting areas. The bushes at the sluice are a notable 'rarity' place and have had Radde's and Pallas' warblers in a week.

WINTER: Bewick's swan, hen harrier, marsh harrier, waders.

SPRING: whimbrel, spotted redshank.

SUMMER: avocet, marsh harrier, common and Sandwich terns, bearded tit, stone curlew, red-backed shrike, nightingale, Savi's sedge and reed warblers, corn bunting, bittern, garganey, shoveler.

AUTUMN: spotted redshank, little stint, curlew sandpiper, black tern, spoonbill, great grey shrike.

Access is by permit in advance only. Full details for the current year are available from the RSPB.

The reserve is approached along a road leaving the Dunwich-Westleton road to the south, threequarters of a mile from Dunwich. This runs into a rough track after 1¼ miles when a small toll may have to be paid. Continue past the Coastguard Cottages to the hill overlooking the reserve. At this point a good look at the sea is often fruitful.

Continue on foot southward between the sea walls until a gate with a notice on the right invites your entry, if a permit holder. For non-permit holders public hides to the south of the official entrance give excellent views of the pools and avocets.

Alternatively visitors may motor in by leaving Westleton eastwards to Eastbridge and thence following sign posts.

ORWELL ESTUARY OS 150; HT +0:21 Harwich

The estuary of the Orwell stretches from Harwich some 8 miles inland to Ipswich. In places it is almost a mile wide and has larger areas of mud than the Deben to the north. Like that water it is narrowest in the lower reaches and most concentrations of birds occur at Pinmill or above. Black-tailed and bar-tailed godwits winter and passage brings large numbers of several species of wader.

WINTER: wigeon, pintail, shoveler, goldeneye, godwits, turnstone, redshank, knot.

SPRING: turnstone, black-tailed godwit.

AUTUMN: redshank, turnstone, whimbrel.

Leaving Ipswich by the A137, turn left after 2 miles on to the A138 and enjoy views of the estuary on your left for 1 mile. The only other point of access is from Pinmill, turn left at Chelmondiston. Footpaths to east and west give views of the best parts.

STOUR ESTUARY   OS 150; HT +0:40 Harwich

The estuary lies on the Essex border and provides not only the largest expanse of tidal water but also the primary resort of wildfowl in Suffolk. Being rather shallow, diving duck are scarce but wigeon and shelduck are particularly numerous on the huge mudbanks on both shores. Wigeon frequently number 4,000 and have reached 13,700. Both species of godwit winter, and the black-tailed builds up to sizeable flocks in spring. The concentration of mute swans, up to 900, at the malthouses at Mistley in autumn is notable.

WINTER: wigeon, pintail, shelduck, brent goose, godwits, grey plover.
SPRING: black-tailed godwit, turnstone.
AUTUMN: waders, mute swan.

There are four basic approaches to the Stour, all start from Manningtree Station on the A137, 10 miles south of Ipswich and north of Colchester.

On the Essex shore:

1. Take the road to Manningtree from the station and continue, joining the B1352 to Mistley to see the autumn gathering of mute swans.

2. Continue through Bradfield and take the second turning left after two miles. There is an inn on the corner. This road passes under the railway and a track leaves to the left after 200 yards to Jacques Bay. Return to and continue along the metalled road to Wrabness Halt where a track leads off to the left for views over Copperas Bay.

3. The section from Copperas to Harwich is the primary haunt of brent geese and is viewed from the Parkston Quay area.

On the Suffolk shore:

4. Leave Manningtree station by the A137 northwards, keep right after 3 miles on the B1080 to Stutton. Turn right and then left to the church. Continue past the church to Holbrook Bay. Returning, turn right past the church to the B1080 then turn right to Holbrook. Turn right past the church and continue to Harkstead in 2 miles. Turn right down to Holbrook Bay.

WALBERSWICK NATIONAL NATURE RESERVE   OS 137

Situated on the coast 1 mile south of Southwold, Walberswick has a variety of habitat that makes it a good centre. The dune beach protects an area of low lying ground that extends inland for some 2½ miles and which is drained by the Dunwich River. The area clearly shows the effects of various degrees of salinity and the principle habitats may be classified as follows: a series of shallow brackish pools behind the sea wall, exposing considerable areas of mud; a huge reed bed with a few open lagoons, which gives way to rough grass and thorn and birch scrub; the final habitat is the dry heathland which is being invaded by birch scrub and which is dotted with old pine and mixed coverts. The Dingle Hills were formerly a rabbit-warren but myxamotosis decimated the rabbits and gorse has grown largely unchecked. The hills are used by the Dingle Bird Club as a bird observatory and ringing station.

Specialities of the area include a large range of breeding birds. In spring and autumn wader passage is often excellent and the Dingle Hills are worth a look for passerines. Winter brings fair numbers of duck, regular hen harriers and good numbers of snow buntings.

Most of the area is within the Nature Reserve and visitors must keep

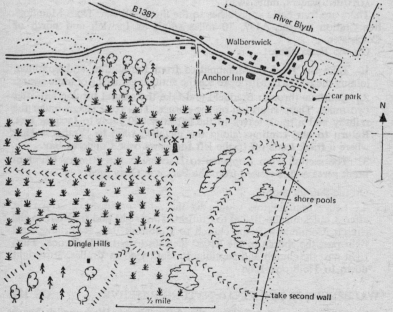

Walberswick Lagoon: walk southward along the shore from the car park and be careful about taking the correct wall. Left at the Wind pump to Hoist Covert and the heath beyond.

to the rights of way and paths which are marked on the very clear notice-board maps. The coverts and heath in particular are sacrosanct, not only because of the breeding birds but because they are preserved as shooting, and well-keepered shooting at that.

WINTER: gadwall, hen harrier, marsh harrier, short-eared owl, great grey shrike, snow bunting, twite, waders.

SPRING: whimbrel, sanderling.

SUMMER: sedge, reed grasshopper and Savi's warblers, long-eared owl, red-backed shrike, nightjar, terns, bittern, bearded tit, redshank, ringed plover.

AUTUMN: ruff, little stint, curlew sandpiper, marsh harrier, snow bunting, twite, shore lark.

Leaving the A12 one mile south of Blythburgh, turn eastwards on to the B387 and continue on to the B1387 after 1 mile. Leave the village south-wards along the beach. Take the second wall past this area to the wind-pump. Head past the windpump towards Hoist Covert, watching out for warblers, and on leaving the marsh, look out for red-backed shrike, and rarities in the bushes. Arriving at a road turn right to the village past collared doves in some well fir-treed gardens. The most interesting species can be seen from this route.

WESTLETON HEATH   OS 137

Westleton Heath, together with the area of heath to the south of the Westleton-Dunwich road which lies within the Minsmere reserve, forms the largest remnant of the East Suffolk heathlands. The area concerning us here, covering 117 acres, is a National Nature Reserve and stretches north of the Dunwich–Westleton road as far as the forestry plantations to the north and east. The area is dominated by heather and scattered clumps of birches. The western boundary consists of a belt of tall trees and tangled bushes which are regularly frequented by shrikes and corn bunting. The open sandy parts are used by stone curlews that fly in in the evenings.

WINTER: corn bunting, great grey shrike.

SUMMER: red-backed shrike, whinchat, nightjar, stone curlew.

Leave the A12 one mile north of Yoxford, turning right signposted Westleton. Leaving the village northwards, take the right-hand fork at the top of the village green towards Dunwich. Watchers should keep strictly to the rights of way, or seek a permit from the Nature Conservancy.

Surrey

CHOBHAM COMMON   OS 170

The common lies between Sunningdale and Chobham, covers 1,648
acres and is one of the largest areas of open heath in this well endowed
county. Apart from the typical heathland birds the area has a number
of specialities.

SUMMER: woodlark, red-backed shrike, redstart, wood warbler.

Take the B383 southwards from Sunningdale or northwards from
Chobham to the cross roads with the B386. Explore, especially to the
north-east.

FRENSHAM COMMON AND PONDS   OS 169

The common lies on either side of the A287 roughly half way between
Farnham and Hindhead and covers 650 acres of heather with Scots pine.
The area is a rough, sandy waste with numerous hills giving wide views
over the surrounding countryside. Birch scrub and plantations of
deciduous trees are more numerous in the eastern part beyond the Little
Pond. The two ponds are not particularly exciting from a wildfowl point
of view but in summer the whole area is alive with small passerines. In
particular the area of pines, birches and scrub near the main road on
the Little Pond side is excellent. Buzzards now breed in the vicinity and
can occasionally be seen soaring.

SUMMER: hobby, stonechat, woodlark, nightjar, warblers, wood warbler,
lesser whitethroat, redstart, nightingale, goldcrest, buzzard.

WINTER: siskin, redpoll, great grey shrike, wildfowl.

Leave the A287 at the Great Pond car park on the northern side. The
whole area can be explored by the numerous tracks.

HANKLEY COMMON OS 169

Situated roughly in the centre of the triangle between Farnham, Hindhead and Milford, Hankley Common extends to 745 acres, it has a larger area of heather than the nearby commons thus making for a more boring and birdless scene. Odd clumps of Scots pine break the monotony while on the western border high on the ridge that runs north to south is a growth of birch scrub and pines that shelters many species.

SUMMER: nightjar, warblers, redstart, goldcrest.

Watch out for signposts along the Tilford–Churt road to the east between the houses. A muddy track at the southern corner leads uphill through woodland to the heath. Continue uphill, no path, for gorgeous views over deserted heather. Explore northwards and end a Sunday stroll watching the cricket on Tilford Village Green from the Barley Mow.

THURSLEY AND OCKLEY COMMONS OS 169

The two commons are to the west of the A3, between Milford and Hindhead. The large area (893 acres) has a variety of habitats from wet bog, through grass, heather, birch scrub, to mature woodland and fir plantations. Apart from its value as a winter haunt of great grey shrike, it has a large variety of breeding species.

WINTER: great grey shrike.

SUMMER: hobby, redshank, curlew, snipe, tufted duck, woodlark, grasshopper warbler, nightingale, redstart, stonechat, tree pipit, wood warbler.

Leave the A3 westwards at Milford on the B3001 to Elstead. Turn left and park near Hammer Pond on the left. Gumboots are essential if one is to explore in all directions. The area is a reserve of the Surrey NT.

Sussex

AMBERLEY WILD BROOKS   OS 182

Situated in the Arun valley near Arundel and together with the levels
between Pulborough and Greatham form the most important area for
wildfowl in Sussex. The new year is the best time. Wigeon sometimes
exceed 4,000, whitefronts, pink-feet and greylags have all been noted,
and Bewick's swans are becoming regular.

WINTER: wigeon, teal, pintail, shoveler, pochard, mute and Bewick's
swans.

Leave A29 six miles south of Pulborough at its junction with A284.
Take the B2139 to Amberley. In the village and round to the east are
several tracks leading to the Wild Brooks.

ARUNDEL REFUGE   OS 182

The Wildfowl Trust has plans to open a refuge on a 60-acre site near
Arundel Castle. Nearly half this area will remain wild and include a
reed-bed.

ASHDOWN FOREST   OS 183

This is a large area of open heathland with some woodland lying
immediately south-east of East Grinstead. The vegetation is mainly rough
grass with areas of heather and gorse.

SUMMER: stonechat, woodlark, nightjar, tree pipit.

The whole of the heathland area is of free public access, but most of the woodland is private. Areas worth a look are:

1. Isle of Thorns, between A22 and A275 south of Wych Cross.
2. The area north-west of Camp Hill on the B2026.
3. The area between B2026 and B2188.

BEACHY HEAD   OS 183

Beachy Head is an excellent place for viewing movements of sea birds offshore because of its geographical position jutting out into the Channel and the extremely good visibility provided by its height (over 500 feet). Divers, terns and gulls are noted in numbers, and in autumn visible movements of hirundines in September, and finches and pipits in October are very heavy. The establishment of an observatory in the area has drawn attention to concentrations of warblers, chats and flycatchers, and Beachy Head is now the most important site in the county for migration studies. The ringing centre is at Whitebread Hollow.

SPRING AND AUTUMN: divers, terns, hirundines, finches, pipits, warblers, chats, flycatchers.

Leave the A259 at Eastdean southwards to Birling and the Head. Alternatively leave Eastbourne southwards along the promenade and turn left on top of the downs after a twisting climb away from the coast.

Whitebread Hollow should not be disturbed by casual visitors; anyone seriously interested in the ringing station should contact The Sussex Ornithological Society.

CHICHESTER GRAVEL PITS   OS 181

There are two main groups of pits north-east and south-east of Chichester, within 4 miles of the sea. Dabbling duck are dominant in autumn and as their number declines with winter so the number of diving duck increase to a peak of several hundred.

During passage periods terns and gulls are numerous with black tern regular, but the ornithology of the pit is dominated by the huge passage of hirundines that use the area as a major staging roost. Over 6,000 sand martins are ringed annually by a group formed to take advantage of the concentration.

WINTER: gadwall, pochard, tufted duck, scaup, great crested grebe.

AUTUMN: teal, sand martin, swallow, sedge and reed warblers.

The A27 round the east and south sides of Chichester passes most of the pits, but at the southern roundabout with the A259 take an obscure unclassified road to Runcton and fork right among the pits. Most can be viewed from the roads and open tracks.

CHICHESTER HARBOUR   OS 181; HT +0:15 Portsmouth

The Harbour lies on the Hants-Sussex border and is closely related to
Langstone and Portsmouth Harbours which lie in Hampshire. Records
for Chichester are published in both county reports though the bulk of
the area lies in Sussex. Wildfowl are quite numerous in winter with
dark-bellied brent geese (up to 500) the main attraction. Waders are
numerous and the usual population includes both godwits (bar-tailed
more numerous). In spring numbers increase, while the huge autumn
numbers reach a peak in September. The occasional ruff is found in
winter and Black Point is a favourite winter haunt of the occasional
little stint.

Divers are present in winter and both black-necked and Slavonian
grebes are regular.

WINTER: brent goose, wigeon, shelduck, eider, merganser, grey plover,
turnstone, knot, godwits, sanderling, divers, grebes.

SPRING: whimbrel, turnstone, godwits, sanderling.

AUTUMN: waders, green sandpiper, spotted redshank, greenshank,
curlew sandpiper, little stint, godwits, grey plover, turnstone.

In Hampshire:

1. Leave the A27 at Havant southwards on the B2149 to Hayling
Island. At Hayling Bay turn left along the coast to Black Point for
excellent views of the mouth.

In Sussex:

2. Leave Chichester southwards on the A286 and after 1½ miles turn
right to Dell Quay.

3. Continue on A286 past Manhood End, once a splendid place now
a marina, and turn right to West Itchenor. Though a sailing resort a
walk westwards along the harbour shore gives good views towards
Thorney Island after a half mile.

4. Continue on A286 to West Wittering where there is a car park
in summer. Walk along the foreshore to East Head.

CUCKMERE HAVEN   OS 183

Cuckmere Haven lies at the mouth of the Cuckmere River between
Seaford and Eastbourne. In the lower part of its course the river meanders
over a flat valley and has left numerous oxbow lakes amongst the water
meadows. The mouth provides a break in an otherwise rocky shore and
attracts a number of waders especially on passage. Migration is often
interesting and to the west Newhaven Harbour has purple sandpipers
in winter.

WINTER: wigeon, waders.

SPRING AND AUTUMN: waders, chats, warblers, wagtails, gulls, terns.

Leave the A259 southwards 1½ miles east of Seaford to South Hill. Continue on foot to the Haven and take the path up the west bank of the river to Exceat Bridge.

LANGNEY POINT AND THE CRUMBLES   OS 183

This spot consists of a shingle peninsula similar to Dungeness and a few quite small pits immediately east of Eastbourne. The point is good for sea-watching and has produced a string of rare and extremely rare birds. Perhaps the sewage outfall here adds attraction to an already well-sited area. Scoter and skuas and divers are regularly seen but terns and gulls are dominant. Mediterranean gull, black and roseate terns are noted most years. Chats are numerous on the shingle on passage and warblers shelter in the few patches of cover, amongst the dense undergrowth in the area between Eastbourne and the new estate, and at the Crumbles.

SPRING: divers, skuas, gulls, terns, roseate tern, chats.

AUTUMN: skuas, gulls, Mediterranean gull, terns, black tern, chats, warblers, rarities.

Leave Eastbourne north-eastwards on the A259. Wallis Avenue runs through a new housing estate out to the point. Further eastward take the B2191 at a roundabout and turn right off the road immediately past King's Caravan Site for the Crumbles. At the point the flying of red flags marks the range area out of bounds. Signs show the whereabouts of the sewage outfall. The area is now much frequented by fisherman and tourists and the housing estate will soon reach the shore.

THE MIDRIPS AND THE WICKS   OS 184

Situated on the Kent boundary on the western side of the peninsula that terminates at Dungeness. A series of shallow pools lie immediately behind the high shingle beach, being flooded by sea water passing through the beach at high tides. Though the water level has always been variable recent improvements to the sea wall may alter the attractiveness of the area. Snow buntings feed on the beach in winter and short-eared owls hunt the rough ground.

During passage periods gulls, terns and skuas are regularly noted offshore. Waders are numerous and the more interesting species are frequently present. Rarities have a habit of turning up here.

WINTER: wigeon, pintail, shoveler, snow bunting, short-eared owl.

SPRING AND AUTUMN: terns, gulls, skuas, waders.

Leave Rye eastwards on the A259 and turn right after 1 mile at Gulde-ford. Pass Camber and where the road leaves the coast park on the left. Walk up a track past some houses on to the sea wall and continue east-wards. If a red flag is flying the Lydd ranges are in use and access is forbidden.

PAGHAM HARBOUR   OS 181; HT —0:01 Portsmouth

The harbour is on the eastern side of the peninsula that ends in Selsey Bill and has been a nature reserve since 1964. Though the harbour was reclaimed in 1876 the sea regained control in 1910 since when the area of approximately 1 square mile has been one of the most notable bird haunts in the county. Wildfowl are never very numerous but include brent geese. Winter waders include both godwits and the pools at Sidlesham are extremely productive during migration.

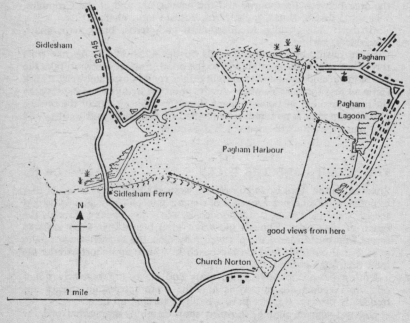

Pagham Harbour: a local nature reserve and interesting bird resort at all seasons

WINTER: brent goose, eider, merganser, scoter, grey plover, turnstone, godwits, sanderling.
SPRING: whimbrel, turnstone, ringed plover.
SUMMER: little tern, ringed plover.
AUTUMN: whimbrel, wood sandpiper, spotted redshank, greenshank, knot, little stint, ruff, warblers, chats, short-eared owl.
Leave Chichester southwards on the B2145 or B2201 to Sidlesham:

1. The pools at Ferry Ho. Sidlesham are worth investigating, and paths run along the eastern side of the main pool, and along the south side of the harbour.

2. Continue to Church Norton and view harbour and sea.

3. Leave Chichester on the B2145 but turn left after 1 mile on to the B2166. After 2 miles turn right to Pagham. Continue right, past the church. A track leads to the right to the harbour wall. Turn left out along the shore line to the sea and Pagham Lagoon, the large water between the caravan site and the sea.

RYE HARBOUR AND PITS
OS 184; HT —0:05 Dover

Near Rye, in the south-eastern corner of the county, on the western bank of the Rother, the large shingle build-up that has separated Rye from the sea has been extensively excavated over many years and an intricate series of pits created. Rye Bay is noted for its huge flocks of scoter and velvet scoter, and eider are regular at Rother mouth. Migrants, waders and chats are numerous and rarities regularly occur amongst the terns and gulls.

WINTER: scoter, velvet scoter, eider, waders.
SPRING: waders, terns, gulls, chats.
SUMMER: black-headed gull, little and common tern, ringed plover, redshank, oystercatcher, wheatear.
AUTUMN: terns, black tern, waders, chats, rarities.
Leave the A259 southwards on the southern side of Rye. Cross the Royal Military Canal and continue past factories to Rye Harbour. A track on the right past the church leads to the main group of pits. Return via the sea and other pits to the harbour mouth. Access to the nature reserve is by permit only but there are hides overlooking some of the best tern islands.

SELSEY BILL
OS 181

Selsey Bill is at the extreme south-western tip of the county and was the site of a bird observatory until bungalow development completely occupied the area. In spite of this, the Bill retains its attraction as a site for sea-watching. Passerines still occur and can be watched flitting through back-garden fences.

In winter divers and sea duck are sometimes numerous, and skuas, terns and fulmars are noted in April. Shearwaters join these species on the return passage, and visible migration is heavy in October.

WINTER: red-throated diver, merganser, scoter.

SPRING: divers, terns, skuas, fulmar, passerines, gull-billed tern, rarities.

SUMMER: collared dove.

AUTUMN: terns, skuas, pomarine skua, fulmar, Manx shearwater, Mediterranean gull, passerines, visible migrants.

Leave Chichester southward on the B2201 or B2145 and continue to the sea at Selsey Bill. The path eastward along the shore is best.

WEIRWOOD RESERVOIR   OS 183

This water is situated 2 miles south of East Grinstead and was created in 1956 by damming the head streams of the River Medway. The 280 acre reservoir has natural banks and is set amongst pleasant woodland and agricultural land. The commoner duck number several hundred, and other species are noted in small numbers.

Waders are regular on passage with a sprinkling of unusual species in autumn. Most concentrate at the shallows at the western end.

WINTER: teal, wigeon, tufted duck, pochard, great crested grebe.

SPRING AND AUTUMN: waders, garganey.

Take the B2110 from East Grinstead centre but immediately turn left. Pass Saint Hill and later turn left on a metalled cul-de-sac to reservoir. A footpath eastward gives good views. Return to road and continue to western end of reservoir for views of marshy shallows.

West Midlands (Staffordshire, Warwickshire and Worcestershire)

WEST MIDLANDS BIRD CLUB.

The Club covers all three counties and holds a regular programme of indoor and field meetings. It is a very active club and is frequently ahead of even national organisations. It got on with an atlas project while others formed committees.

WEST MIDLANDS TRUST FOR NATURE CONSERVATION.

READ: *The Birds of Staffordshire*, J. Lord and A. R. M. Blake. *Atlas of Breeding Birds of the West Midlands*, ed J. Lord and D. J. Munns. *The Birds of Worcestershire*, A. J. Harthan.

ALVECOTE POOLS (Warwick) OS 120

The pools lie east of Tamworth, 2 miles north of the A5. Extensive areas of mining subsidence along the River Tame have created a series of shallow pools that provide a wealth of rich habitat including open water, reed-marsh, damp bog and thorn. The 100 acre area is a local nature reserve of the West Midland Trust for Nature Conservation.

The commoner duck are frequently present in large numbers. Wader passage is heavy, especially in autumn when black and commic terns also pass through. The reserve is extensively used by school parties for field work and by fishermen in winter, and is an excellent example of co-operation of differing interests.

WINTER: teal, wigeon, tufted duck, pochard, snipe.

SPRING: waders, terns.

SUMMER, snipe, redshank, reed warbler, lesser whitethroat, kingfisher.

AUTUMN: little ringed plover, common sandpiper, greenshank, ruff, black and commic terns.

Leave Tamworth eastwards on the A51 and turn left under the railway viaduct on to an unclassified road signposted 'Amington'. Continue to the pools, most of which can be seen from the road. Excellent bird-watching with a permit from West Midland Trust for Nature Conservation.

AQUALATE MERE (Stafford) OS 119

The mere is 10 miles west of Stafford and just over 1 mile from Newport. It is a natural lake, rather shallow, with reeds and some muddy edges surrounded by a boggy area of wet pasture on three sides. To the south lies Aqualate Park and Hall, of which it is part.

WINTER: wigeon, shoveler, pochard, tufted duck, goosander, Canada goose.

The mere and park are strictly private and entry is only by permission of The Estate Office, Aqualate Hall, Newport.

BARTLEY RESERVOIR (Warwick) OS 131

The reservoir is some 5 miles from central Birmingham and is used for storing pure water prior to direct distribution. For this reason all birds have been discouraged by the Water Department by the use of bangers. Though this has had an effect on the wildfowl population, it has not prevented the water being used by passing migrants, including waders and terns, especially black terns in autumn.

WINTER (erratic): wigeon, goosander, goldeneye.

SPRING AND AUTUMN: ringed plover, greenshank, dunlin, black tern.

Leave Birmingham south-westwards to Selly Oak, then right through a maze of lanes to Bartley Green. Take the narrow lane from the roundabout southwards past the western end of the water and view from the road. See OS.

BELVIDE RESERVOIR (Stafford) OS 119

This water lies north of Wolverhampton alongside the A5. It is a natural banked reservoir set among low lying agricultural land. There are large numbers of common duck as well as smew in late winter. The water collects the odd rare grebe and diver, and wader passage is regular. Black and commic terns are frequent and occasionally numerous.

WINTER: wigeon, shoveler, pochard, goldeneye, goosander, smew, Canada goose, snipe.

SPRING: waders, black and commic terns, garganey.

SUMMER: redshank, yellow wagtail.

AUTUMN: whimbrel, green sandpiper, greenshank, ruff, black and commic terns, garganey.

Leave Cannock westwards on the A5. The reservoir is to the south after 6 miles and can be seen from the road and from a track at the western end. Permits can be obtained from the West Midland Bird Club.

BITTELL RESERVOIRS (Worcester) OS 131

Situated south of Birmingham and west of the A441 near Barnt Green.

The largest pool which is half a mile long is the most attractive to wild-fowl which are regular in good numbers. Great crested grebes breed and sometimes form large flocks, and the occasional rarer grebe turns up from time to time. Small numbers of waders are regular along the natural edges in autumn.

WINTER: teal, wigeon, pochard, goldeneye, Canada goose.

SPRING AND SUMMER: great crested grebe.

AUTUMN: grebes, ringed plover, jack snipe, greenshank, dunlin, terns.

Leave Birmingham southwards on the A441, turn right towards Barnt Green a quarter of a mile past Hopwood. At the causeway across the smaller pool stop, and then turn sharp right up a narrow lane to view the upper reservoir.

BLITHFIELD RESERVOIR (Stafford) OS 120

This is an 800 acre water, 2½ miles by half a mile, between Rugeley and Uttoxeter. It was flooded in 1952 and is now ranked third amongst English reservoirs. Teal and wigeon both have peaks over 1,000, and pochard and tufted over 500. Shoveler, goosander and Canada goose all reach three figures, and flocks of goldeneye are quite large. Great crested grebes are numerous and the rarer grebes and divers turn up regularly.

Wader passage is the best in the West Midland area and black terns are present on both passages along with commic terns, and little gulls in autumn.

WINTER: wigeon, pochard, shoveler, goosander, goldeneye, pintail, Canada goose, Bewick's swan, great crested grebe, snipe, jack snipe.

SPRING: waders, black and commic terns.

AUTUMN: little ringed plover, turnstone, whimbrel, sandpipers, spotted redshank, little stint, curlew sandpiper, ruff, black and commic terns, little gull.

Leave Rugeley northwards on the B5013 to the reservoir causeway in 4 miles. A road southwards on the east side gives good views but only early in the morning because of light conditions.

BRANSTON GRAVEL PITS (Stafford) OS 120

The pits lie 2 miles south-west of Burton-upon-Trent on either side of the A38. They are still being extended, are rather bare, and the main attraction is wildfowl and other aquatic species. Diving duck are numerous and a few waders pass through on both passages.

WINTER: tufted duck, pochard, teal, goosander, Canada goose.

Leave Burton-upon-Trent southwards on the A38. Pass through Branston and the gravel pits lie on either side of the road. The pit on the eastern side can be seen from the road.

CANNOCK CHASE (Stafford) OS 119 and 120

This is a large stretch of infertile sandy heath, covering 25 square miles between Stafford, Rugeley and Cannock. Its natural vegetation is largely heather and bracken, though large areas have been planted with conifers by the Forestry Commission. Typical heathland and woodland birds breed freely and a few red grouse still survive. The area is partly common land and partly privately owned, and is the best in the West Midlands for oddities like harriers and shrikes.

WINTER: redpoll, siskin, stonechat.

SUMMER: nightjar, whinchat, redstart, wood and grasshopper warblers, long-eared owl, red grouse.

Within such a large area cover is generally inadequate and watchers are urged to explore unknown sites. For a casual visit the area in the west around Brocton Field and Anson's Bank is very rewarding with special interest along the Sherbrook Valley, though Brownhills Common in the south is conveniently near the urban areas.

CANNOCK RESERVOIR (Stafford) OS 120

The reservoir lies just north of the A5 one mile from Brownhills and is set in an industrial landscape of slag heaps and desolate waste ground. Even its regular species which are mainly numbers of diving duck do not hold much excitement. It does, however, attract a number of unusual species fairly regularly, and oddities like snow buntings seem to turn up here more often than anywhere else in the area.

WINTER: tufted duck, pochard, sea duck, divers, grebes, oddities.

SPRING: waders, black tern.

AUTUMN: little ringed plover, turnstone, common sandpiper, greenshank, black and commic terns, oddities.

Leave the A5 just east of its junction with the A452 near Brownhills. Turn northwards into Wilkin or Hednesford Roads. After half a mile turn right on an industrial track just before a small pool. Continue across grey clay to the bare reservoir. There are plans for a leisure centre.

COOMBS VALLEY, LEEK (Stafford) OS 111

An RSPB reserve covers 191 acres of this beautiful valley. The Coombs Brook is a swift flowing, boulder strewn stream beloved by dippers, and is flanked on both sides by stands of mixed woodland. There are also some area of open bracken heath with birches. Breeding birds include black grouse, little owl and sparrow hawk.

SUMMER: sparrow hawk, little owl, dipper, kingfisher, grey wagtail, red and black grouse, woodcock, wheatear, stonechat, whinchat, redstart.

Free access by permit from RSPB from April to July, Saturday, Sunday, Tuesday, Thursday. There is a nature trail and a guide is available from the warden.

COPMERE (Stafford)   OS 119

Copmere lies 9 miles north-west of Stafford and 2 miles west of Eccleshall. It is a beautiful little reed fringed lake about a quarter of a mile square set in deciduous woodland and is a notable haunt of wildfowl regularly attracting a variety of species that can be seen at close range.

WINTER: teal, wigeon, tufted duck, pochard, goldeneye, goosander, water rail.

Leave Stafford north-westwards on the A5013 to Eccleshall. Turn left on to the B5026 and in 1½ miles turn left, following the signpost to Offley Hay and Bishops of Fley. Pass a pool and view the mere between the trees.

GAILEY RESERVOIRS (Stafford)   OS 119

These three pools lie alongside the A5 north of Wolverhampton, just west of Cannock. They are artificially embanked pools built to feed the nearby Staffordshire and Worcester Canal and surrounded by woodland. Diving duck predominate and cormorants are present through the winter and can be seen sitting on the pine trees on the tiny island.

WINTER: pochard, tufted duck, goldeneye, cormorant.

SUMMER: tufted duck, cormorant.

Leave Cannock westwards on the A5. The reservoirs can be seen to the north of the road between the trees but permits can be obtained from the West Midland Bird Club. Park in lay-by on the south side of the very busy road.

WYRE FOREST (Worcester)   OS 130

The forest is placed 5 miles west of Kidderminster and is 3 miles by 2 miles. It is an old forest of predominantly deciduous species but with an interesting sprinkling of conifers. It is bisected by a railway which runs alongside the attractive Dowles Brook.

SUMMER: kingfisher, redstart, pied flycatcher, tree pipit, wood warbler, warblers.

Leave Kidderminster westwards on the A456 and turn right at Bewdley on to the B4194. In 2½ miles stop at Buttonoak and explore southwards on footpaths.

Wiltshire

BY BROOK
OS 156

This beautiful stream runs through a deep, wooded valley for several miles but is at its best on either side of Castle Combe, voted the most beautiful village in England, north of the A420, 5 miles west of Chippenham.

A wide variety of woodland species breed.

SUMMER: dipper, grey wagtail, redstart, wood warbler.

Leave Chippenham westwards on the A420. Fork right on to the B4039 after 2½ miles and in 3 miles turn left at Castle Combe. Cross the bridge and walk north or south along the river.

COATE WATER
OS 157

The lake is threequarters of a mile long and lies in a public park on the south-east outskirts of Swindon. It is a notable haunt of wildfowl regularly holding several hundred birds. There is a sizeable roost of hirundines in autumn.

WINTER: teal, wigeon, pochard, Canada goose, snipe, jack snipe.

SPRING: garganey.

SUMMER: sedge and reed warblers.

AUTUMN: common sandpiper, black tern, swallow, sand martin.

Leave Swindon south-eastwards on the A345 and fork right in the outskirts to view the lake from the south. Access is straightforward from Coate village to the north.

CORSHAM LAKE
OS 156

The lake lies in the grounds of Corsham Court, which were laid out by

'Capability' Brown, some 3 miles south-west of Chippenham. Though quite small it holds numbers of wildfowl and black and commic terns occur irregularly on passage.

WINTER: teal, wigeon, tufted duck, pochard, shoveler.
SUMMER: sedge and reed warblers, lesser spotted woodpecker.
AUTUMN: black tern.

Corsham is open to the public on Sundays throughout the year and daily, except Monday, during the summer. Leave Chippenham westwards on the A4.

LONGLEAT LAKE AND SHEARWATER   OS 166

Longleat Lake is set in the grounds of the mansion of that name, one of the finest Elizabethan houses in Britain with grounds by 'Capability' Brown, and is really a chain of lakes, the largest being half a mile long. Shearwater is a larger lake, lying 3 miles to the east and separated from Longleat by an extensive area of woodland. Wildfowl of a fair variety are present and there is usually a good collection of winter finches.

WINTER: teal, shoveler, pochard, tufted duck, redpoll, siskin.
SUMMER: buzzard, sparrowhawk, redstart, wood warbler.

Leave Frome southwards on the B3092 and after 4 miles turn left towards Horningham. Longleat is a well known safari park and open to the public daily, except on Christmas Day. On leaving take the right fork of the two lanes opposite and in 1¼ miles turn left. After 2 miles fork left and in 1¼ miles view Shearwater on the left.

MARLBOROUGH DOWNS   OS 157

This area is to the north-west of Marlborough, and covers 25 square miles of high chalk downland. There is no common land though access is frequently unrestricted. The area is full of old field systems, earthworks, etc., and the wide horizons are interrupted by the occasional clump of trees. Like Salisbury Plain, its birds are rare and no one is going to publish details of where to find what. In autumn harriers and golden plover enliven the scene.

SUMMER: buzzard, hobby, stone curlew, quail, wheatear.
AUTUMN: buzzard, harriers, golden plover.

Explore with OS map. The casual visitor motoring over the top from Marlborough to Broad Hinton might well see something.

RODBOURNE SEWAGE FARM   OS 157

Situated in the north-western suburbs of Swindon on the south side of the mainline railway. Its sludge lagoons are the best wader haunt in the county, regularly attracting a considerable variety of species.

SPRING: waders.

AUTUMN: ringed and little ringed plovers, wood and green sandpipers, dunlin, ruff.

The entrance to the farm is clear on the OS map. This area is of no use to the casual observer; local watchers should seek the permission of the Farm Manager.

SALISBURY PLAIN   OS 167

Salisbury Plain is roughly enclosed by a line drawn from Amesbury west to Deptford, to Warminster, to Westbury, east to Market Lavington, and on to Upavon. The area is chalk downland interrupted by belts and clumps of trees. There are very few roads and most of the area west of the Shrewton–West Lavington road is occupied by the military and to all intents closed. The Plain has long been known as the breeding haunt of a number of scarce birds. The first weekend in June sees the egg collectors clambering around the copses after hobby's eggs – against the law but still much practised.

SUMMER: hobby, buzzard, stone curlew, quail, wheatear.

The A360 between Shrewton and West Lavington is good and so is the minor road to the east.

SAVERNAKE FOREST   OS 157

Savernake lies south-east of Marlborough between the A4 and A346 and is the remnant of a royal deer forest. Its old oaks and beeches with their clearings can only be appreciated on foot. Though famous for fungi its birds include a variety of woodland species.

SUMMER: nightjar, redstart, nightingale, wood warbler.

Leave Marlborough on either the A4 or A346 south-eastwards and explore numerous tracks and paths.

Yorkshire

The Union consists of over forty natural history societies and has sections covering most aspects of natural history. Field and indoor meetings are held in each vice-county.

READ: *Yorkshire Birds*, R. Chislett.

BEMPTON CLIFFS   OS 93

These cliffs lie immediately north of Flamborough Head and rise higher (450 feet). They have been noted for many years as the only mainland breeding site of the gannet in Britain – now booming and increasing. They are, however, easy to miss amongst the vast numbers of kittiwakes (possibly 40,000 pairs between Flamborough and Bempton). Rock doves, indistinguishable from pure wild stock, breed.

SUMMER: gannet, kittiwake, guillemot, razorbill, puffin, fulmar, rock dove.

Leave Bridlington eastwards on the B1255 and turn left in Flamborough to Bempton. A public footpath from Cliff Lane runs along the cliff-tops. The RSPB has a summer warden whom visitors are asked to contact at the reserve.

BOLTON ABBEY AND WOODS   OS 96

The woods lie in the Wharfe Valley, 7 miles north-west of Ilkley, and are part of the Chatsworth Estate, open to the public. The area lies alongside the Wharfe between Barden Bridge and the car park opposite the entrance to Park House, and up the tributary Valley of Desolation to the north.

SUMMER: pied flycatcher, redstart, woodcock, common sandpiper, dipper.

Leave Ilkley westwards on the A65 and turn right after 3 miles on to the B6160. Join and leave the A59 and continue for 1 mile past Bolton Abbey to the car park on the right.

BRIDLINGTON–SEWERBY   OS 93; HT +0:45 Middlesbrough

This stretch of coast runs immediately south of Flamborough Head. Between the Humber and the Tees estuaries hardly a single river of any consequence reaches the sea, and Bridlington Bay holds the only large numbers of waders. These are unexceptional but include a thousand plus of the common species. Little gulls are noted most winters.

WINTER: redshank, dunlin, sanderling, little gull, scoter, scaup.

Access direct from Bridlington northwards to Sewerby.

DERWENT FLOODS   OS 98

In the Derwent Valley between Wheldrake and Bubwith, 6 miles northeast of Selby. The floods usually last for 6–8 weeks in February–March and then hold a huge population of several thousand wildfowl, including up to 100 Bewick's swans. Whooper swans and geese are sometimes seen.

WINTER: wigeon, teal, pintail, shoveler, pochard, goldeneye, Bewick's swan.

Leave Selby northwards on the A19 and turn right 1 mile past Barlby on to the A163. Continue to Bubwith and inspect the river northwards just before the village. In 1 mile turn left on the B1228. Most of the area can be seen from this and minor roads leading to Aughton, Ellerton, East Cottingwith and Storwood. The Yorkshire Naturalists' Trust has created a reserve between the river and the canal at West Cottingwith. Access is unrestricted but visitors must keep to the footpaths. At Aughton the floods lap picturesquely against the churchyard walls.

ECCUP RESERVOIR AND HAREWOOD PARK LAKE   OS 96

Situated 5–8 miles north of Leeds to the west of the A61, Eccup is just over a mile long, has natural banks and a mixed winter population of duck, including goosander, which reach a maximum in March. Harewood Lake is set in mixed woodland and has a large flock (once 750) of Canada geese. Black tern, waders, etc., turn up mainly in autumn in small numbers.

WINTER: wigeon, shoveler, tufted duck, smew, goosander, Canada goose, Bewick's swan.

AUTUMN: waders, terns.

Access to both places is by permits which are only issued to members of the Leeds and District Bird Watchers Club. Membership is limited to 80. All enquiries to the Honorary Secretary, c/o The City Museum, Leeds.

FAIRBURN INGS   OS 97

The Aire subsidences are a series of marshes up to 600 yards wide between

Swillington and Newton, and form one of the most important wetlands in England, in spite of considerable disturbance from industrial activities. The area at Fairburn has been declared a local nature reserve. Duck, many of which breed, are numerous and both wild swans occur regularly. Passage brings waders, black terns, water rails and in early September, the number of sand martins and swallows coming to roost has been estimated at well over a million birds.

WINTER: wigeon, shoveler, pochard, goldeneye, gadwall, Bewick's and whooper swans.

SPRING: garganey.

SUMMER: sedge and reed warblers, shoveler, pochard, gadwall.

AUTUMN: sand martin, swallow, black tern, water rail, waders, garganey.

Leave the A1 westwards at Fairburn, 2 miles north of Ferrybridge. This road runs along the northern side of the reserve, and there is a footpath across the marsh along a raised wall with hides, etc.

FILEY BRIGG   OS 93; HT +0:40 Middlesbrough

This is a mile-long reef which juts into the sea 7 miles south of Scarborough. At low tide the Brigg is a mass of rock pools which hold the usual species of waders. In autumn the area is excellent for sea watching, and in winter sea duck are noted offshore together with the rarer grebes.

WINTER: scoter, eider, black-necked and Slavonian grebes, snow bunting.

AUTUMN: divers, Manx shearwater, gannet, skuas, terns, auks, Lapland bunting.

Straightforward public access northwards from Filey.

FLAMBOROUGH HEAD   OS 93

The Head is the largest projection from what is otherwise a generally smooth coastline. The chalk cliffs rise to 250 feet and provide nesting sites for large numbers of kittiwakes and a fine vantage point for observing sea birds, including unusual species. Passerines, including warblers, chats and flycatchers, are regular and occasionally large falls occur.

SPRING: divers, fulmars, terns, auks.

SUMMER: kittiwake, scoter.

AUTUMN: divers, fulmar, Manx and sooty shearwaters, gannet, skuas, terns, auks, passerines.

Leave Bridlington eastwards on the B1255. Continue straight on the B1259 at Flamborough and drive to the Head.

GOUTHWAITE RESERVOIR   OS 91

This water is 2 miles long, lies in Nidderdale beyond Pateley Bridge, and is a beautiful setting in which to watch wildfowl in winter. Up to 25 whooper swans are regularly present, and a few passage waders and the odd black tern are noted annually.

WINTER: wigeon, pochard, goldeneye, whooper swan.

SUMMER: dipper, grey wagtail, Canada goose.

Leave Harrogate northwards on the A61 to Ripley, turn left on to the B6165 to Pateley Bridge. Continue northwards on unclassified roads. Views along whole length of reservoir from the western side.

HORNSEA MERE   OS 99

Lying less than a mile from the sea behind the village of Hornsea, the mere covers 300 acres, and has extensive areas of reed-bed. Hornsea would be a good haunt anywhere in Britain but its geographical position makes it quite outstanding. Large numbers of wildfowl winter and wild swans are regularly present. Passage can bring almost anything to the area but bittern, black tern, little gull, Slavonian grebe and a number of sea birds are all annual visitors.

WINTER: wigeon, shoveler, pochard, goldeneye, goosander, Bewick's and whooper swans.

SPRING: black tern, garganey, bittern.

SUMMER: pochard, tufted duck, shoveler, heron, warblers.

AUTUMN: Slavonian grebe, water rail, waders, black tern, little gull, gannet.

A road signposted 'To the Mere' leads westwards out to a peninsula from Hornsea, car park, etc. The B1244 along the northern side gives good views at several points. Escorted visiting by arrangement with the RSPB warden, Mr D. Ireland, The Bungalow, The Mere, Hornsea, Yorks.

HUMBER WILDFOWL REFUGE   OS 98; HT +0:39 Hull

The refuge stretches 4 miles downstream from where the Rivers Trent and Ouse open out into a tidal estuary with shoals, saltings and an island. The area covers 3,130 acres between Faxfleet and Brough which are strictly preserved and wardened. The main species protected is the pink-foot of which 10,000 are usually present in early autumn with smaller numbers in winter. The birds roost on Whitton Sand and flight out to feed in the surrounding countryside. Other species include thousands of duck and small numbers of waders. Controlled shooting is allowed by permit but is generally unsuccessful.

WINTER: pink-footed goose, wigeon, teal, shoveler, shelduck, waders.

AUTUMN: pink-footed goose.

Do not trespass on the reserve. The birds are best seen flighting in from several vantage points:

1. FAXFLEET: leave A63 one mile west of Newport and drive southwards four miles to the estuary.

2. WHITTON: leave the A1077 six miles west of South Ferriby. Two miles past South Ferriby view the estuary out towards Read's Island.

INGLEBOROUGH
OS 90

Amongst the many Pennine walks the three peaks walk taking in Pen-y-ghent, Ingleborough and Whernside is the most famous. It is a long trek over open moorland but there is a variety of birds to be seen by the fit and experienced.

SUMMER: dipper, grey wagtail, redshank, golden plover, curlew, wheatear, raven, peregrine, buzzard.

Stainforth, north of Settle, is the start and Dent, south-east of Sedbergh, the finish. Walk up to Horton-in-Ribblesdale and make direct ascent of Pen-y-ghent. Return and head for Ingleborough, over the top, through Chapel-le-Dale and along the ridge of Whernside and down to Dentdale. This is a long walk and map, compass and experience are essential. For the less energetic, train to Horton, walk halfway up Pen-y-ghent. Train to Dent Station and walk down the beautiful valley to Dent.

KNARESBOROUGH RINGING STATION
OS 96

The station is south-east of Knaresborough and covers the area enclosed between a large loop of the River Nidd and the B6164. Two large Heligoland traps, and other smaller traps account for several thousand birds ringed every year, including a variety of warblers. Interesting birds are present and caught at all seasons.

AUTUMN: warblers.

Leave Knaresborough eastwards on the A59 and fork right after 1 mile on to the B6164. After a quarter of a mile cross Grimbald Bridge and turn left down the first track to the car park and notice. All enquiries to The Warden, 44 Aspin Lane, Knaresborough, nr Harrogate, Yorks.

MALHAM TARN FIELD CENTRE
OS 90

Though better known to geologists than ornithologists, Malham Tarn and the surrounding moorland and rough pasture provides an ideal base for getting to know the commoner moorland birds. Lying immediately north of the Aire-Ribble gap Malham is easy to reach via the A65. Both peregrine and merlin have bred in recent years, and over 140 species have been recorded.

SUMMER: redstart, wheatear, ring ouzel, dipper, common sandpiper, redshank, curlew, golden plover, red grouse, peregrine, merlin, black-headed gull.

A general exploration of the area is advised with the Field Centre serving as base. An excellent round trip involves a train to Horton-in-Ribblesdale, climbing Pen-y-ghent direct and turning south over Fountain's Fell down past the Tarn to the Cove and Malham. The whole is energetic and should not be undertaken without some experience of mountains. Mists can come down very suddenly here.

Field Centre: details from Field Studies Council, 9 Devereux Court, Strand, London WC2.

## ROMBALDS MOOR	OS 96

North-west of the industrial complex of the West Riding, between Airedale and Wharfedale, this is largely open moorland with bracken and rough grass, but with some areas of heather, and patches of woodland along the streams.

SUMMER: red grouse, golden plover, redshank, snipe, dunlin, curlew, ring ouzel.

Access is unlimited to the main bulk of the moor and there are numerous paths. A good start would be to take the road between the two valleys south from Ilkley.

## SKIPWITH COMMON	OS 98

The common lies 5 miles north-east of Selby and covers 857 acres of rough grass and scrub, with some quite extensive areas of mixed woodland. There are a large number of ponds set in boggy ground which are the haunt of a sizeable population of wildfowl and 130 species have been noted, 90 of them breeding.

WINTER: teal, wigeon.

SUMMER: teal, shoveler, pochard, tufted duck, nightjar, willow tit, three woodpeckers, five owls, black-headed gull.

Leave Selby northwards on the A19 and turn right 1 mile past Barlby on to the A163. In 2¼ miles turn left and stop in 1 mile where a track leads left over the common. The Yorkshire Naturalists' Trust runs the reserve and has erected noticeboards.

## SPURN BIRD OBSERVATORY	OS 105; HT —0:10 Grimsby

The observatory lies at the south-eastern corner of the county at the mouth of the Humber. It is a 3 mile long peninsula little more than 250 yards wide and is also a nature reserve of the Yorkshire NT. In winter the huge flats along the western side of the Spurn are a notable haunt of waders and wildfowl.

Migrants include a large range of diurnal species coasting in both spring and autumn, and terns, skuas, divers and waders are present in good variety. Migrant chats, warblers and flycatchers are often involved in 'falls' in autumn, and there are always a few rarities each season including regular great grey shrike, barred and yellow-browed warblers and bluethroat.

WINTER: wigeon, teal, knot, redshank.

SPRING: divers, bar-tailed godwit.

SUMMER: little tern, ringed plover.

AUTUMN: spotted redshank, bar-tailed godwit, wood sandpiper, greenshank, curlew sandpiper, divers, terns, skuas, chats, warblers, flycatchers, great grey shrike, barred and yellow-browed warblers, bluethroat, rarities.

Leave Hull eastwards on A1033 and fork right in Patrington on the B1445 to Easington. Continue on unclassified roads to Kilnsea, and then south to Spurn. The reserve is private and there is an admission fee, there is also a public footpath. Accommodation is available at the Observatory. There is a resident warden with whom bookings should be made: Spurn Observatory, Kilnsea, via Patrington, Hull, E. Yorks.

STOCKS RESERVOIR   OS 95

High up in Bowland Forest in the extreme west of the county, this is a large water which holds a fair range of wildfowl species in no great numbers, other than flocks of goosander which total over 100 on occasion in March.

WINTER: goosander, Bewick's and whooper swans, wigeon, pochard, goldeneye.

Leave Skipton westwards on the A65. Turn left at Long Preston on the B6478, and turn right after 6 miles. The view of the reservoir along the causeway and along the road between the trees is limited.

WASHBURN VALLEY AND RESERVOIRS   ·   OS 96

The valley is a tributary of the Wharfe and lies 12 miles north of Leeds. Three natural banked reservoirs have been created by damming the river and a fairly large area of the surrounding hillsides has been afforested.

WINTER: wigeon, pochard, goldeneye, whooper swan.

SUMMER: curlew, redshank, snipe, pied flycatcher, warblers.

Leave Otley northwards on unclassified roads to Newall. Turn right over the bridge on the B6451 and then left still on B6451 outside Farnley Hall. At Farnley continue to Lindley Bridge.

There are many footpaths in the valley, including one on the north side of Lindley Wood Reservoir, and on the south side of Swinsty Reservoir.

Permits for the reservoirs can be obtained from the General Manager and Engineer, Leeds Waterworks Dept., 182 Otley Road, West Park, Leeds 16.

Part 2
Wales

READ: *The Naturalist in Wales*, R. M. Lockley

Anglesey

CAMBRIAN ORNITHOLOGICAL SOCIETY.

MERSEYSIDE NATURALISTS.

NORTH WALES NATURALISTS' TRUST.

BULKELEY LAKE   OS 106

The lake, which lies 1 mile from Beaumaris and only a little more from Lavan Sands, is very small but still holds sizeable flocks of duck in winter. In summer the extensive reed beds and sedges hold a mixed population of the commoner marsh species.

WINTER: wigeon, teal, shoveler, tufted duck.

SUMMER: marsh species.

Leave Beaumaris on the B5109 and turn right on to an unclassified road flanked by woodland after 1 mile. In 600 yards pass the Bulkeley Memorial on the right and park. A footpath signposted Llwyr Cyhoeddus (Welsh for Public Footpath) climbs over a wall almost opposite the memorial and leads along the eastern side of the lake.

CEMLYN BAY   OS 106

The bay is on the north coast of Anglesey and consists of a brackish lagoon separated from the sea by a shingle bar, the sheltered bay, the rocky and weedy shore, and some wet pasture fields. The whole area is very attractive to birds, in spite of the construction of the nuclear power station on nearby Wylfa Head, and is owned and managed as a bird reserve by the National Trust.

WINTER: wigeon, shoveler, pochard, goldeneye, whooper swan, turnstone, grey plover, redshank, bar-tailed godwit, golden plover.

SPRING AND AUTUMN: waders.

Leave the A5025 one mile west of Cemaes Bay at Tregele westwards to Cemlyn. Past Plas Cemlyn a signpost on the right marks the track to Trwyn Cemlyn. The whole area can easily be enjoyed from this track and visitors should respect the reserve.

LLYN CORON
OS 106

This lake lies just over a mile from the tidal Cefni Estuary and is most important as a roost for the winter wildfowl of the area. The water is much shot over and the number of duck are erratic. Wigeon have numbered 7,000 and are regularly over 1,000.

WINTER: wigeon, shoveler, pochard, tufted duck, Canada goose, geese.

Watch out for the lake northwards over a rough heath about a mile east of Aberffraw. A footpath leads across the eastern edge of the heath to the lake. Otherwise Coron is surrounded by private land, even the footpath is probably not a right of way.

LLYN LLYWENAN
OS 106

This is the best inland water in Anglesey for wildfowl. Several species of duck breed in the surrounding reed beds, and in winter a large population often includes whooper swan.

WINTER: wigeon, teal, shoveler, pintail, pochard, goldeneye, whooper swan, Canada goose.

SUMMER: tufted duck, shoveler, black-headed gull.

Leave the A5 on to the B5112, 1½ miles west of Gwalchmai. In 2 miles turn left at Trefor and take the third right after 2 miles. This unclassified road runs along the west and north side of the lake and gives very good views.

NEWBOROUGH WARREN NATIONAL NATURE RESERVE
OS 106; HT —0:53 Holyhead

The Reserve lies at the southern extremity of Anglesey, covers 1,566 acres, and is one of the best bird watching areas in Wales. The dune system of the Warren proper is the finest in Wales and is biologically very rewarding. A large area is now planted with conifers but open dunes and slacks, as well as part of the Cefri Estuary known as the Malltraeth Sands, are included in the Reserve. These sands are thronged by wildfowl and waders at all seasons. On passage the pool at the head of the estuary and separated from it by the sea wall, called The Cob, is excellent and regularly holds one of the best collections of waders in Wales. Unusual birds frequently appear.

WINTER: Slavonian grebe, curlew, oystercatcher, wigeon, shelduck, pintail, peregrine.

SPRING: waders.

SUMMER: curlew, oystercatcher, herring gull, shag.

AUTUMN: whimbrel, spotted redshank, godwits, little stint, sandpipers. The whole area lies to the west of the A4080 and is reached from it.

A track from the village of Newborough leads right through the reserve to the tip of the rugged Llanddwyn Island. At Malltraeth there is straight-forward access at the sluices on to The Cob for good views over Malltraeth Sands and the Pool. The Cob even has cast iron seats for viewing the estuary. Apart from these and other rights of way marked on Reserve notice boards, permits are required for visitors and are obtainable from the Nature Conservancy Penrhos Road, Bangor, but for ordinary bird-watching, the rights of way are quite adequate.

PENMON POINT   OS 106

The cliffs of this area in the south-east of Anglesey hold quite large numbers of the commoner sea birds though the south stack on Holyhead Island is undoubtedly better.

SUMMER: razorbill, guillemot, kittiwake.

Leave Beaumaris northwards on the B5109 and turn right on any one of a number of unclassified roads to Penmon. The road continues to the point (toll), then walk along the northern shore.

PUFFIN ISLAND   OS 106

Puffin Island lies less than a mile off Penmon Head towards the south-eastern corner of Anglesey. It is under a mile long but exposes some quite large lengths of cliffs that provide breeding sites for a good variety of sea-birds.

SUMMER: puffin, razorbill, guillemot, gulls, kittiwake, raven, shag, cormorant.

Cross the Menai bridge and turn right on to the A545 to Beaumaris where boats can be arranged.

SOUTH STACK, HOLYHEAD ISLAND   OS 106

This is the westernmost point of Anglesey and one of the best sea bird areas on the island. Though apparently ideally situated for sea-watching in autumn, there are no reports to date.

SUMMER: razorbill, guillemot, kittiwake, puffin.

AUTUMN: sea birds.

Leave Holyhead westwards on unclassified roads with OS map as guide.

Breconshire

READ: *The Birds of Brecknock*, Ingram and Salmon, available from the County Museum, Brecon.

BRECON BEACONS   OS 141

The Beacons lie to the south of Brecon and reach a maximum height of just under 3,000 feet. Though merely a desolate and comparatively birdless moor in winter, summer brings a wealth of species including the occasional merlin and peregrine. The wooded valleys hold the typical species.

SUMMER: wheatear, buzzard, peregrine, merlin, red grouse, ring ouzel, pied flycatcher, wood warbler, tree pipit, dipper, nuthatch.

Hundreds of acres are 'open' but large areas belonging to the Forestry Commission and to various Municipal Water Boards. It is accessible from the A470 near the Storey Arms, and from the minor roads from Brecon, Tal-y-bont, and Pontsticill in the south.

DDERW POOL   OS 141

Dderw Pool lies in the Wye Valley near the village of Llyswen, 9 miles north-east of Brecon. Though only a farmland pool it holds a variety of species, including all three species of swan in winter. A few migrating waders appear in autumn.

WINTER: mute, whooper and Bewick's swans, duck, golden plover.

SUMMER: yellow wagtail, heron.

AUTUMN: waders.

Leave Brecon north-eastwards on the A438 and after 6 miles turn left on to the A4073 to Llyswen. The pool can be viewed from the A479.

FFOREST FAWR   OS 140 and 141

This area is the westward extension of the Brecon Beacons and has a series of peaks over 2,000 feet. The ground is mainly open moorland but there are large areas that have been afforested. Typical moorland birds breed, and a variety of species is found in the wooded valley.

SUMMER: buzzard, merlin, red grouse, ring ouzel, raven, pied flycatcher, wood warbler, tree pipit, dipper.

Several roads cross the range from the Usk Valley into Glamorgan, but Senny-bridge is the best starting point, and the minor road along the Afon Senni is probably the best route.

LLANGORSE LAKE OS 141

The lake is situated at over 500 feet, 6 miles east of Brecon near the Usk Valley. It is the largest natural lake in South Wales and is surrounded by extensive reed-beds that give shelter to waterfowl. Recent developments include motor boats, yachts, canoes, and water-skiing, and many former residents are being driven away.

The reed-beds hold a large fringe colony of reed warblers which outnumber the sedge warblers. Yellow wagtails too are on the edge of their range here. Migration is surprisingly good and a large roost of sand martins gather in autumn.

WINTER: wild swans, pintail, goosander, Canada goose, gulls.

SUMMER: great crested grebe, reed warbler, yellow wagtail.

AUTUMN: oystercatcher, greenshank, green sandpiper, dunlin, ringed plover, commic and black terns.

Leave Brecon south-eastwards on the A40 and turn left on to the B4560 at Bwlch. Continue to Llangorse village. Though the land surrounding the lake is private, there are access points at Llangorse village and Llangasty Church.

LLWYN-ON-RESERVOIR OS 141

The reservoir lies 5 miles north of Merthyr Tydfil in the Taff Valley and is surrounded by coniferous plantations. The summer population is augmented by passage waders in autumn, and there are wildfowl in winter.

WINTER: wild swan, goldeneye.

SUMMER: buzzard, raven, dipper, heron, great crested grebe, long-eared owl, common sandpiper.

AUTUMN: wood and green sandpipers, greenshank.

Leave Merthyr northwards on the A470 to the reservoir on the left. There are public highways all round the lake.

TAL-Y-BONT RESERVOIR OS 141

The water covers over 300 acres and lies at over 500 feet, 7 miles southeast of Brecon. It is the major haunt of wildfowl in the county. Cormorants are present in winter, and there is a small passage of waders in spring and autumn.

WINTER: wigeon, pochard, tufted duck, goldeneye, goosander, wild swans, cormorant.

SUMMER: common sandpiper, dipper, yellow wagtail, grasshopper warbler.

AUTUMN: greenshank, spotted redshank, oystercatcher, ruff.

Leave Brecon south-eastwards on the A40 but turn right after 2 miles on to the minor road running along the southern side of the Usk. Turn right at Tal-y-bont and view the reservoir from the road in 2 miles.

Caernarvonshire, Denbighshire and Flintshire

CAMBRIAN ORNITHOLOGICAL SOCIETY.
The Society holds indoor and field meetings.

FLINTSHIRE ORNITHOLOGICAL SOCIETY.

MERSEYSIDE NATURALISTS.

NORTH WALES NATURALISTS' TRUST.

BARDSEY ISLAND BIRD OBSERVATORY (Caernarvon)   OS 115

Bardsey is just under 2 miles south-west of the western tip of the Lleyn Peninsula. The island is 1¾ miles by three quarters of a mile and the main features are the 500 foot mountain in the east, the farmland area immediately west, and the southern lighthouse end joined to the main part by a narrow isthmus. The island has a varied breeding population and migrants are good on both passages, usually including a number of rarities. There is a resident warden.

SUMMER: chough, Manx shearwater, storm petrel.

SPRING AND AUTUMN: migrants, chats, warblers, flycatchers, melodious warbler.

Boats leave from Aberdaron and there is an island landing fee. Accommodation must be booked in advance. Full board is available at peak periods.

CLWYD HILLS (Denbigh/Flint)   OS 108

These hills run between the Vale of Clwyd and the Dee Estuary. Though well below 2,000 feet the area is of significant ornithological interest and not to be by-passed on the way to Snowdonia.

SUMMER: merlin, red grouse, wheatear, ring ouzel, grasshopper warbler, whinchat, pied flycatcher, raven, buzzard.

The best area is around Moel Vammau and the best access is off the Ruthin-Mold summer road via Bwlch Pen Barras.

COLWYN BAY (Denbigh)   OS 107 and 108

Colwyn Bay stretches east of Rhos Point to Llanddulas. In spite of its heavily commercialised sea front, the area is a most important wintering ground for sea duck and a watch point for waders coasting westwards in autumn. Scoter (10,000) are dominant but velvet scoter are always present with up to 300 scaup.

WINTER: scoter, velvet scoter, merganser, scaup, wigeon, knot, turnstone, purple sandpiper, red-throated diver.

AUTUMN: waders.

The promenade at Colwyn stretches westwards all the way to Rhos Point, which is probably the best observation point. The coastal railway is crossed to the east at Llanddulas and Abergele, both good points for sea duck.

CONWAY ESTUARY (Caernarvon)   OS 107; HT —0:40 Liverpool

The estuary flows into the sea to the west of Great Ormes Head near Llandudno, and at Llandudno Junction is almost a mile wide. The commoner waders are numerous and reach a peak in autumn. This season also brings the rarer grebes most years.

WINTER: wigeon, teal, shelduck, pintail, oystercatcher, curlew.

SPRING: waders.

AUTUMN: whimbrel, greenshank, grebes.

The estuary can be worked from the eastern shore but only where there is access across the Conway Valley Railway. The three major vantage points are Glan Conway, Llandudno Junction, and Deganwy. A comprehensive view of the estuary may be had by taking the Llanrwst road (A496) a quarter of a mile east of Llandudno Junction. Proceed a quarter of a mile and park in the lay-by on the right of the road.

FFORYD (Caernarvon)   OS 106; HT —0:30 Holyhead

The bay lies at the western end of the Menai Straits and is almost enclosed by the Morfa Dinlle dune system. The inter-tidal sand holds a good population of winter wildfowl and the commoner waders.

WINTER: wigeon, teal, shelduck, oystercatcher, redshank, curlew.

SPRING: waders.

AUTUMN: sandpipers, greenshank.

Leave Caernarvon southwards on the A499 and turn right at Bontnewydd into a maze of lanes to Fforyd. The road runs right alongside the bay and good views over the entire area can be obtained.

GREAT ORMES HEAD (Caernarvon)   OS 107

This is a tourist site of note and a very good cliff breeding sea bird colony. Though these species are the main attraction autumn brings an interesting passage of other sea birds.

SUMMER: guillemot, razorbill, puffin, kittiwake, fulmar, raven.

AUTUMN: Manx shearwater, gannet, scoter, terns.

Leave Llandudno northwards along the esplanade and continue along the coast road to the Head where there is a car park. Alternatively use the Great Orme Railway from Church Walks.

LAVAN SANDS (Caernarvon)   OS 107; HT —0:30 Liverpool

The sands lie at the eastern end of the Menai Straits and stretch from Bangor 6 miles to Llanfairfechan, and 4 miles out to sea. The estuary of the Ogwen at the eastern end is predominantly mudflats but the rest is mainly sand. As on most open shores the waders are best in late autumn and winter. Duck are most plentiful at the Ogwen Estuary.

WINTER: wigeon, teal, goldeneye, oystercatcher, curlew, bar-tailed godwit, knot.

AUTUMN: oystercatcher, knot, grey plover, sanderling, bar-tailed and black-tailed godwits.

There are four main means of access:

1. Leave Bangor southwards on the A5 and turn left after 1 mile on to the A55. In a little under a mile cross a railway bridge and turn left on to an unclassified road to the mouth of the Ogwen.

2. Leave the A55 northwards at Aber church and bear left under the railway to the shore.

3. Leave the A55 northwards 1 mile west of Llanfairfechan across the railway to Glan-y-mor Elias.

4. Leave the A55 northwards at Llanfairfechan.

SHOTTON POOLS (Flint)   OS 109; HT +0:27 Liverpool

At the head of the Dee Estuary amongst a huge area of saltings and mud flats is a large steel works covering in all 1,000 acres. Amongst the buildings lie several natural freshwater pools and reed beds, and to the west are brackish lagoons, saltings and mud flats. In this uninspiring setting over 35 species regularly breed and a great many more visit. Dominating these visitors are large numbers of waders on both passages, though in August the reed beds provide a roost for up to 25,000 swallows. A high tide wader roost is best seen from the end of the ramp running westwards from the slag tip with 29 foot tides.

SPRING: waders.

SUMMER: shelduck, oystercatcher, common tern, reed warbler, wheatear, whinchat.

AUTUMN: greenshank, spotted redshank, ruff, green sandpiper, curlew sandpiper, little stint, swallow, sand martin.

Leave Chester westwards on the A548 and continue until it joins the A550. Turn left and enter works approach road, second on right, a quarter of a mile north of Queensferry Bridge.

The whole area is private land but permits are obtainable from The Works Relations Manager, John Summers and Sons Ltd, Hawarden Bridge Steelworks, Nr Chester.

Do not venture into the tidal area when tides exceed 30 feet.

SNOWDONIA (Caernarvon)   OS 107

Snowdonia is contained within a rectangle joining Conway, Betws-y-coed, Portmadoc and Caernarvon, yet to the climber and fell walker there is almost no need to look any further than the Llanberis pass and Ogwen Valley. It is a beautiful rugged landscape with bare grass and heather moors in the north, the peaks and mountain passes in the centre, and the beautiful wooded valleys to the south. Over such a vast area there are many good bird-watching places and the visitor is urged to make his own explorations.

The heather moor north of the Llyn-y-mynydd Reservoir west of Bethesda is worth a try for waders and grouse, and the Glaslyn valley south of Beddgelert is good for woodland species.

Choughs breed in some of the slate quarries, ring ouzels are found on the high screes, and a peregrine might be seen anywhere. Whooper swans are the only wildfowl of interest and almost the only inhabitants of the large lakes.

WINTER: whooper swan, buzzard, raven, peregrine, dipper.

SUMMER: buzzard, raven, dipper, grey wagtail, pied flycatcher, chough, redstart, wood warbler, wheatear.

Walking over the area is generally permitted, though the usual courtesies are as important as anywhere. There are numerous paths which should be used wherever possible. The list of areas which follow is only intended as an outline guide:

1. Llyn Dinas, Llynan Mymbr, Cwm-y-Glo, often hold whooper swans.

2. The oak woods at Capel Curig, with their entrance across the bridged stream opposite Cobden's Hotel, are both beautiful and full of birds.

3. The A498 between Beddgelert and Prenteg is good for buzzards.

4. The moors north of Llyn-y-mynydd Reservoir and west of Bethesda for possible grouse, golden plover etc.

5. The first bridge north of Bethesda on the Nant Ffrancon for dipper and grey wagtail.

6. Cwm Idwal in the Ogwen Valley for wheatear, ring ouzel, beautiful scenery, and alpine flowers.

7. The woods around Betwys-y-coed for woodland species.

8. Vale of Ffestiniog for delicious and extensive oakwoods for pied flycatcher, etc.

There are several hotels to choose from at Llanberis, Capel Curig, and Beddgelert, all are splendidly central. Climbers and walkers camp all over the place and there are many cheap 'barns' for those who rough it.

Cardiganshire and Carmarthenshire

WEST WALES NATURALISTS' TRUST.

BLACK MOUNTAIN (Carmarthen) OS 140 and 153

The Black Mountain lies on the eastern county boundary and is a large upland area reaching a peak of 2,632 feet at Carmarthen Van. Some areas of old oakwood remain along the major valleys and these hold the usual upland species, as do the swiftly flowing streams. The open tops are rather bare and probably do not now hold red grouse though black grouse may soon move into the plantations from Brecon.

SUMMER: buzzard, dipper, grey wagtail, wood warbler, redstart, whinchat, wheatear.

The A4069 crosses the range and reaches a maximum height of 1,600 feet and some of the wooded streams in the west are worth following.

CORS TREGARON (Cardigan) OS 127 and 140

This area was declared a National Nature Reserve in 1955 and now extends to 1,898 acres. It is probably the finest example of a raised bog in England and Wales and is the only resort of Greenland white-fronts south of the Solway. Other wildfowl are regular in good numbers, as are hen harriers and other predators. Both otter and polecat live here among a great variety of bog flowers. Ridges along the edges have been left by peat cutters.

WINTER: white-fronted goose, wigeon, gadwall, pintail, shoveler, pochard, tufted duck, goldeneye, whooper swan, hen harrier, red kite, merlin.

SPRING: garganey.

SUMMER: buzzard, curlew, snipe, red grouse, black grouse.

Tregaron lies on the A485 between Lampeter and Aberystwyth, and the bog between the A485 and the B4343 along the River Teifi. Permits are required but a great deal can be seen from the roads and rights of way. A walk along the disused railway track from the derelict station at Ystrad Meurig is an excellent way of seeing the northern half of the bog. The warden lives at Ty Coed, Nr Tregaron and advises visitors.

DOVEY ESTUARY (Cardigan)   OS 127; HT —2:22 Holyhead

The estuary stretches inland for 5 miles and is nowhere less than a mile wide. The inter-tidal area is largely sand but with some extensive areas of mud and a good growth of salting, especially at the head of the estuary and around the Leri outfall near the mouth. The northern shore is bordered by hills with oak woods, while to the south there are extensive water meadows and nearer the mouth the peaty Borth Bog. The mouth is sheltered by the dune system of Twyni Bach. This variety of lowland makes the Dovey the most important centre for wildfowl in this part of Wales. Duck are numerous and Borth Bog, which is largely impassable, holds a flock of Russian white-fronts (maximum 500 in February–March). The usual sandy shore waders are present. The RSPB reserve at Ynys-hir at the head of the estuary has most of the typical species as well as some beautiful wooded landscapes full of the birds of the Welsh oakwoods. Shelduck, merganser and common sandpiper can all be found and in winter there is a chance of a harrier or peregrine.

WINTER: wigeon, pintail, shelduck, merganser, white-fronted goose, redshank, oystercatcher, buzzard, hen harrier, peregrine.

SPRING: waders.

SUMMER: warblers, pied flycatcher, redstart, buzzard, redshank, shelduck, common sandpiper.

AUTUMN: whimbrel, greenshank, spotted redshank.

Using Aberdovey as a base, it is probably best to use the passenger ferry to Twyni Bach and cross Borth Bog on foot along the B4353 to see the geese.

Good views of the estuary proper can be obtained at many places from the A493 along the northern shore; and there are good views of the oak woods especially where that road turns north east at the head of the estuary, or around Tre'r-ddol in the south. The RSPB reserve at Ynys-hir lies near the village of Eglwysfach on the A487. Permits are available from April to September 4 days each week.

THE GWENFFRWD (Carmarthen)   OS 140

High up in the sheep walks above Llandovery and covering 1,200 acres lies the RSPB reserve of The Gwenffrwd. Beautiful old oak woods cling to the hillsides and high above them hang the most exciting and masterful of British raptors – the kites. Reduced to a few pairs by a combination of circumstances the red kite survived in this and adjacent valleys and has now spread back over central Wales. With a population of over twenty pairs the kite is no longer the great rare bird of prey, though it would be foolish to think that these 1,200 acres afford protection to the species. Buzzard, kestrel and merlin find a home here along with the

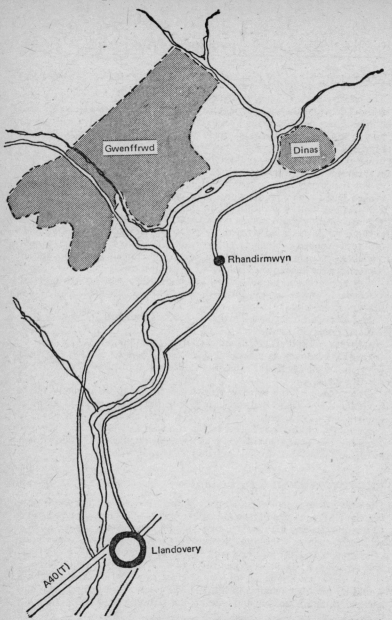

Gwenffrwd and Dinas: two RSPB reserves offering excellent chances to see red kites in one of their strongholds

delightful pied flycatchers and wood warblers of the woods. Dipper and grey wagtail along with common sandpiper haunt the streams.

The nearby hill of Dinas has similar species.

SUMMER: red kite, buzzard, merlin, pied flycatcher, redstart, wood warbler, dipper, grey wagtail, common sandpiper.

Access by permit from the RSPB four days each week during the summer. There is a nature trail at the Dinas where admission is unrestricted. Leave Llandovery northwards on unclassified roads to Rhandirmwyn – contact warden. See map.

TAF, TOWY AND GWENDRAETH ESTUARIES (Carmarthen)
OS 152; HT —0:11 Milford Haven

The three rivers share a communal estuary at the head of Carmarthen Bay. There is an area of salting on the southern side of Gwendraeth, but the outstanding area of the Witchett Pool in the Laugharne Burrows is occupied by the military. There are fair sized flocks of the commoner dabbling duck, notably on the Taf, and sea duck are often numerous off Pendine. Waders are not outstanding but there is a good variety especially on passage. Turnstones occur at Salmon Point Scar, blacktailed godwits at Ferryside and both godwits on the Gwendraeth, where there is the occasional wintering greenshank.

WINTER: wigeon, shoveler, pintail, godwits, grey plover, greenshank.
AUTUMN: golden plover, godwits, knot, turnstone.

The following are all good spots:

1. LAUGHARNE: leave the A40 southwards on the A4066 at St Clears.

2. GINST POINT: leave the A4066 southwards via the Brill Road checkpoint when range not in use.

3. LLANSTEPHAN: leave the A40 1 mile west of Carmarthen southwards on the B4312.

4. FERRYSIDE: leave Carmarthen southwards on the A484 and turn right on unclassified roads after 6 miles to Ferryside.

5. GWENDRAETH AND SALMON POINT SCAR: leave the unclassified road between Ferryside and Kidwelly southwards on several tracks that pass under or over the railway. That at Tan-y-lan is good for both main areas.

TEIFI ESTUARY (Cardigan)   OS 139; HT —3:13 Holyhead

The estuary lies north-west of Cardigan and is 1½ miles long. It forms the only substantial inter-tidal area for a considerable length of coastline and though not outstanding it does hold the commoner waders that are otherwise not generally seen in the area. Wildfowl are not numerous though wigeon have topped a thousand.

WINTER: wigeon, teal, waders.

AUTUMN: waders, grebes, divers.

View from east or west from B4548 and B4546 respectively out of Cardigan.

Glamorganshire

THE CARDIFF NATURALISTS' SOCIETY, ORNITHOLOGICAL SECTION.
The Society is a strong and active body that holds a regular programme of indoor and field meetings.

GOWER ORNITHOLOGICAL SOCIETY.
The Society co-operates with the Cardiff Naturalists' Society to produce a County Bird Report. It has its own programme of indoor and field meetings and publishes Field Notes thrice yearly. It is particularly active in the protection of birds in the beautiful Gower Peninsula.

GLAMORGAN COUNTY NATURALISTS' TRUST.

EGLWYS NUNYDD RESERVOIR   OS 153

This is an industrial reservoir covering 260 acres within the Steel Company of Wales' Margam site. It has part natural and part concrete banks and holds a good winter population of wildfowl, including several hundred diving duck. A small passage of waders is noted in spring and autumn and black terns are regular. A number of rarities have occurred including spoonbill, purple heron and white-winged black tern.

WINTER: pochard, tufted duck, gadwall, goldeneye, scaup, smew, whooper and Bewick's swans, divers.
AUTUMN: sandpipers, spotted redshank, greenshank, black tern.

Leave the A48 on to the B4283 at Water Street, 4 miles east of Port Talbot. The reservoir is half a mile on the right through a private entrance. Permits are available from the Steel Company of Wales Ltd, Port Talbot, Glamorgan and are only issued to the following Societies: Ornithological Section Cardiff Naturalists' Society; Gower Ornithological Society; Glamorgan Naturalists' Trust; Monmouthshire Naturalists' Trust; local WAGBI association; and the Nature Conservancy.

FLATHOLM   OS 154

Flatholm is an island of 30 acres, 3 miles off Lavernock Point in the Bristol Channel. It has a mainly rocky shore with cliffs up to 100 feet high on the south and east sides. The past 10 years have seen the establishment of a large gullery consisting of 1,000 pairs of lesser black-backed and 600 pairs of herring gulls.

SUMMER: lesser black-backed and herring gulls, shelduck, rock pipit.

Access is by motor boat from Penarth by arrangement (usually available daily in summer) with the lessees of the island. The island is owned by Trinity House.

KENFIG POOL　　　　　　　　　　　　　　　　　OS 153

Kenfig is a 70 acre freshwater pool amongst the coastal sand dunes between Margam Steelworks and Porthcawl. The pool is best in winter with small numbers of whooper and Bewick's swans and in autumn a few waders, as well as black terns, appear.

There is regular sailing at weekends and the disturbed wildfowl fly out to sea or to the nearby Eglwys Nunydd Reservoir.

WINTER: Bewick's and whooper swans, coot, goldeneye, wigeon.

AUTUMN: green and wood sandpipers, little stint, black tern.

Leave Porthcawl northwards on the B4283 and turn left at Nottage after 1 mile. Continue to Kenfig and car park.

LAVERNOCK POINT　　　　　　　　　　　　　　OS 154

The point lies at the south-east corner of the county on the Bristol Channel 1 mile south of Penarth and consists of farmland with some scrub and open areas near the cliff tops. It is almost exclusively a migration spot with spring passage of a variety of species in small numbers from February to June. June and July see various sea birds offshore including Manx shearwater and gannet with occasional skuas and storm petrel, largely depending on the weather. Autumn passage from July to November brings various warblers, a heavy and often dramatic hirundine and finch passage, and later the passage of winter thrushes. Rarities occur annually and have included kite, hobby, hoopoe, icterine and Bonelli's warblers, red-breasted flycatcher and ortolan bunting in recent years.

SPRING: visible migrants, chats and warblers.

SUMMER: Manx shearwater, gannet, raven.

AUTUMN: chats, warblers, flycatchers, hirundines, finches, thrushes, skuas.

Leave Penarth southwards on the B4267. Turn left half a mile past Lower Penarth and follow Fort Road to the coast. A coastal path leads from Penarth to the Point. The scrubland on cliff top is open to the public and this is the best spot.

LLANISHEN AND LISVANE RESERVOIRS　　　　OS 154

These two reservoirs lie in the northern suburbs of Cardiff and cover 60 acres and 20 acres respectively. They are artificially stone banked pools separated by a narrow embankment and are a winter haunt of wildfowl, with divers and grebes being regularly noted. There is some local movement between the reservoirs and the public boating lake at Roath Park 1 mile to the south. Spring usually brings a few common sandpipers and black terns.

WINTER: pochard, tufted duck, goldeneye, sawbills, grebes.

SPRING: common sandpiper, black tern.

The main entrance is from Rhydypenau Road, Cyncoed, and there is another from Station Road, Llanishen. Access is by permit only available from Cardiff Corporation, Water Engineer's Office, Greyfriars Road, Cardiff and these are only available to members of the Ornithological Section of the Cardiff Naturalists' Society or similar society.

OXWICH BAY   OS 153

The bay lies on the south side of the Gower Peninsula and consists of a 2 mile expanse of sand bounded by limestone cliffs and backed by sand-dunes, salt-marsh, fresh marshes and woodlands. An area of 542 acres is now a National Nature Reserve. Wildfowl are quite numerous and the small numbers of waders include sanderling. Birds of prey are regularly noted. The variety of habitats enables a large range of species to find a niche including reed warblers that here reach their most westerly breeding haunt.

WINTER: wigeon, shoveler, sanderling.

SPRING AND AUTUMN: waders, warblers.

SUMMER: woodland and marsh species, sedge and reed warblers.

Leave the A4118 on the eastern road to Oxwich. This provides a transect of the various habitats and should be walked, many species can be seen from the road. Access to the east salt marsh is by a footpath on the left of the marsh road from the Oxwich Towers. Assistant Wardens are present in summer and a Nature Trail is laid out. Access to the fresh marsh is by permit.

TAFF ESTUARY, PENARTH FLATS   OS 154; HT at Cardiff

This area lies between Cardiff and Penarth and is surrounded by the docks of these towns. In winter it holds several thousand of the commoner waders, and, occasionally, numbers of sea duck.

WINTER: redshank, knot, curlew, oystercatcher, shelduck, pochard, scaup, raven.

SPRING: ringed plover, turnstone, grey plover.

AUTUMN: redshank, knot, curlew, oystercatcher, ringed plover, turnstone, grey plover.

Much of the perimeter including the docks, is accessible to the public.

The coastal road in Grangetown is known as Ferry Road and is an excellent place to watch waders return from their roost on Penarth Moors soon after high tide.

WHITEFORD BURROWS   OS 152; HT —0:08 Milford Haven

This is an extensive area of sand dunes and fir plantations on the north-western tip of the Gower peninsula at the mouth of the Burry Inlet. The Burrows belong to the National Trust and have been declared a National Nature Reserve. On the west side is the 2 mile stretch of Whiteford Sands and on the east Berges Island, the area of saltings around Landimore Marsh, and the Llanrhidian Sands. The wildfowl population is of great importance and includes large flocks of the commoner duck with small flocks of eider and brent geese. Waders can be exceptionally numerous especially on passage and hen harriers and peregrines are present most winters.

WINTER: brent goose, wigeon, pintail, shelduck, divers, black-necked and Slavonian grebes, turnstone, bar-tailed godwit, knot, sanderling, oystercatcher, hen harrier, peregrine.

SPRING AND AUTUMN: bar-tailed godwit, turnstone, sanderling, grey plover, terns, merlin, jack snipe.

Leave Swansea westwards on the A4118. At the suburb of Killay turn right on to the B4396 and in 2½ miles join the B4296 to the left. Past Penclawdd this road runs along the shore and the area holds large flocks of shoveler. Continue to Llanrhidian and a maze of lanes to Cheriton. In a quarter of a mile this road merges with another on the left. Stop here. Take Frog Lane on the right hand side of the road. The track leads downhill above Burry Pill, past an old quarry, along the footpath to Pill House, across the sea wall, then turns north, skirting the sand dunes on the west. Continue along the path to the end of the Burrows, turn left for Whiteford Point, east for Berges Island.

WORMS HEAD   OS 152

A mile long rocky promontory at the south-western tip of the Gower peninsula near Rhossili, and is separated from the mainland at high tide. The Head is a National Nature Reserve and breeding birds include auks and gulls. Passage bring numbers of shearwaters, terns and skuas offshore, and there are usually large rafts of scoter in Rhossili Bay, and a few purple sandpipers on the Crabart in winter.

WINTER: scoter, purple sandpiper.

SPRING: Manx shearwater, terns.

SUMMER: guillemot, razorbill, greater black-backed and herring gulls, puffin.

AUTUMN: shearwaters, terns, skuas.

Leave the A4118 14 miles west of Swansea on to the B4247 to Rhossili. A footpath leads along the cliff top to the Coastguard Station which overlooks the head. The path continues down to the rocky causeway which is uncovered for approximately $5\frac{1}{2}$ hours, from $3\frac{1}{2}$ hours after, to $3\frac{1}{2}$ hours before high tide. Consult the tide tables at the Coastguard Station before crossing. While crossing keep to northern side on approach, work across to the middle of the causeway and veer again to the northern side near Inner Head. Follow the easy footpath on the southern side of Inner Head across the rocks at Low Neck and proceed to Outer Head. There is no camping and birds and flowers should not be disturbed.

Merionethshire and Montgomeryshire

WEST WALES NATURALISTS' TRUST.

MONTGOMERYSHIRE FIELD SOCIETY.

BROAD WATER (Merioneth)   OS 127; HT —2.15 Holyhead

This is the small tidal estuary of the Dysynni River lying immediately north of Towyn, and holds a small population of wildfowl and waders. A large area of low-lying marshes extends inland along the Dysynni and this holds a few geese and numbers of duck in winter. In summer buzzards are frequently seen and several waders breed. The Bird Rock, 5 miles up the valley from Towyn, is well known as a breeding site of cormorants.

WINTER: white-fronted goose, duck, waders, gulls, buzzard, peregrine.
SUMMER: buzzard, cormorant, grey wagtail, warblers, redstart.

For Broad Water; leave the A493 threequarters of a mile east of the point where it leaves the coast and turns directly inland at Rhoslefain. Follow this narrow lane southwards round Talygarreg avoiding the military establishment and the quarries. Good views over the sands can be had from the road and keep an eye on the hill to the north. Continue back to the main road trying to follow an approximately constant direction at difficult lane junctions.

For Bird Rock; leave the A493 up the Dysynni Valley at Bryncrug, marshes on the left and Bird Rock on the right where the marshes end.

COED Y BRENIN (Merioneth)   OS 116

Five fast flowing streams join together in the forest to form the River Mawddach. Though the trees are predominantly planted conifers there are natural oak woods especially along the streams, and the National Trust owns a large area near Ganllwyd.

SUMMER: buzzard, dipper, grey wagtail, pied flycatcher, wood warbler, redstart.

There are numerous unclassified roads and tracks through the area and the A487 cuts right through the middle.

DOVEY FOREST (Merioneth)   OS 116 and 127

The River Dulas has its source high in the forestry plantations of the

Dovey Forest. Throughout its short length it runs through woodland forming an exceptionally beautiful valley. The Dovey Forest is approximately 5 miles square and though it consists largely of planted conifers there is a sprinkling of natural or semi-natural oak and birch woods. There are certainly as many buzzards as anywhere in Britain and merlins can be found on the tops.

SUMMER: buzzard, merlin, curlew, common sandpiper, dipper, grey wagtail, pied flycatcher, whinchat, redstart, wood warbler, warblers, ring ouzel, redpoll.

There are two roads up the Dulas Valley, the A487 and an unclassified road on the eastern side. This road continues upstream past Corris to Aberllefenni and beyond.

DULAS VALLEY (Montgomery)   OS 127

The Dulas runs south-east of Machynlleth and is a tributary of the River Dovey. A number of smaller streams join the Dulas from the south and east and together make an attractive and rewarding area. Old oak woods and new plantations are quite extensive.

SUMMER: buzzard, pied flycatcher, redstart, tree pipit, ring ouzel, wheatear, whinchat.

Leave Machynlleth eastwards on the A489 and turn right up the Dulas Valley. Explore up to the tops by the mountain road to Bryn y Fedwen. Return and cross northwards into the Ffernant valley.

MAWDDACH ESTUARY (Merioneth)   OS 116; HT —2:15 Holyhead

The estuary stretches inland for some 5 miles to the Toll bridge at Penmaenpool. The seaside resort of Barmouth lies on the northern shore opposite the narrow outlet. The expanse of inter-tidal sand holds numbers of duck and occasional parties of whooper swans, as well as numbers of the commoner waders. The woodland along both banks, and especially the beautiful old oak woods, makes the area scenically outstanding.

WINTER: wigeon, teal, shelduck, whooper swan, oystercatcher, redshank, curlew, buzzard.

SUMMER: pied flycatcher, redstart, wood and other warblers, buzzard.

The A496 winds in and out among the woods and hills along the northern shore and gives excellent views at several spots across the estuary and to the sombre and impressive Cader Idris.

MOCHRAS (Merioneth)   OS 116; HT —2:15 Holyhead

The sandy pool at Mochras is over 1 mile long and is out of all proportion to the tiny Artro River that is its parent. The dune system of Morfa

Dyffryn all but encloses the pool which is no more than 200 yards wide at its mouth.

WINTER: wigeon, teal, shelduck, redshank, oystercatcher, curlew.

SPRING AND AUTUMN: waders.

Turn westwards off the A496 immediately south of the bridge in Llanbedr. Follow the road over the railway, past the airfield to the pool.

TRAETH BACH (Merioneth)   OS 116; HT —2:14 Holyhead

This is the largest part of the estuaries of the Glaslyn and the Dwyryd. The inter-tidal area stretches inland for 5 miles and though over 2 miles wide in parts, the mouth is little more than half a mile across because of the huge dune system of Morfa Harlech. The area supports a good population of waders of the commoner species in winter and a more varied population in autumn.

The wildfowl of the area are mainly found on the salt marsh of Glastraeth near Ynys Gifftan Island. The Glaslyn Pool, formed by the ballast bank at Portmadoc, is a regular haunt of whooper swans and the estuary mouth has a small flock of eider.

WINTER: wigeon, teal, shelduck, whooper swan, eider, oystercatcher, curlew, redshank.

SPRING AND AUTUMN: waders.

Glaslyn Pool and Traeth Mawr can be seen from the toll road (A497) along the ballast bank at Portmadoc.

Continue eastward on the A497 and in 1½ miles take the unclassified road across the Llandecwyn Railway Bridge—pay toll for cars. Continue south on the A496 but turn right 1 mile past Talsarnau on to the B4573. Cross the river and turn sharp right where the road turns left. This metalled road leads to the shore.

VYRNWY LAKE (Montgomery)   OS 117

This is a 5 mile long reservoir constructed to serve Liverpool. Its shores and the surrounding hillsides have been afforested and there are now woodlands of all ages, though very few old oak woods remain. Birds include the usual upland species with moorland species above the tree line.

SUMMER: buzzard, dipper, ring ouzel, grey wagtail, wheatear, redstart pied flycatcher.

The lake is marked on most maps and the B4393 runs all the way round. At the northern end a mountain road climbs up to 1,500 feet before dropping down to Bala Lake. To the north west another road rises to 1,790 feet and passes an extensive area of oaks on its way to the same place.

Monmouthshire

CALDICOT LEVEL   OS 155

This area lies alongside the Severn to the west of the Severn Tunnel and consists of flat grazing land that is often flooded in winter and spring. Wild swans and a variety of duck are regular and quite large numbers of waders are often present.

WINTER AND SPRING: Bewick's and whooper swans, pintail, wigeon, shoveler, turnstone.

Leave the A48 between Newport and Chepstow southwards on the B4245 to Rogiet. Cross the railway at Severn Tunnel Junction and, keeping right, follow farm tracks toward Undy. The flooded area is on the right and can be inspected from a car.

There is access down lanes to the sea wall and coast for the Severn mudflats.

LLANDEGFEDD RESERVOIR   OS 155

Llandegfedd is a new reservoir covering some 400 acres, 3 miles south-east of Pontypool. Although its bird population has not settled down it has quickly become the most important inland water in the county. Large numbers of duck are noted together with great crested grebe. Passage is as yet little studied.

WINTER: wigeon, teal, pochard, tufted duck, coot.

SPRING AND AUTUMN: greenshank, knot, oystercatcher.

Leave Pontypool southwards on the A4042 and watch for signposts at New Inn. The reservoir lies to the left. Park at the dam and walk along the easterly shore. Access is by permit and these are held for members only by the Monmouth Ornithological Society and Monmouthshire Naturalists' Trust.

LLANTHONY VALLEY   OS 141 and 142

The valley lies 6 miles north of Abergavenny off the A465. The B4423 runs along this beautiful valley as far as Llanthony and a narrow lane continues into the heart of the Black Mountain country to Hay. The beautiful Honddu stream runs between steep hillsides and old oak woods. The typical upland birds are found and the Sugar Loaf and Blorenge are worth climbing.

SUMMER: dipper, grey wagtail, pied flycatcher, buzzard, red grouse, raven, ring ouzel.

Leave Abergavenny northwards on the A465 to Llanvihangel Crucorney, turn left on the B4423 up the valley.

PETERSTONE AND ST BRIDES WENTLOOG
                              OS 154 and 155; HT at Cardiff

This stretch of shore lies between Cardiff and the Usk and consists of 4 miles of mud flats, a sea wall, and a large area of grazing. It is probably the best area in the county for waders and white-fronts sometimes fly down from Slimbridge.

WINTER: knot, curlew, grey plover, wigeon, shelduck, white-fronted goose.

Leave the A48 between Cardiff and Newport southwards at Castleton to Marshfield. Continue crossing the grazing meadows to a T junction. Park here and take a lane through the gate to the sea wall.

RHYMNEY OUTLET   OS 154; HT at Cardiff

Immediately east of Cardiff and adjacent to the important Peterstone Wentloog area, the area is one of inter-tidal mud with quite extensive reed beds. Waders are generally more interesting than along the open shore and there are more records of passage migrants.

WINTER: knot, curlew, wigeon, shoveler.

SUMMER: reed warblers.

AUTUMN: greenshank.

Leave Cardiff north-westwards on the A48. Immediately after crossing the Rhymney River turn right and after half a mile through houses turn right over a narrow railway bridge. This leads on to the sea wall along the eastern side of the outlet.

USK ESTUARY   OS 155; HT —0:11 Avonmouth

The Usk enters the sea south of Newport at the mouth of the Severn. A large area of inter-tidal foreshore is exposed at low tide providing feeding for wildfowl and waders. Though waders are most plentiful in winter, passage should not be ignored.

WINTER: teal, wigeon, pochard, scaup, turnstone.

Leave Newport south-eastwards through Somerton to Goldcliff and view from the sea wall. Permission to walk along the wall must be obtained at the farmhouse.

Pembrokeshire

WEST WALES NATURALISTS' TRUST.
The Trust is the only organisation to cover several of the western counties of Wales. It administers several of the outstanding Pembrokeshire sea-bird areas, and holds field and indoor meetings.

READ: *The Birds of Pembrokeshire*, R. M. Lockley.

DINAS ISLAND   OS 138/151

Dinas Head is 4 miles north-east of Fishguard and provides the motorist with an excellent round walk of 2 miles and the sight of some of the highest cliffs in Pembroke.

SUMMER: razorbill, raven, shag, buzzard, stonechat.

Leave Fishguard eastward on the A487. At Dinas turn left to Bryn-henllan, pass through the village and continue to a small cove on the west of the headland. From here take the cliff-top footpath round the coast.

GRASSHOLM   OS 138/151

The island of Grassholm lies 10 miles west of the mainland and, covering 22 acres, is the smallest of the famous Pembrokeshire islands. It is a RSPB reserve and is famous as the second largest colony of gannets in Britain, numbering 15,500 pairs.

SUMMER: gannet, kittiwake, guillemot, razorbill.

Landing arrangements must be made with the RSPB, 18 High Street, Newtown, Montgomeryshire, SY161 AA. Landing is exceedingly difficult and infrequent but Grassholm remains one of the most accessible gannetries and well worth the effort.

GWAUN VALLEY   OS 138/151

The valley stretches south-east from Fishguard inland toward the Presely Hills and is lined with old oak woods. The usual upland species are found in beautiful surroundings and a marshy flat valley bottom area near Sychbant is worth a look.

SUMMER: buzzard, redstart, wood warbler, dipper, grey wagtail.

Leave Fishguard south-eastwards on the B4313. Turn left after 3 miles to Cilrhedyn Bridge and continue eastwards along the valley.

MILFORD HAVEN OS 138/151; HT at Milford Haven

The Haven is a huge tidal network stretching inland for 20 miles. The main bird-watching centres are on a series of shallow subsidiary channels at Gann mudflats, Angle Bay, Pembroke River, Cresswell River, Carew River and the two Cleddau Rivers. Wildfowl are present in some numbers, and the tiny Bicton Irrigation Reservoir regularly holds a number of duck and waders. Divers and grebes come into the Haven, especially during rough weather when they can be found at Dale Roads, Angle Bay and Pennar Gut. Waders of the normal estuarine species occur in winter and on passage but there are sometimes wintering black-tailed godwit, common sandpiper, and greenshank on the Gann.

WINTER: wigeon, pintail, shoveler, goldeneye, shelduck, divers, grebes, black-tailed godwit, common sandpiper, greenshank.

SPRING: whimbrel.

AUTUMN: whimbrel, turnstone, spotted redshank, ruff.

Access is at many good points:

1. RIVER GANN: can be seen from the B4327 north of Dale.

2. BICTON IRRIGATION RESERVOIR: can be seen from the road east of St Ishmaels.

3. ANGLE BAY: view from the footpath that runs all the way round, starting at Angle, B4320.

4. PEMBROKE RIVER: view from Lambeeth where a footpath leads east and west. Leave the B4320 northwards to Pwllcrocham and turn right at Wallaston Cross.

5. COSHESTON PILL: access from Waterloo on the north east side of Pembroke.

6. CAREW RIVER: access from West Williamson off A4075.

7. CRESSWELL RIVER: view from the road south of Lawrenny.

8. GARRON PILL: access at Garron north of Lawrenny.

9. LANDSHIPPING QUAY can be reached via a maze of lanes from Cross Hands on the A4075 where it joins A4115.

10. HOOK: leave Haverfordwest southwards on the A4076. Fork left at Merlin's Bridge and turn left in 3 miles. Walk along by river to Fowborough Point.

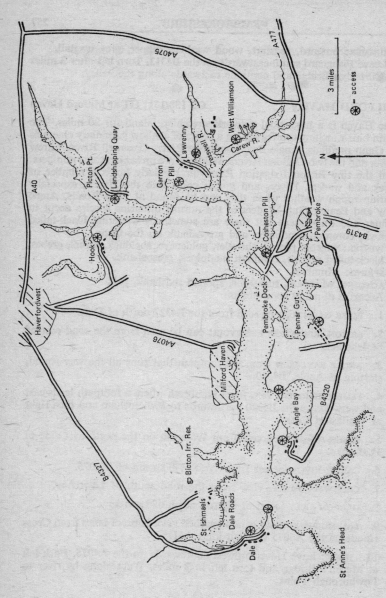

Milford Haven: showing the main access points grouped along the tributary valleys and bays

⊛ = access

3 miles

N

A40

A4075

A477

B4319

B4320

B4327

A4076

Haverfordwest

Hook

Picton Pt.

Landshipping Quay

Garron Pill

Lawrenny

Cresswell R.

West Williamson

Carew R.

Cosheston Pill

Pembroke Dock

Pembroke

Pennar Gut

Angle Bay

Milford Haven

Bicton Irr. Res.

St Ishmaels

Dale Roads

Dale

St Anne's Head

Accommodation is available for individuals and groups who wish to study birds in the area at Dale Fort and Orielton Field Centres under the auspices of the Field Studies Council. A number of courses on birds are organised every year and there are many opportunities for birding in the neighbourhood.

MINWEAR AND CANASTON WOODS   OS 138/151 and 152

These woods lie 7 miles east of Haverfordwest immediately south of the A40. Minwear is mainly deciduous and Canaston consists of conifers of varying ages. The Forestry Commission have opened a marked trail.

SUMMER: wood warbler, redstart, nightjar, tree pipit.

Leave the A40 southwards on the A4075. The first on the right leads to Minwear, on the left to Canaston.

RAMSEY ISLAND   OS 138/151

The island lies half a mile off the northern arm of St Bride's Bay, covers 650 acres, and is a RSPB reserve with a resident warden. It is an attractive island with cliffs rising to 170 feet on which choughs breed.

SUMMER: chough, razorbill, guillemot, kittiwake, fulmar, stonechat, wheatear, buzzard.

Permits including a landing fee are obtainable from the official boatman, but do not include the cost of transport. Boats leave from the lifeboat station at St Justinian's, 1½ miles west of St David's, where the name of the boatman and times of departure are displayed. A furnished bungalow is available and the warden will give you a free map and route guide.

ST ANN'S HEAD   OS 138/151

St Ann's Head lies at the entrance to Milford Haven and is remarkably convenient to Dale and Dale Fort Field Centre, should visitors to Skokholm have to wait for the swell to subside. Gannets and Manx shearwaters are frequently noted just offshore and there are interesting breeding species.

WINTER: divers, grebes.

SUMMER: chough, fulmar, shag, gannet, Manx shearwater.

Leave Dale, at the end of the B4327, southward to the Head – only one road. See Map.

ST BRIDE'S   OS 138/151

St Bride's is on the southern shore of St Bride's Bay, 7 miles west of

Milford Haven. In a comparatively short stretch of coast an excellent variety of species can be seen in beautiful scenery. The area is wonderful for flowers.

SUMMER: chough, fulmar, peregrine, buzzard.

Join the B4327 and head westwards for Dale. 1½ miles north of Dale turn westward to Marloes, and once past the village take the footpath to Musselwick Sands. Walk northwards along the cliff tops to Nab Head and on to St Bride's Haven.

ST MARGARET'S ISLAND   OS 152

The island is a quarter of a mile long, formed of limestone, and lies just offshore from Caldy Island near Tenby. It is a West Wales Naturalists' Trust reserve and holds a large breeding colony of cormorants as well as other sea birds.

SUMMER: cormorants, razorbill, kittiwake.

Permits to land from the Secretary of the West Wales Naturalists' Trust. Many summer boat trips round the island from Tenby.

SKOKHOLM BIRD OBSERVATORY   OS 138/151

Skokholm lies 2 miles west of the mainland, the same distance south of Skomer, and is 1 mile by half a mile. Emphasis on the island is on migration and the work is organised by the West Wales Naturalists' Trust in conjunction with the Edward Grey Institute, Oxford. Sea bird movements are interesting and migration of chats, warblers and flycatchers is often heavy. The October migration of finches and thrushes is sometimes dramatic and this month is usually very good for rarities, such as red-breasted flycatcher, yellow-browed warbler and Lapland bunting. Breeding birds include storm petrel and well studied Manx shearwater.

SPRING: migrant passerines.

SUMMER: Manx shearwater, guillemot, razorbill, storm petrel.

AUTUMN: shearwaters, gannet, kittiwakes, skuas, waders, thrushes, finches, chats, warblers, flycatchers, rarities.

Access is on Saturdays from Dale and full-board accommodation is available. Arrangements are made to meet the night train from Paddington at Haverfordwest and transport visitors to Dale Fort for breakfast. All visitors must become members of the West Wales Naturalists' Trust. Usual conditions concerning delays and weather. Enquiries to 4 Victoria Place, Haverfordwest, Pembrokeshire.

SKOMER ISLAND   OS 138/151

The island lies 1 mile off the coast and is the largest, most accessible and in many ways the best of the four Pembrokeshire islands. Covering 752 acres, its towering cliffs surround a flat plateau at about 200 feet. It is composed of grey, igneous rocks like Grassholm but unlike Skokholm, which is old red sandstone. The island was declared a National Nature Reserve in 1959 and is administered by the West Wales Naturalists' Trust, who appoint a warden. Manx shearwaters and puffins are the most abundant birds but others include storm petrel and chough.

Migrants are exciting and include sea birds, passerine falls and rarities but are not intensively studied as they are at Skokholm.

SUMMER: Manx shearwater, storm petrel, fulmar, puffin, razorbill, guillemot, kittiwake, stonechat, chough, buzzard, short-eared owl, peregrine.

A guide and trail is laid out for visitors and the island is open daily during the summer. Visitors who are not members of the West Wales Naturalists' Trust pay a landing fee. A boat normally runs from Martins Haven leaving at 10.30 am. Intending visitors should contact the boatman before departure, especially outside the main season, though weather permitting the boat leaves daily Whitsun–August. Limited accommodation is available to West Wales Naturalists' Trust members on a hostel basis, enquiries to the Trust Secretary.

STACK ROCKS, FLIMSTON   OS 138/151

These rocks are limestone cliffs and stacks 6 miles south-west of Pembroke, and hold good colonies of sea birds.

SUMMER: chough, guillemot, razorbill, kittiwake, fulmar, herring gull.

Leave Pembroke southwards on the B4319 and turn left after 7 miles to Flimston. Access to the coast is allowed across the tank range when the red flag is not flying. Also good cliff walk to St Govan's Head.

STRUMBLE HEAD   OS 138/151

Situated on the north Pembroke coast, 4 miles north-west of Fishguard, the steep cliffs hold numbers of sea birds as do the offshore stacks. Choughs have a stronghold here and auks are quite numerous. Good sea watching in autumn.

SUMMER: chough, guillemot, razorbill, kittiwake, fulmar, cormorant, stonechat.

AUTUMN: sea birds.

From Fishguard a maze of roads leave westward to the Head. There is an excellent walk southwards to Pwll Deri and back up the path by the Youth Hostel. The lighthouse area is closed before sunset till after sunrise.

Part 3

Scotland

THE SCOTTISH ORNITHOLOGISTS' CLUB.
Scottish Centre for Ornithology and Bird Protection.
Secretary: 17 Regent Terrace, Edinburgh EH7 5BN.
Journal: Scottish Birds, quarterly.
In the general absence of natural history or ornithological societies the
Scottish Ornithologists' Club has established a number of branches and
groups in different parts of the country. *Scottish Birds* maintains the
highest standard of recording accuracy.

NATURE CONSERVANCY.
Scottish Office: 12 Hope Terrace, Edinburgh 9.

ROYAL SOCIETY FOR THE PROTECTION OF BIRDS.
Scottish Office: 17 Regent Terrace, Edinburgh EH7 5BN.

READ: *The Birds of Scotland*, E. V. Baxter and L. J. Rintoul (2 vols).

Part 6

Scotland

Aberdeenshire, Banffshire, Kincardineshire, Morayshire & Nairnshire

CULBIN BAR AND FOREST (Nairn/Moray)

OS 29; HT —0:05 Inverness

This area lies on the Nairn–Moray border 3 miles east of the town of Nairn. A 5 mile long sand bar has been built up offshore and areas of salting flank either side of the channel between the bar and the mainland. Culbin Forest covers most of the land away from the shore and is 6 miles by 1½ miles. At its western end are Loch Loy and Cran Loch, two large freshwater pools among the pines.

The bar holds a variety of breeding birds, including all the British terns except roseate. The pine forest has an excellent collection of species that bird-watchers flock to see at Speyside. Crossbill, crested tit, capercaillie and siskin all breed, as do nightjars in some of the more open spaces. The wildfowl of the area are centred on the channel and include large numbers of sea duck, while the forest lochs hold fresh species and whooper swans.

WINTER: wigeon, scoter, velvet scoter, merganser, pintail, tufted duck, goldeneye, whooper swan, redshank, curlew, dunlin.

SPRING: waders, crossbill.

SUMMER: eider, shelduck, merganser, common, Arctic, Sandwich and little terns, crossbill, crested tit, capercaillie, siskin, goldcrest, nightjar.

AUTUMN: waders, gannet, Arctic skua.

Leave Forres westwards on A96 and immediately after crossing the Findhorn River, fork right on minor roads to Kintessack village. Continue through the village to Welhill gate and park, continuing on foot. The bar is accessible at most states of the tide if the county boundary is followed exactly. *No smoking* in the forest – *absolutely essential.*

FINDHORN BAY (Moray)

OS 29; HT —0:07 Inverness

The bay is on the Moray coast, 2 miles north of Forres and is the almost land-locked tidal estuary of the Findhorn River. The basin is about 2 miles square and is bordered on the western side by the extensive Culbin Forest and on the east by the Findhorn dune system. This is a quite exceptional area for migrant waders particularly in early autumn when knot and bar-tailed godwits are numerous.

WINTER: greylag goose, wigeon, long-tailed duck, knot, curlew, little stint, divers.

SPRING: scoter, velvet scoter, waders.

AUTUMN: scoter, velvet scoter, whimbrel, greenshank, little stint, knot, bar-tailed godwit.

Leave Forres eastwards on the A96 and fork left outside the town on to the B9011. At Kinloss, turn left to Findhorn. The road runs alongside the bay. Northward from Forres there are a number of lanes leading to the south side of the bay.

LOCH FLEMINGTON (Nairn/Inverness)   OS 28

Flemington is a small, reed-fringed loch lying south of the Inverness–Nairn road (A96) that is mainly noted as a winter duck haunt particularly in November.

WINTER: wigeon, tufted duck, goldeneye, scaup, whooper swan.

Leave the A96 southwards on to the B9090. After half a mile turn left along a small road beside the loch.

FOWLSHEUGH CLIFFS (Kincardine)   OS 43

The cliffs stand 3 miles south of Stonehaven, immediately north of Henry's Scorth which is marked on the OS map. Though not high, they are one of the most important sea bird stations on this coast, and their rubbly and indented nature make for easy viewing.

SUMMER: razorbill, guillemot, kittiwake, fulmar.

Leave Stonehaven southwards on the A92 and turn left after 3½ miles to Crawton. Walk northwards on cliff footpath for threequarters of a mile.

JOHNSHAVEN–GOURDON (Kincardine)   OS 43

This is a 3 mile stretch of rocky coastline, 8 miles north of Montrose. For most of the year there is little to distinguish it from any other stretch of this coast but in July–August it is the moulting ground of up to 3,000 eider.

AUTUMN: eider, scoter.

There are several access points off the A92 between Johnshaven and Gourdon that enable a car to be taken to the foreshore.

PENNAN HEAD (Banff)   OS 31

Situated 9 miles west of Fraserburgh and half a mile east of the small coastal village of Pennan. The main attraction is the breeding sea birds on the 350 foot high cliffs. Peregrines are often seen and house martins nest on the cliffs and in caves.

SUMMER: guillemot, razorbill, puffin, kittiwake, fulmar, peregrine, house martin.

Leave Fraserburgh on the A98 and turn right on to the B9032 at Ardlaw. After 1½ miles continue on the B9031 and after a further 7½ miles turn right to Pennan. Access along cliff tops eastward to the Head. The cliffs are dangerous.

PETERHEAD BAY (Aberdeen) OS 31; HT —0:40 Aberdeen

The bay is enclosed by two long breakwaters forming Peterhead's outer harbour and provides sheltered water for storm driven sea birds. Sea duck in particular are present throughout the winter and the usual waders are noted in season.

WINTER: goldeneye, eider, merganser, long-tailed duck, divers, grebes, turnstone.

Straightforward access on the south side of Peterhead.

LOCH OF SKENE (Aberdeen) OS 40

The loch lies 10 miles west of Aberdeen between the A944 and A974. It is a shallow loch 1 mile by half a mile, set amongst pine and mixed woods. It is a major haunt of duck with wigeon in autumn numbering up to 6,000 and occasional pink-feet.

WINTER: wigeon, goldeneye, pochard, tufted duck.

AUTUMN: wigeon, goldeneye, pink-footed goose.

Leave Aberdeen westwards on the A944. In 10 miles view southwards from the road. Permission to approach closer should be sought at the Lodge.

SPEY MOUTH (Moray) OS 29 and 30; HT —0:12 Inverness

For its final 4 miles, the Spey is a network of channels and islands with areas of alder swamp. As it enters the sea there is a sand bar and a considerable inter-tidal area. The bar and offshore area holds numbers of sea duck in spring. Terns breed on the shingle islands with a wealth of small birds, and autumn passage brings waders and sea birds offshore.

WINTER: wigeon, teal, turnstone, bar-tailed godwit, cormorant.

SPRING: goldeneye, long-tailed duck, merganser.

SUMMER: common and Arctic terns, stonechat, corn bunting.

AUTUMN: whimbrel, greenshank, merganser, velvet and common scoter, red-throated diver, gannet.

Access is simple from Spey Bay village on the east side. On the western and more interesting side, access is from Garmouth and Kingston via the B9015 from Mosstodloch, 1½ miles west of Fochabers. At Garmouth cross the golf course past the club house to reach the river. Viewing from Kingston is excellent.

LOCH SPYNIE (Moray)   OS 29

The loch is situated between Elgin and Lossiemouth 2½ miles from the sea and was formed in the sixteenth century by the extension of a shingle spit across the former estuary mouth. It has since been reduced to 80 acres but is surrounded by extensive reed beds. Though a variety of birds breed, the loch is mainly known as a winter haunt of geese.

WINTER: greylag and pink-footed geese, wigeon, pochard, tufted duck, goldeneye, shoveler.

SUMMER: pochard, tufted duck, black-headed gull, water rail.

Leave Lossiemouth on the B9103. Turn right after 2 miles and take the farm track to Scarffbank Farm. Park and continue on foot. Access is strictly by permission obtained in advance from Captain Dunbar, Pitgaveney.

LOCH OF STRATHBEG (Aberdeen)   OS 31

The loch lies at the easternmost corner of Scotland near Rattray Head between Fraserburgh and Peterhead. A storm in 1715 closed the Crimond Burn and formed this 500 acre loch, 2 miles by half a mile. It is separated from the sea by less than half a mile of sand and shingle and is surrounded by marshy vegetation and reeds. All of these factors combine to make the Loch of Strathbeg one of the most attractive and exciting places to watch birds in Scotland.

The winter population of wildfowl is varied and includes up to 8,000 mallard, the largest flock in Britain (see Rostherne Mere, Cheshire). Greylags and pinkfeet number up to 2,000 in autumn with the latter reaching 5,000 in spring. Up to 600 whooper swans have been noted in autumn and a pond at nearby Pittenheath has the only regular Bewick's swans in Scotland.

In summer a wide variety of species breed, and eider and great crested grebe can be seen together. Passage brings terns and waders.

WINTER: mallard, wigeon, pochard, tufted duck, goldeneye, goosander, greylag and pink-footed geese, whooper swan.

SPRING: pink-footed goose.

SUMMER: terns, eider, great crested grebe.

AUTUMN: marsh harrier, greylag and pink-footed geese, whooper and mute swans, terns, green sandpiper.

Leave the A952 between Fraserburgh and Peterhead eastwards on un-classified roads 1 mile south of Crimond. Views of the loch can be obtained northwards near the old chapel and there is general access along the dunes. The North Sea oil industry has already cast its greedy eyes at this splendid wildlife site.

TROUP HEAD (Banff) OS 31

Troup Head is 10 miles east of Banff and forms 350 feet high cliffs that are the haunt of large numbers of sea birds. House martins breed in caves at the extreme eastern end of the area. The long sea tunnel known as Hell's Lum with its enormous blow holes some distance inland is a non-ornithological must.

SUMMER: guillemot, razorbill, puffin, fulmar, house martin.

Leave Banff eastwards on the A98 and turn left after 2 miles on to the B9031. 1¾ miles past the Gardenstown signpost turn left to Northfield Farm and park. Walk northwards to the head of a large gully and follow its left bank to the headland.

YTHAN ESTUARY (Aberdeen) OS 40; HT +2:07 Aberdeen

Situated 13 miles north of Aberdeen between Newburgh and Ellon. Though 3 miles long the estuary is nowhere much more than quarter of a mile wide and birds can be seen at close range. The 1774 acre expanse of the Sands of Forvie borders the northern side of the estuary for its lower half and was made a National Nature Reserve in 1959. Sand dunes also border the estuary on the southern shore and both areas hold breeding colonies of terns, gulls and eider.

Upstream mud flats and mussel beds are frequented by eider and flocks of wintering waders and wildfowl, including about 1,000 each of greylag and pinkfeet. The lochs to the north, including Cotehill and Sand inside the Reserve, and Meikle, threequarters of a mile to the north, hold duck. Autumn brings hordes of waders and Arctic skuas frequently come up stream to chase the numerous terns.

WINTER: greylag and pink-footed geese, wigeon, scaup, goldeneye, long-tailed duck, tufted duck, pochard, goosander, eider, common and velvet scoter, divers, knot, golden plover, redshank, snow bunting.

SPRING: terns, waders, eider.

SUMMER: eider, shelduck, common, Arctic, Sandwich and little terns, black-headed gull, ringed plover, red grouse, stonechat, red grouse.

AUTUMN: terns, skuas, grey plover, turnstone, bar-tailed and black-tailed godwits, whimbrel, green sandpiper, spotted redshank, curlew sandpiper, ruff, warblers, chats, flycatchers.

Leave Aberdeen northwards on the A92 and fork right after 12 miles

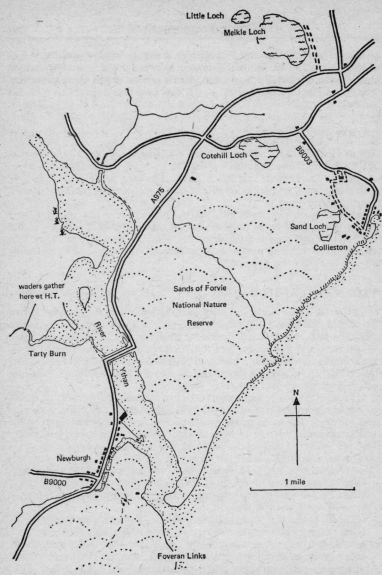

Ythan Estuary: the A975 provides ideal vantage points to north and south of the bridge, and the lochs to the north of the Sands of Forvie are not to be missed

on to the A975 to Newburgh. The road then runs alongside the estuary, crosses it, and continues along the eastern bank. At high tide waders congregate around the Tarty Burn, which can be approached along the estuary on the west side.

The Reserve is approached via Collieston on the B9003, though Cotehill and Meikle Lochs can be seen from roads and tracks. Authority to enter the Reserve must be obtained during the summer and autumn from the Nature Conservancy Scottish Office.

Angus, Clackmannanshire, Fifeshire, Kinross-shire & Perthshire

BLAIRGOWRIE LOCHS (Perth) · OS 49

The lochs lie to the south and west of Blairgowrie and form an important and attractive area in this part of the Tay Valley. The two lochs of Drumellie and Stormont are the best, the latter being very marshy, though Loch of Clunie to the west is worth a look. Up to 2,000 greylags and 100 whooper swans are regular, and the shingle islands in the Tay near Meikleour hold another 3,000 greylags.

WINTER: wigeon, shoveler, pochard, tufted duck, goldeneye, goosander, greylag goose, whooper swan.

Loch of Clunie and Drumellie can be seen from the A923 4 and 2 miles west of Blairgowrie. For Stormont Loch leave Blairgowrie southwards on the A923. In 1½ miles cross the level crossing and after 600 yards turn right, cross the railway and view to the south.

CAMERON RESERVOIR (Fife) · OS 56

Its position 4 miles south-west of St Andrews places the reservoir strategically between the Firths of Forth and Tay. The reservoir is under a mile long, covers 100 acres, and is flanked by plantations. It is a noted haunt of wildfowl with several thousand each of greylag and pinkfeet in autumn and smaller numbers through the winter.

WINTER: gadwall, wigeon, pochard, tufted duck, goldeneye, greylag and pink-footed geese, whooper swan.

SUMMER: gadwall.

AUTUMN: greylag and pink-footed geese, whooper swan.

Leave St Andrews southwards on the A915. After 3½ miles turn right and in half a mile turn left to the reservoir.

EDEN ESTUARY (Fife) · OS 56; HT +1.00 Aberdeen

The estuary of the Eden is 2 miles north of St Andrews with the famous golf links on the sand bar at its mouth. It is 3 miles long and for most of its length under 1 mile wide. The expanse of mud is frequented by vast numbers of wildfowl and waders in winter. The area at the mouth holds huge rafts of scoter almost throughout the year. Eiders too are numerous, and both species come inshore to shelter on the east side of Shelly Point in rough weather. This shingle spit is the main wader roost and holds colonies of breeding terns. It is, however, unprotected and is becoming a bathing beach and doubtless the terneries will now decline. The bay between the point and the mainland is a haunt of passage waders and little gulls are noted in spring.

WINTER: wigeon, teal, pintail, shoveler, goldeneye, velvet scoter, eider, long-tailed duck, knot, oystercatcher, godwits, curlew.

SPRING: black-tailed godwit, grey plover, little gull.

SUMMER: common, Arctic, Sandwich and little terns.

AUTUMN: black-tailed and bar-tailed godwits, grey plover, whimbrel, spotted redshank, ruff, terns.

Leave St Andrews northwards along the coast on the seaward side of the golf links to Out Head which is half a mile from Shelly Point. Views can also be obtained from Cable Shore, 3 miles north-west of St Andrews, and from the outer bridge across the Mottray Water at Guard Bridge.

FIFE NESS (Fife)   OS 56; HT —0:21 Leith

This is one of the most prominent headlands on the east coast of Scotland and is attractive to migrants, particularly chats, warblers and flycatchers; the overgrown garden between the farmhouse and the cottages being a particularly notable site. Waders and sea birds are present on both passages.

SPRING: waders, divers, terns, roseate tern, fulmar.

AUTUMN: curlew sandpiper, little stint, divers, terns, skuas, auks, shearwaters, chats, warblers, flycatchers, rarities.

Leave Crail north-eastwards to Craighead and walk to Fife Ness.

FLANDERS MOSS AND LAKE OF MENTEITH (Perth)   OS 54

The area lies south-east of Aberfoyle between the arms of the A81. Flanders Moss is a great peat bog, in many places impassable, that shelters a variety of breeding and wintering birds. The Lake of Menteith is 1½ miles long and is known as a haunt of wildfowl. Recent disturbance by water-skiing has reduced its attractiveness and geese are now more often found on the Moss and on Loch Rusky.

WINTER: greylag and pink-footed geese, goldeneye, whooper swan, great grey shrike, hen harrier.

SPRING: greylag and bean geese.

SUMMER: black-headed and lesser black-backed gulls, woodcock, heron, golden plover, curlew, goosander, red and black grouse, raven.

AUTUMN: pink-footed goose, hen harrier.
Leave Aberfoyle southwards on the A821, at its junction with the A81.

1.   Turn right and stop in 1 mile at the bridge over the railway and the River Forth. Walk eastwards along the old railway track to the river and follow bank out on to West Moss. This land is private and permission should be sought locally.

2.   Turn left and view Lake of Menteith in 2½ miles. Continue and turn right in a further mile on to the B8034 for further views.

3.   Turn left and leave the A81 southwards at Thornhill on the B822. At the bend in the road walk westwards for 2½ miles on to East Moss. Anywhere on the moss is heavy and wet going, gumboots are essential.

FORFAR LOCHS (Angus)   OS 50

Immediately west of the town is the Loch of Forfar, while 3 miles to the east are Rescobie and Balgavies Lochs. All are good for wildfowl, can be seen from the road, and are thus ideal for the casual visitor. Geese are generally absent but mute and whooper swans are regular with a wide variety of duck.

WINTER: wigeon, shoveler, pochard, tufted duck, goldeneye, goosander, mute and whooper swans.

LOCH OF FORFAR: leave Forfar westwards on unclassified roads.

RESCOBIE LOCH: leave Forfar eastwards on the B9133 view to the south after 3 miles.

BALGAVIES LOCH: As for Rescobie but continue eastwards and turn right. In threequarters of a mile view westwards and turn right at the A932 and view to the north.

GARTMORN DAM (Clackmannan)   OS 55

This is a mile long reservoir extending to 140 acres, 2 miles north-east of Alloa. Though mainly known as the haunt of diving duck, up to 200 whooper swans and a resident winter flock of greylags, the reservoir also attracts numbers of passage migrants including the commoner waders. In this respect Peppermill Dam, 3 miles to the south-east, is better known.

WINTER: wigeon, pochard, tufted duck, goldeneye, greylag goose, whooper swan.

AUTUMN: waders.

Leave the centre of Alloa north-eastwards on the A908. Pass under three railway bridges and turn right into New Sanchie immediately after the third. Continue straight through to the reservoir's north bank.

KINCARDINE (Fife)
OS 55; HT +0:20 Leith

The area centres on Kincardine Bridge, covering the north and south shores of the Forth. The mud flats are narrower here than downstream at Grangemouth and Culross and wildfowl include large numbers of diving duck. Waders are numerous at high tide and will probably increase with the disturbance at Longannet Point.

WINTER: pochard, tufted duck, goldeneye, merganser, whooper swan, knot, bar-tailed godwit, merlin.

AUTUMN: merganser, knot, bar-tailed godwit, whimbrel, grey plover, turnstone, curlew sandpiper.

In Kincardine a level crossing by the old station leads out westwards to the sea wall. On the southern shore turn west just before the bridge leading to the shore.

LARGO BAY, KILCONQUHAR LOCH AND ELIE NESS (Fife)
OS 56; HT —0:10 Leith

These three spots lie in a compact area on the northern shore of the Forth east of Leven. Though waders occur at all seasons the area is mainly noted for wildfowl and sea birds. Largo Bay holds several hundred scoter in winter, and there is a notable double passage of up to 200 long-tailed duck. Kilconquhar Loch covers 100 acres and is nowhere deeper than 6 feet. Its winter population includes numbers of duck and 300 greylag geese. Both the loch and Largo Bay are haunts of little gulls in autumn. Lundin Links is the most reliable but the loch has held over 500 of these birds. Elie Ness usually has a few in autumn and this is the best place to watch for divers, auks, terns, skuas and shearwaters on both passages.

WINTER: scoter, tufted duck, pochard, goldeneye, shoveler, wigeon, greylag goose.

SPRING: long-tailed duck, waders, divers, terns.

SUMMER: pochard, grasshopper warbler.

AUTUMN: little gull, black tern, divers, waders, auks, terns, roseate tern, skuas, shearwaters, long-tailed duck.

LUNDIN LINKS: leave the A915 half a mile west of Lower Largo southwards to the station. Turn right and pass under the railway.

LARGO BAY: leave Lower Largo eastwards along the front and continue on foot around the Bay.

ELIE NESS: directly accessible on the eastern side of Elie.

KILCONQUHAR LOCH: visible from roads on north side and from churchyard.

SHELL BAY: leave the A917 westwards near Kilconquhar Loch on minor road and track. Ruddons Point is accessible when firing is not taking place on nearby ranges.

LOCH LEVEN (Kinross)   OS 55

Loch Leven lies midway between the Firths of Forth and Tay immediately east of Kinross. The National Nature Reserve covers 3,946 acres and is the most important inland water in Britain for wildfowl. It is the main arrival area for pinkfeet which number 12,000 in autumn, and several hundred greylags and a few bean also use the loch as a staging post. Pinkfeet decline to a winter level of 1,000 but build up again in spring,

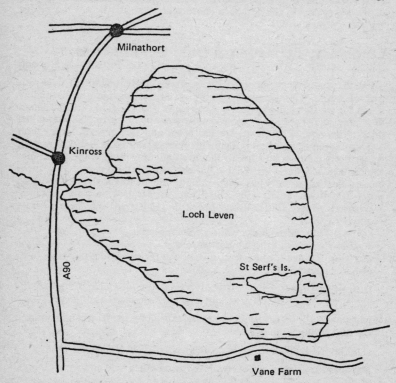

Loch Leven National Nature Reserve with Vane Farm Nature Centre in the south: autumn landing point of large concentrations of geese entering the UK

when greylags sometimes number 3,000. Wigeon, teal, pochard and tufted have all topped 1,000 and breeding ducks are important.

A great variety of other species occur including waders, terns and gulls. Whooper swans number 400 in autumn. The RSPB have a reserve and nature centre at Vane Farm at the south of the loch where geese can be seen in comfort.

WINTER: greylag and pink-footed geese, wigeon, pochard, tufted duck, shoveler, goldeneye, goosander, whooper swan.

SPRING: greylag and pink-footed geese, waders.

SUMMER: tufted duck, shoveler, gadwall, mute swan.

AUTUMN: greylag, pink-footed and bean geese, mute swan, waders, terns.

Access to the reserve is confined to:

1. KIRKGATE PARK, Kinross.

2. BURLEIGH SANDS, 2 miles north-east of Kinross on the A911.

3. FINDATIE, in the south-eastern corner of the Loch off the B9097 adjoining Vane Farm.

4. LOCH LEVEN CASTLE.

5. VANE FARM, the RSPB reserve in the south-eastern corner of the loch on the B9097, opposite St Serf's Island. It is open the year round every day except Monday and Friday. There is a nature centre and an observation room with displays. See Map.

LOCH OF LINTRATHAN (Angus)   OS 49

A reservoir lying at 700 feet 8 miles north-east of Blairgowrie. It is surrounded by pine plantations, open moorland and some agricultural land. Its 300 acres act mainly as a roost for wildfowl though there is an area of marshy feed at the northern inlet. A large and varied duck population is augmented by up to 3,000 roosting greylags and 50 whooper swans.

WINTER: wigeon, pochard, tufted duck, goldeneye, goosander, greylag goose, whooper swan.

Leave the A926 between Blairgowrie and Forfar northwards on the B954 or B951. Take unclassified roads to Bridgend of Lintrathen. Minor roads run along all sides.

ISLE OF MAY (Fife)   OS 56

The island stands at the mouth of the Firth of Forth, 5 miles south-east of Anstruther and covers 140 acres. Though known since 1907 as a migration watch point, this attractive island holds a good population of breeding sea birds on the cliffs.

Migrants include large numbers of thrushes, pipits, goldcrests and finches in early spring and late autumn. The commoner warblers, chats and flycatchers occur in largest numbers in autumn when most rarities turn up. These have included barred warbler, bluethroat, ortolan bunting and vagrants like Raddes' warbler, yellow-breasted bunting, etc. Waders are usually quite numerous and the passage of shearwaters sometimes includes sooty.

SPRING: thrushes, finches, goldcrest, warblers, chats.

SUMMER: razorbill, guillemot, puffin, kittiwake, fulmar, shag, gulls, rock pipit, wheatear.

AUTUMN: turnstone, whimbrel, purple sandpiper, little stint, spotted redshank, Manx and sooty shearwaters, Arctic and great skuas, warblers, chats, flycatchers, barred warbler, bluethroat, ortolan, snow and Lapland buntings, thrushes, finches, rarities.

The island is reached by boat from Anstruther. Accommodation is available on hostel lines. Enquiries to Scottish Ornithologists' Club.

MONTROSE BASIN (Angus)   OS 50; HT +0:50 Aberdeen

This is in fact the estuary of the River South Esk, immediately inland from Montrose. It is 2 miles by 1 mile and its 2,000 acres are almost empty at low water. The exposed mud is a resort of numerous wildfowl, including a large autumn population of geese. Waders include the usual variety of winter and passage species.

Unfortunately the Basin is of straightforward access and is much disturbed by shooting.

WINTER: wigeon, pintail, shelduck, eider, goldeneye, greylag and pink-footed geese, knot, dunlin, redshank.

SPRING: waders.

AUTUMN: greenshank, green and curlew sandpipers, bar-tailed godwit, spotted redshank, little stint, ruff, mute swan.

Several points of access from the A935 along the northern shore, and from the A934 and the unclassified road at the south-western corner.

MORTON LOCHS (Fife)   OS 56

The lochs, 1 mile south of Tayport, are a National Nature Reserve covering 59 acres. They lie in the area that includes Tentsmuir Point also a National Nature Reserve, Earlshall Moor and Shelly Point which is dealt with under the Eden Estuary. The lochs are known as a wintering and breeding haunt of many duck. In spring and autumn waders, including 'fresh' species, are abundant, if the water level is low. Nearly 130 species have been recorded, including 45 breeding.

WINTER: wigeon, teal, shoveler, tufted duck, whooper swan.

SPRING: waders, little gull.

SUMMER: shoveler, tufted duck, gadwall, waders, stonechat, sedge warbler, corn bunting.

AUTUMN: godwits, green sandpiper, spotted redshank, little stint, curlew sandpiper, ruff.

Leave Tayport southwards on the B945 and turn left after 2 miles on to the track that separates the lochs. Though a great deal can be seen from this road, permits enabling one to use the hides on either side of the northern loch can be obtained from the Nature Conservancy Scottish Office.

RANNOCH AND STRATH TUMMEL   OS 48

The area includes the Black Wood of Rannoch, one of the largest areas of natural pine outside the Spey Valley, and a good place to find capercaillie and Scottish crossbill. Some of the lochs contain more duck than most Highland waters. Dunalastair Reservoir has a few whooper swans and wigeon and Loch Kinardochy and Loch Faskally are admirable places to see goosander and goldeneye in winter. Birch woods clothe most of their banks.

SUMMER: capercaillie, black grouse, common sandpiper, dipper, crossbill, buzzard, redstart, redpoll, woodcock.

WINTER: capercaillie, black grouse, dipper, crossbill, buzzard, goldeneye, goosander, whooper swan, snow bunting.

Access to the whole area is by turning west from the A9 above Pitlochry and driving along the B8019 and the B846: the unclassified roads on the south of the lochs are even more enjoyable. The Black Wood of Rannoch on the south side of Loch Rannoch belongs to the Forestry Commission, and is subject to their usual rules of access. Most other areas are viewable from the roads.

FIRTH OF TAY (Fife)   OS 50, 55 and 56; HT +1:30 Aberdeen

The Firth cuts deep into the Scottish coast and between Budden Ness to Perth there are nearly 30 miles of tidal water and some of the most outstanding bird haunts in Scotland. For our purpose the whole area is divided into three parts:

1. The Flats at the mouth west of Tentsmuir.
2. The Buddon Burn area on the north shore.
3. The estuary above Dundee along the northern bank.

1. **Tentsmuir** (OS 50 and 56) lies at the mouth of Tay on the southern shore with extensive flats to the west. Flocks of sea duck occur immediately offshore including a large gathering of long-tailed duck in early spring.

Waders are numerous and snow buntings are often abundant in autumn.
WINTER: eider, scoter, scaup, wigeon, merganser, pink-footed goose,
knot, bar-tailed godwit, snow bunting.
SPRING: long-tailed duck, little gull.
SUMMER: eider, scoter.
AUTUMN: bar-tailed godwit, whimbrel, greenshank, curlew sandpiper,
little stint.
Leave Tayport southwards and turn left after 2 miles past Morton
Lochs to Morton and on to Fetterdale. A maze of forest drives leads to
the point. No access for vehicles within the reserve.

2. **Buddon Burn** (OS 50; HT +1:20 Aberdeen) lies on the northern
shore at the mouth of the Tay 1 mile east of Monifieth. The small stream
enters the sea through a tiny bay amongst the dunes at the western end
of Buddon. The fresh water attracts a number of species but is outstanding as a haunt of little gulls particularly in spring, but the species
is present throughout the summer and autumn. Over 50 have been
recorded.
SPRING: little gull, sanderling.
SUMMER: little tern.
AUTUMN: little gull.
Walk eastwards along the shore from Monifieth.

3. **Tay Estuary** (OS 55 and 56), west of Dundee the Estuary is up to 3
miles wide with extensive mud banks along the northern shore. Above
Powgavie the shore is fringed by large reed beds that shelter a variety
of breeding birds. The mud banks are an important roost for pink-feet,
up to 20,000 appearing in autumn and 5,000 remaining for the winter.
Greylags (up to 2,000) also occur but prefer the area around Mugdrum
Island. Goldeneye are especially numerous off Newburgh in spring and
vast assemblages of waders occur on passage and in winter.
WINTER: pink-footed and greylag geese, tufted duck, goosander,
merganser, goldeneye, knot, dunlin, bar-tailed godwit.
SPRING: goldeneye, waders.
AUTUMN: knot, godwits, grey plover, whimbrel, little stint.
There are several access points, as follows:

1. KINGOODIE: leave Dundee westwards on the A85 and turn left
on to the B958 at Invergowrie.

2. POWGAVIE: continue on the B958 to Powgavie and take the road
straight to the shore.

3. PORT ALLEN: continue on the B958 and turn left.

4. NEWBURGH: take the ferry from Dundee to Newport and turn
westwards on the A914. At its junction with the A913 turn right to
Newburgh and view Mugdrum Island.

Argyllshire, Inverness-shire and Inner Hebrides

CAIRNGORMS (Inverness)　　　　　　　OS Tourist Map Cairngorms

The mountains between the Spey and its tributary the Feshie River, and the Dee and its tributary the Geldie Burn. The area forms a geographical unity some 10 miles square which constitutes one of the largest nature reserves in Europe. The main peaks are all about 4,200 feet mark and the high plateau forms the most extensive 'alpine-arctic' habitat in Britain. Ptarmigan, dotterel and snow bunting are found in that order of abundance, but it is possible to tramp over all the tops for a day and still not see a sign of any of these birds. Further west the country becomes more rugged and golden eagle, buzzard, peregrine and merlin become more numerous along with greenshank and red grouse.

WINTER: snow bunting.

SUMMER: ptarmigan, dotterel, snow bunting, golden eagle, peregrine, merlin, greenshank.

Restrictions on access are confined to parts of Mar and Glenfeshie in August–October, otherwise the visitor is free to walk the 58,000 acres as he will.

The opening up of the Cairngorms as a tourist area has made the high tops easily accessible to all via the chair-lift at the head of Glen More.

No matter how strong and energetic the bird-watcher the Cairngorms are no place for the beginner. Day walkers should carry a one inch OS map, preferably cloth, compass and be suitably equipped with food and clothing.

Speyside has a range of accommodation, but try Braemar which is also convenient for the Forests of Mar and Derry with crested tit, etc.

CANNA (Inverness)　　　　　　　　　　　　　　　　OS 33

The island lies 3½ miles north-west of Rhum and 25 miles west of Mallaig. It is over 4 miles long by 1 mile and reaches a maximum height of 690 feet. It is less grand and impressive than its neighbours Rhum and Eigg and with its rich soil on a basalt base, can grow the earliest potatoes in Scotland. Like Rhum and Eigg it is a big Manx shearwater station but is also very good for many other species including cliff breeding sea birds. The cliffs west of Tarbert hold shearwaters and nearby Sandy and Hykseir are very good generally. Amongst a comparative wealth of land birds, corncrakes are still numerous.

SUMMER: Manx shearwater, fulmar, kittiwake, razorbill, guillemot, black guillemot, puffin, eider, corncrake.

MacBraynes run a regular steamer service to Canna from Mallaig. Accommodation is available in crofts.

COLONSAY AND ORONSAY (Argyll) OS 51

The two islands are 8 miles west of Jura, 10 miles long, and in spite of their position open to the Atlantic they are a wonderful example of what can be done in the face of apparently insurmountable difficulties. There are natural woodlands of a variety of species and plantings that have succeeded in overcoming the harsh conditions. The result is a wealth of small birds that is unparalleled in the Hebrides. Yet the open moors, cliffs, sand dunes and lochs all have their own bird life. Barnacle geese winter on Eilean nan Ron at the southern tip of Oronsay.

WINTER: barnacle goose.

SUMMER: razorbill, guillemot, kittiwake, fulmar, common, Arctic and little terns, Canada goose, corncrake, passerines.

MacBraynes' steamers sail regularly from West Loch Tarbert to Colonsay with connections to Gourock and Glasgow. Oronsay is connected to Colonsay for 3 hours at low tide. There is a hotel at Scalasaig and many cottages take in visitors.

ISLAY (Argyll) OS 57

Islay is one of the most beautiful and varied of Scottish islands. It measures 26 miles from north to south and is large enough for a long holiday of exploration. Its varied habitats include woodland, moors, cliffs, dunes, machair, lochs and sea lochs. Winter is probably the best season, for by February Islay holds 10,000 barnacle geese or one sixth of the world's population. Greenland white-fronts reach 3,000 about the same time, and 500 greylags winter. Most of these geese can be seen on the huge shallow sea loch, Loch Indaal, but the biggest flocks are on the north-western part of the island. Loch Indaal also holds most of the sea duck that winter, great northern divers are numerous, and whooper swans and glaucous gulls regular.

Over 100 species breed, including the occasional scoter; black guillemot at Port Askaig for instance; golden eagle and outstandingly one of Scotland's two colonies of chough on Oa (the other is on nearby Jura). Perhaps the Arctic skua breeds.

WINTER: barnacle, white-fronted and greylag geese, scaup, eider, merganser, wigeon, shelduck, whooper swan, glaucous gull, great northern diver.

SPRING: great northern diver, whimbrel, turnstone.

SUMMER: merganser, eider, auks, black guillemot, kittiwake, terns, golden eagle, buzzard, chough.

AUTUMN: Manx shearwater, skuas, black-tailed godwit, greenshank, sanderling, curlew sandpiper, little stint.

MacBraynes run a daily (except Sunday) service between Gourock/Tarbert/Islay which is on two steamers and a short bus ride. This is increased to twice daily two days each week during July–August. Western Ferries run daily throughout the year from Kennocraig to Port Askaig.

Between West Loch Tarbert and Gigha in winter the sea holds velvet scoter, long-tailed duck, Slavonian grebe, and huge numbers of great northern divers.

BEA run a daily service from Glasgow (Renfrew) and by air Islay is 4½ hours from London. Choughs are frequently seen at the airport.

There is plenty of accommodation and cars can be hired. Write to Islay, Jura and Colonsay Tourist Association, District Offices, Bowmore.

MULL (Argyll)   OS 45, 51 and 52

Mull is, apart from Skye, the largest of the Inner Hebrides and overlaps three different OS maps. Rising to over 3,000 feet the island offers most of the habitats found on the mainland within a confined and explorable area. Outstanding are the cliffs of the Gribun which hold colonies of sea birds and a good population of golden eagles. The woodlands are attractive, especially those on the south coast at Carsaig, while the nearby Loch Buie is a haunt of whooper swans in winter. Barnacle geese winter on the neighbouring Staffa, which is a famous sea bird resort and tourist spot (for instance Fingals Cave and Basalt Columns). The island is best visited on an excursion from Tobermory or Oban in summer.

WINTER: barnacle goose, whooper swan, great northern diver, eider.

SUMMER: golden eagle, buzzard, razorbill, guillemot, puffin, kittiwake, fulmar, common and Arctic terns, eider, ptarmigan.

MacBraynes' steamers call daily at Craignure and Tobermory and bus services connect the main parts of the island. Steamers carry cars at quite cheap rates from Oban to Craignure and there is a good choice of accommodation. By selecting the right sailing, either the outward or homeward journey can include a call at Staffa. Write to: Mull and Iona Council of Social Service, 48 Main Street, Tobermory.

RHUM (Inverness)   OS 33

This was for long a forbidden island but since 1957 has been a National

Nature Reserve covering 26,400 acres, or about 8 miles square. It rises to 2,659 feet and is one of the wettest places in Britain, lying 15 miles west of Mallaig and immediately south-west of Skye. The island is grass covered, with patches of heather, mountain lichens and mosses, and some areas of trees around Loch Scresort and Papadil Lodge. It is now used as an outdoor laboratory and research includes an intensive study of the population of red deer.

Birds include an interesting colony of several thousand pairs of Manx shearwaters, near the top of Askival, at a height of 2,500 feet as well as cliff breeding sea-birds. Two or three pairs of golden eagles and peregrines breed annually.

SUMMER: Manx shearwater, guillemot, razorbill, puffin, fulmar, black guillemot, kittiwake, eider, golden eagle, peregrine, golden plover, merlin, red-throated diver, merganser, corncrake, rock dove, common gull, Arctic tern, goldcrest, twite, tree creeper.

Day visitors are free to land at Loch Scresort and explore the area on the south side of the loch. Permission to go beyond this must be sought from the Wardens at White House, Kinloch or Bayview Kinloch. Bird-watchers, and other naturalists, wishing to study any particular feature of the island's natural history should write to the Nature Conservancy Scottish Office as far in advance as possible. Every effort will be made to provide facilities for research, but there is no accommodation. Only scientists, naturalists and climbers can stay on Rhum.

MacBraynes' steamers leave Mallaig three times a week for Rhum. The crossing takes 3–3½ hours.

SPEYSIDE AT ABERNETHY FOREST AND LOCH GARTEN
(Inverness)   OS Tourist Map Cairngorms

The forest and loch lie on the eastern side of the Spey valley 8 miles downstream from the more renowned Rothiemurchus, near Nethybridge and Boat of Garten. Bird-watchers have for too long concentrated on Rothiemurchus, and Abernethy has been consequently neglected though it is almost as rich in birds.

Basically the area is much the same as Rothiemurchus with scattered growth of old Scots pines and new plantations, with birches and juniper bushes, and heather and small berry plants. The small passerines include the specialities, crested tit, crossbill and siskin, but Abernethy has the ospreys at Loch Garten as a unique attraction. Capercaillies are numerous and the only large-scale display ground of this species in the country is in Abernethy.

In spring many northern species stay very late, displaying and look as if they are settling down to breed. Goldeneye, redwing, brambling are all regular in May.

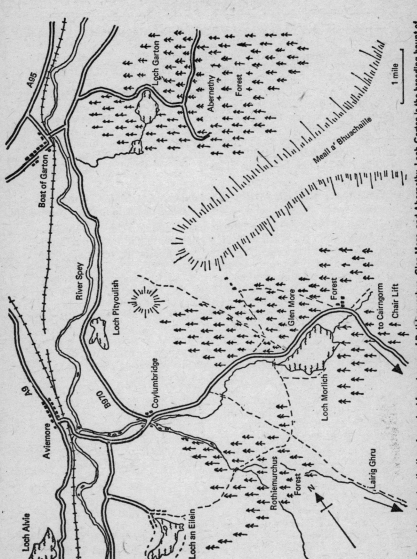

Speyside: showing the three important forest areas of Rothiemurchus, Glen More, and Abernethy. Loch Garten is the breeding haunt of ospreys and Loch Mortich a favourite fishing ground, while Loch an Eilean is a celebrated nineteenth-century haunt. Glen More is an excellent centre and has a Youth Hostel and camp site

WINTER: whooper swan, goldeneye, hen harrier, short-eared owl, cross-bill.

SPRING: redwing, goldeneye, brambling, crossbill.

SUMMER: crested tit, siskin, grouse, capercaillie, long-eared owl, golden eagle, peregrine, merlin, greenshank, woodcock.

Leave the A95 eastwards to either Nethybridge or Boat of Garten on the B970. A ring road runs from both up to Loch Garten which is 'osprey signposted' in summer. This road makes an excellent basis for exploration which is facilitated by a series of forest tracks heading up into the mountains east of Abernethy proper. Excellent views of breeding ospreys can be obtained from the RSPB hides near the Loch Garten eyrie from 10.00 to 20.00 hours during the season.

SPEYSIDE AT ROTHIEMURCHUS AND GLEN MORE (Inverness)
OS Tourist Map Cairngorms

This is one of the outstanding bird haunts in Britain. The area stretches from Aviemore in the north to Insh, 9 miles south and up to the Cairn-gorms east of Loch Morlich. The Forest of Abernethy, including Loch Garten and the Cairngorms, are treated separately. The whole can be divided into several quite distinct parts, all of which should be visited. The Spey Valley itself and the large Loch Insh with its marshy inlet are the haunt of wildfowl in winter. To the west lie the birch woods of Craigellachie (250 acres) which have been incorporated into a National Nature Reserve and which abound with birds, indeed Rothiemurchus seems deserted in comparison. From the top of Craigellachie the huge basin of Rothiemurchus lies before one, mingling in to the Glen More Forest further north with Meall a' Bhuachaille separating the whole from Abernethy, and the Cairngorms massively enclosing the area from the east. This basin is the chief haunt of the crested tit and Scottish crossbill and holds many other interesting species. The area also lies on the line separating carrion from hooded crow and though neither is numerous, both forms breed.

SPRING: goldeneye, whooper swan, golden eagle, crossbill.

SUMMER: crested tit, crossbill, siskin, capercaillie, black grouse, golden eagle, woodcock, greenshank, willow and wood warblers, redstart, carrion and hooded crows.

The Spey is flanked on the west by the A9 and on the east by the B970 and there are railway stations at Aviemore and Kincraig. The whole area is comparatively open and free of access though it is advisable to keep to the established tracks wherever possible. These are numerous out of the Aviemore–Coylumbridge area and from the shore of Loch Morlich. Places worth visiting include Loch an Eilean where the castle is an old and famous osprey haunt; Loch Morlich where ospreys regularly fish;

and a walk through the heart of Rothiemurchus. The Forestry Commission publishes a booklet of 'Walks in the Queen's Forest' dealing with Glenmore Forest Park. As a growing resort the area is well served by hotels. See Map, page 285.

TIREE (Argyll) OS 44

Tiree lies in the Inner Hebrides immediately west of Mull. It is, however, not protected from the Atlantic by the Outer Hebrides and so receives the full force of gales. Because of this it has a landscape closely akin to that of the outer islands with extensive beaches of shell sand and a generally fertile mixture of sand and peat. Whereas Coll, its easterly neighbour, is sheltered from the ocean and is to a large extent bare rock and peat. Wildfowl find the island attractive and Loch a' Phuill and Loch Bhasapoll are major centres, though white-fronts are found on the Reef, a marshy area in the centre of the island. Sea duck are numerous in the bays, and Gunna between Tiree and Coll, holds 400 barnacle geese. The vast beaches hold waders on passage and the island is renowned as the best snipe shooting in Europe! The cliffs at Ceann a'Mhara in the south-west hold breeding sea birds, and Gunna has terns.

Nearby Coll holds Arctic skua and red-throated diver.

WINTER: whooper swan, wigeon, gadwall, tufted duck, goldeneye, eider, merganser, barnacle and white-fronted geese, snipe, jack snipe.

SPRING: whimbrel, turnstone, sanderling.

SUMMER: common and Arctic terns, ringed plover, guillemot, razorbill, black guillemot, red-throated diver, wheatear, stonechat, hooded crow, Arctic skua, snipe, shag, fulmar, rock dove, chough.

AUTUMN: bar-tailed godwit, sanderling, greenshank.

MacBraynes' steamers leave Oban 3 days a week to Coll and Tiree. Tiree has an airport and there are frequent services from Glasgow. A range of accommodation is available – but book in advance. There are hotels at Arinagour on Coll and Scarinish on Tiree.

TRESHNISH ISLES (Argyll) OS 44

The islands lie within the arms of Mull and 2 miles south-west of Treshnish Point on that island. They are composed of basalt and are mainly steep sided and flat topped. There are large colonies of sea birds particularly on the Harp Rock off Lunga.

WINTER: barnacle goose.

SUMMER: storm petrel, Manx shearwater, fulmar, razorbill, guillemot, puffin, common tern, eider.

At present the isles are used as seasonal grazing. There is no permanent settlement and visitors should be prepared to camp, and make local arrangements for transport. The Treshnish Isles seem, however, to be well worth the efforts involved in getting there. They were the property of the late Niall Rankin.

WEST LOCH TARBERT (Argyll) OS 58

This is a 10 mile long sea loch that almost separates Kintyre from the mainland. Because of its geographical position it is used as the major shipping route between Glasgow and the Highlands by MacBraynes with a shuttle bus service between it and East Loch Tarbert. Its convenience as a transport centre makes the winter concentrations of sea duck, grebes, and especially great northern divers easily accessible. A flock of white-fronts winters on the flats opposite Gigha, and numbers of barnacles are noted at the loch mouth in spring.

WINTER: great northern diver, Slavonian grebe, velvet scoter, eider, long-tailed duck, white-fronted goose.

SPRING: barnacle goose.

Frequent steamers from Gourock to Tarbert and coaches on the A83 along the southern side of the loch. Alternatively, and better, explore by car. The steamer trip to Gigha and back is outstanding.

Ayrshire, Dunbartonshire, Lanarkshire, Renfrewshire & Stirlingshire

AILSA CRAIG (Ayr) OS 72

A precipitous hump in the Firth of Clyde threequarters of a mile long and rising to 1,110 feet. It lies 10 miles west of Girvan and is quarried commercially. Ailsa is one of Britain's foremost sea bird breeding stations. Recent counts suggest that about 13,500 pairs of gannets breed, together with large numbers of the commoner species, including both northern and southern guillemots. The quarries are particularly noted for the quality of their granite which is used to make curling stones.

SUMMER: gannet, razorbill, guillemot, puffin, kittiwake.

A boat leaves Girvan harbour every Monday and Friday, cost £1.00, to land and take off quarrymen; this trip does *not* allow sufficient time to visit the sea bird colonies. However it is possible to camp on the island with the permission of Mr. I. Girvan, 'Millcraig', Henrietta Street, Girvan, who is also the boatman. Other boats make trips during summer allowing other camping arrangements – but time does not permit a worthwhile exploration without staying overnight. Consult the Publicity Department, Town Clerk's Office, Girvan.

British Railways run a steamer trip round the island three times each summer and this gives good views not normally available from small boats.

Under no circumstances should the gannetry be closely approached after 15th July. By this date the young birds are well grown and tend to leave their nests at human approach. Such action is inevitably fatal.

CASTLE SEMPLE LOCH (Renfrew) OS 60

The loch lies to the south-west of Glasgow, immediately east of Lochwinnoch. Though over 1½ miles long it is extremely shallow, being nowhere deeper than 5 feet. It is a first class wildfowl water and both diving and dabbling duck are numerous. A small flock of greylags has been regular for almost 30 years, and whooper swans have topped 100.

WINTER: wigeon, pintail, shoveler, pochard, tufted duck, goldeneye, goosander, greylag goose, whooper swan.

Leave Glasgow westwards on the A8 but fork left on to the A737 to

Paisley. Continue and turn right on to the A760 2½ miles past Howwood. Cross the railway, two rivers and then turn right on to an unclassified road into Lochwinnoch. View the southern end of the loch. Pass under the railway and immediately turn right parallel to it and in half a mile fork right over the railway back to the loch shore.

HUNTERSTON SANDS (Ayr)   OS 59; HT —0:27 Greenock

The sands lie on the eastern shore of the Firth of Clyde 2½ miles south of Fairlie, where the foreshore widens to almost threequarters of a mile. On a rising tide large numbers of sea duck are present with eider and merganser reaching a peak in late summer. Waders can usually be seen, and there is a good selection in autumn.

WINTER: wigeon, eider, merganser, shelduck, waders.

AUTUMN: eider, merganser, waders.

Leave Fairlie southwards on the A78 and turn right after 1½ miles on the road to Hunterston Nuclear Power Station.

FIRTH OF CLYDE (Dunbarton/Renfrew)

OS 59 and 60; HT at Greenock

The Firth is not outstanding for birds. The only extensive areas of fore-shore are between Dunbarton and Cardross on the northern shore and Langbank on the southern. A fair variety of duck occur especially off Cardross, but scaup gather off Helensburgh. Knot are regular but the flocks are much smaller than on the east coast. At passage times the Clyde and the Solway are the best west coast wader sites.

WINTER: wigeon, pintail, goldeneye, merganser, shelduck, scaup, knot.

AUTUMN: knot, curlew, sandpipers, little stint, greenshank.

Leave Glasgow north-westwards on the A82 and fork left on to the A814 to Dunbarton. Continue to Cardross. Cross the railway west of the station and walk along the shore.

Alternatively, leave Glasgow westwards on the A8 and view the estuary between West Ferry and Langbank.

GRANGEMOUTH (Stirling)   OS 61; HT +0:30 Leith

Grangemouth lies on the southern shore of the Forth above Edinburgh. Between Kincardine Bridge and Bo'ness the mudflats are up to 1½ miles wide and are interrupted only by the Grangemouth Docks extension. Though this central area is an industrial sprawl the birds are outstanding. Wildfowl usually number several thousand and include roosting greylags and pinkfeet, December–March. Vast numbers of knot are present with other waders in winter when the main roosts are at Longannet Point and

Kincardine Bridge on the Fife shore. The present industrial developments on both sites will doubtless change this situation. In autumn a large range of waders pass through including most of the fresh species, especially at Skinflats to the west of Grangemouth. High tide visits advised.

SPRING: wigeon, pintail, goldeneye, goosander, merganser, shelduck, greylag and pink-footed geese, knot, bar-tailed godwit, turnstone, merlin.

SPRING: waders.

AUTUMN: knot, bar-tailed godwit, whimbrel, curlew sandpiper, little stint, green sandpiper, spotted redshank, grey plover, ruff.

The dockland area of Grangemouth provides excellent, if unsavoury, views over large areas of mud. Leave the town centre northwards up the eastern side of the docks.

For Skinflats, leave Grangemouth northwards on the A905, cross the River Carron and take the first turning right past Skinflats village. Continue on one of several tracks to the sea wall.

HAMILTON LOW PARKS (Lanark)   OS 61

The parks lie between the industrial developments of Hamilton and Motherwell. The Clyde here flows through a flood plain dotted with numerous pools and backwaters, a large part of which has been declared a bird sanctuary. In winter 2,000 duck, 200 greylags and 30 whooper swans are regularly present and a large number of these can be seen from Bothwell Bridge. Passage of waders is very good for an inland locality.

WINTER: wigeon, pintail, shoveler, pochard, tufted duck, goldeneye, greylag goose, whooper swan.

SPRING: waders.

AUTUMN: ruff, wood and green sandpipers, greenshank, spotted redshank.

Leave Glasgow eastwards on the A74. This road passes over Bothwell Bridge on the far side of the town. The M74 passes to the east. Permits can be obtained from the Town Clerk, The Town House, Hamilton.

HORSE ISLAND (Ayr)   OS 59

This is a 5 acre island in the Firth of Clyde, 1 mile west of Ardrossan. It has sandy beaches, rock shorelines, and is a breeding site of five species of gull and three species of tern. The island is an RSPB reserve.

SUMMER: common, Arctic and Sandwich terns, gulls.

Free permits are available from the Honorary Warden at Ryesholm, 26 Caldwell Road, West Kilbride, Ayrshire, and visits should be arranged with the official boatman, Mr R. Arnott, 10 Mayville Street, Stevenston, Ayrshire.

LENZIE LOCH (Gadloch) (Lanark) OS 60

The loch is 4 miles north-east of central Glasgow and immediately south of Lenzie. Its western banks consist of mudflats in summer made up of coal silt brought down by a stream from a nearby pit. Wildfowl are the most interesting birds especially in spring and autumn, though up to 300 greylags are resident in winter. The coal mudflats attract waders on passage and eighteen species have been reported to date.

WINTER: greylag goose, wigeon, teal, golden plover.
SPRING: whooper swan, geese, duck, waders.
SUMMER: pochard.
AUTUMN: wildfowl, green sandpiper, snipe, spotted redshank.

Leave Glasgow northwards on the A803 and turn right after 4 miles on to the B819. The loch is on the right after 2 miles. It is surrounded by farmland but can be seen from the road at many points at distances down to 50 yards.

LOCH LOMOND (Dunbarton-Stirling) OS 53

Loch Lomond lies north-west of Glasgow and is a wonderful, open playground for the people of the industrial lowlands. It is an extremely beautiful area and the lochside and many islands are well wooded with semi-natural oaks and recent conifers. Though mergansers and capercaillie breed and the woodlands hold the usual highland summer species, the main attraction is the wildfowl in winter. These concentrate around the mouth of the Endrick in the south-east, the west bank of which forms part of a National Nature Reserve. Numerous duck, up to 1,000 greylag geese as well as the occasional small flocks of Greenland white-fronts are found in the area.

WINTER: wigeon, pochard, tufted duck, merganser, goldeneye, greylag and white fronted geese, whooper swan.
SUMMER: heron, merganser, grey wagtail, grasshopper and other warblers.
AUTUMN: waders.

Leave Glasgow northwards on the A809. Turn left on to the A811 at Drymen Bridge. Turn right on to an unclassified loop road half a mile before Gartochorn. Continue on foot from the post box. All enquiries to Nature Conservancy Scottish Office or the Warden at Drymen. Arrangements to visit the islands can be made at the boat house, Balmaha.

Berwickshire, The Lothians (East, West and Mid), Peeblesshire, Roxburghshire and Selkirkshire

ABERLADY BAY (East-Lothian)　　　　OS 62; HT —0:11 Leith

This is a tidal estuary lying north of Aberlady Village on the A198 between Edinburgh and North Berwick. Its 1,400 acres of foreshore and dunes have been made a local nature reserve. Several hundred duck use the bay and pinkfeet are frequently present. Waders include the usual species in winter and a wider variety on passage, especially autumn. Aberlady is the most regular place in Scotland for wood sandpipers.

Gullane Point on the northern side of the bay is an excellent place for sea birds, notably red-necked grebes, at all seasons.

WINTER: pink-footed goose, wigeon, scoter, velvet scoter, merganser, long-tailed duck, knot, bar-tailed godwit, red-necked grebe, divers.

SPRING: waders, red-necked grebe, divers.

SUMMER: long-eared owl, common, Arctic and little terns, dunlin, redshank.

AUTUMN: skuas, terns, green, wood and curlew sandpipers, grey plover, black-tailed godwit, little stint, ruff, red-necked, black-necked and Slavonian grebes, divers.

Leave Aberlady eastwards and stop at the head of the bay where a timber bridge crosses the small stream. There are no limitations on access except to a small part in summer.

ALMOND ESTUARY (Mid-Lothian and West Lothian)　　　　OS 62

The river runs through a wooded gorge to its mouth at the village of Cramond, 6 miles from the centre of Edinburgh. The western shore of the estuary reaches almost to Queensferry and contains the most waders (up to 8,000 in winter) and duck (up to 2,000). Some 15,000 gulls use the flats as a roost; several hundred merganser flock here in autumn, while pinkfeet and other geese are casual in small numbers. The woodlands of the Dalmeny estate stretch from Cramond to Queensferry and are full of small birds. Cramond Island is tidal, and though it has no seabird colonies it deserves more study than it gets. 157 species have been recorded for the area.

WINTER: mallard, pintail, merganser, knot, oystercatcher, dunlin, curlew, bar-tailed godwit.

SUMMER: common tern, woodcock, dipper, grey wagtail, shelduck.

AUTUMN: roseate and 'commic' terns, skuas, redshank, merganser.

Public paths give access to the eastern side of the river and estuary. The western side is reached by rowing-boat ferry over the Almond from Cramond and there is a fine walk through the woods edging the foreshore all the way to Queensferry (five miles). Cramond Island is accessible for not more than two hours each side of the low tide.

BASS ROCK (East Lothian)   OS 56

Bass Rock lies 1½ miles offshore and 3 miles north-east of North Berwick at the mouth of the Firth of Forth. It is a quarter of a mile by 300 yards and is a large gannetry. Nearly 6,000 breeding pairs were counted in a recent survey.

SUMMER: gannet, fulmar, shag, kittiwake, guillemot, razorbill, puffin.

Access is by permission of the owner and by boat from North Berwick. The Scottish Ornithologists' Club run organised excursions most summers. Because of the risk of disturbance to this valuable sanctuary, all visitors should enquire first to the Scottish Ornithologists' Club. There are regular boat trips round the island during the summer.

CHEVIOT HILLS (Roxburgh)   OS 70 and 71

The Cheviots form the border between England and Scotland and rise to 2,676 feet. The vast area of heather and grass moorland is as lonely as any could wish and does not even attract climbers, walkers and tourists to any great extent. The hills have been long famous as a haunt of birds, including the usual moorland species. Almost every plantation holds woodcock, and black grouse are numerous.

SUMMER: golden plover, dunlin, woodcock, merlin, short-eared owl, ring ouzel, dipper, red grouse, black grouse.

There are several roads leading into the heart of the hills, notably on the northern and eastern sides. All are public except that from West-newton up the College Valley on the northern side, 1 mile west of Kirk-newton on the B6351. Permission to motor up must be obtained from D. M. Campbell, Estate Agent, Wooler. Wooler is a good centre with accommodation and good roads up Harthorpe Burn. There are foot-paths throughout the area and no restrictions on the open moor.

COBBINSHAW RESERVOIR (Mid-Lothian)   OS 61

The reservoir lies in the Pentland Hills 17 miles south-west of Edinburgh and 11 miles north-east of Lanark. It covers 300 acres at 850 feet, and holds small numbers of duck and a regular flock of up to 30 whooper swans. Greylag geese total 150 but are outnumbered by the 1,500 plus pinkfeet that flight in to roost from the Lanark area. The water is usually deserted by the end of the year.

WINTER: greylag and pink-footed geese, wigeon, teal, tufted duck, goldeneye, whooper swan, gulls.

SUMMER: black-headed gull.

Leave the A71 1¼ miles south of West Calder southwards on to the A704. After 1¼ miles turn left and follow through till a road on left leads to reservoir. View from the road and causeway. Permission to go round the reservoir should be sought at the local farm.

DUDDINGSTON LOCH, DUNSAPPIE LOCH, ARTHUR'S SEAT (Mid-Lothian)   OS 162

These three localities lie within 1½ miles of the centre of Edinburgh inside Holyrood Park. Duddingston Loch extends to 30 acres and includes a large reed bed; it is the venue of several thousand pochard and tufted duck in winter, and a good place for marsh birds all the year. Dunsappie is much smaller, but in winter almost always has wigeon and gadwall that can be seen at very close range. Arthur's Seat is a grass covered hill with gorse flanks attractive to migrants; wheatears are found on the top in the summer, and snow buntings in winter.

WINTER: pochard, tufted duck, gadwall, wigeon, shoveler, water rail, snow bunting, corn bunting.

SUMMER: great crested grebe, little grebe, tufted duck, pochard, long-eared owl, grasshopper warbler, wheatear.

PASSAGE: warblers, redstarts, tree pipit.

Access to Duddingston is prohibited, but the reserve can be overlooked from many points on the road in Holyrood Park, and where the loch nears the road on the north side outside the park. Access to Dunsappie and Arthur's Seat is unrestricted.

FIDRA, EYEBROUGHTY AND THE LAMB (East Lothian)   OS 56

These are three small rocky islets lying less than a mile off the East Lothian shore of the Firth of Forth and covering a total of 6 acres. Fidra is the largest and supports breeding colonies of terns, including a few pairs of roseate. The Lamb has the only colony of cormorants in the Forth, and Eyebroughty is the smallest island and mainly noted as a moulting ground for up to 2,000 eiders in June and July. The rocks opposite Fidra are one of the best places in Scotland to see roseate terns without a boat journey.

SUMMER: common, Arctic, Sandwich and roseate terns, cormorant, shag, eider, kittiwake, fulmar, gulls.

The islands are managed as reserves by the RSPB and arrangements to land should be made through the Society's Scottish Office, 17 Regent Terrace, Edinburgh EH7 5BN. To see the moulting eiders from the mainland, leave the A198 at the eastern end of Dirleton village northwards to Yellowcraig car park. Walk along the coast 1½ miles westwards.

GLADHOUSE RESERVOIR (Mid-Lothian)   OS 62

The reservoir lies in the Moorfoot Hills 13 miles south of Edinburgh at 900 feet and covers 400 acres. The water is a major roost of greylag (1,000) and pinkfeet (8,000) from October to December, and is then used again in the spring. Gulls, too, use it as a secure base. Snow buntings are regular and the passage of waders is excellent for an inland locality.

WINTER: pink-footed and greylag geese, wigeon, teal, tufted duck, goldeneye, goosander, gulls, snow bunting.

SPRING: waders.

SUMMER: duck, grasshopper warbler, black grouse.

AUTUMN: greenshank, oystercatcher, ruff, green sandpiper.

Leave Edinburgh south-eastwards on the A7 and turn right on to the B6372 just past Gorebridge. Follow this past Rosebery Reservoir on the left and where the road turns sharp right take the half left up to the fir wood. Turn sharp left on emerging and view the reservoir round the north-western side. Access is strictly prohibited, and trespassers are doing bird-watching a great deal of harm.

THE HIRSEL (Berwick)   OS 64

The Hirsel is the traditional home of the Earls of Home and is one of the best areas for birds in Scotland south of the Highlands. 156 species have been noted and 96 have bred. The 27 acre Hirsel Lake holds a winter concentration of over 2,000 duck, and the Scottish Ornithologists' Club organises a summer excursion.

WINTER: shoveler, goldeneye, wigeon, scaup.

SUMMER: marsh tit, pied flycatcher, warblers.

Leave Coldstream westwards on the A698. In half a mile turn right at Coldstream Lodge on to the main carriage drive which leads past the lake. There is a footpath round the edges giving excellent watching in the woodland area.

HULE MOSS (Berwick)   OS 63

This spot lies 750 feet up, 2 miles north of Greenlaw. It is set in an area of sheep farming and consists of a loch and a surrounding area of bog. Pinkfeet are the main attraction with up to 6,000 in autumn, 1,500 in winter and 3,000 in spring. A total of 80 species has been noted.

WINTER: pink-footed goose, goldeneye, pochard, tufted duck.
SPRING: pink-footed goose.
AUTUMN: duck, pink-footed goose, black-tailed godwit, knot, spotted redshank.

Access is direct from the A6105, 2 miles north of Greenlaw, but permission should be obtained from Hollyburton Farm which is 3 miles north-west of Greenlaw on an unclassified road.

INCHMICKERY (Mid-Lothian)   OS 62

This is an island lying in the middle of the Firth of Forth about 4 miles from the centre of Edinburgh. It covers 3 acres and was heavily built up by the military during 1939. Its colony of 450 pairs of roseate terns is the largest in the Forth and other terns breed in good numbers.

SUMMER: roseate, common, Arctic and Sandwich terns.

The island is an RSPB reserve and access is by permit obtainable from the Society's Scottish Office, 17 Regent Terrace, Edinburgh EH7 5BN. The roseate terns return in the middle of May.

LINLITHGOW LOCH (West Lothian)   OS 61

The loch lies on the north side of the A9 at Linlithgow. The loch is natural, covers 100 acres with several small reed beds and in spite of sailing activities is a virtual sanctuary. There are good numbers of wintering duck.

WINTER: wigeon, pochard, tufted duck, goldeneye.

Access is straightforward from the centre of the town.

PORTMORE LOCH (Peebles)   OS 62

The loch is 1 mile east of the A703 between Penicuik and Peebles, and has been described as 'a little gem' by Baxter and Rintoul in their *Birds of Scotland*. Though basically a natural loch the water level has been raised by a dam and the loch is now nearly threequarters of a mile long. It is set at 1,000 feet and is surrounded by pines with open moors rising to 2,000 feet in the east. Winter brings many duck and a roosting flock of greylags. In summer many upland species breed and great crested grebes usually make an attempt.

WINTER: tufted duck, goldeneye, goosander, greylag goose.

SUMMER: black grouse, common sandpiper, tree pipit, whinchat, great crested grebe.

Leave the A703 eastwards at Fala Toll and turn right on track in 1 mile. Access is to the east side of the loch only. The path continues through the hills to Eddleston where there is a convenient hotel.

ST ABB'S HEAD (Berwick)   OS 64

St Abb's Head is on the coast 12 miles north of Berwick-upon-Tweed.
Though the cliffs at the Head rise to over 300 feet they stretch westwards
almost to Cockburnspath and reach a maximum height of 500 feet.
Breeding sea birds are the main interest, including a small number of
puffins, and there are 8 miles of cliff to explore.

SUMMER: razorbill, guillemot, puffin, kittiwake, fulmar.

Several tracks leave the A1107 eastwards between Cockburnspath and
Coldingham that lead to the cliff top. That to Dowlaw is easy to find and
has a footpath at the end over Telegraph Hill to Fast Castle which is a
good spot.

SEAFIELD, LEITH (Mid-Lothian)   OS 62; HT at Leith

Seafield consists of a long sea wall to the east of Leith Docks with some
sandy shores further east. There is a sewage outfall that attracts vast
numbers of sea duck in winter and numerous other species at all seasons.
Scaup, up to 30,000, are dominant but other large numbers include 2,000
goldeneye, 1,500 scoter, and hundreds of eider and long-tailed duck. Up
to 400 great crested grebe have been counted and large numbers of
mergansers congregate at the mouth of the Esk at Musselburgh in
autumn. On passage many species are noted.

WINTER: scaup, scoter, eider, long-tailed duck, great crested grebe,
knot.

SPRING: waders, terns.

AUTUMN: gannet, waders, terns, skuas.

Take the bus from Leith to Portobello and alight at Seafield. Cross the
railway to the north.

THREIPMUIR RESERVOIR AND BAVELAW MARSH
(Mid-Lothian)   OS 62

The area lies in the Pentland Hills some 8 miles south-west of Edinburgh
at 800 feet and covers 220 acres. The marsh is at the south-western inlet
end of the reservoir and is mainly noted as a breeding ground of duck.
In winter whooper swans are regular, and several hundred greylag geese
roost in autumn and early winter.

WINTER: wigeon, teal, whooper swan, greylag goose.

SUMMER: teal, shoveler, tufted duck, black-headed gull, great crested
grebe.

Leave Edinburgh south-westwards on the A70 and turn left after 8
miles to Balerno. Fork left and continue past Marchbank Hotel. As the
road turns right a track leads downhill. Fork left at the firwood and

continue along the north-western shore. A causeway back on the road overlooks the Bavelaw marsh, otherwise the area is private.

TYNE MOUTH (East Lothian)   OS 63; HT —0:08 Leith

The river mouth lies immediately west of Dunbar and forms a small estuary 1½ miles by half a mile. It has areas of saltings and holds up to 1,000 pinkfeet and the odd greylag and brent. Duck are both numerous and varied and the usual estuary waders winter and are augmented by passage species.

    WINTER: pink-footed goose, wigeon, shelduck, goldeneye, eider, waders.
    SPRING: green sandpiper.
    SUMMER: eider, shelduck, ringed plover, short-eared owl.
    AUTUMN: green and curlew sandpipers, ruff, whimbrel, greenshank, little stint.

Leave Dunbar westwards on the A1087. Turn northwards in West Barns and follow footpath along the south side of estuary. The reefs

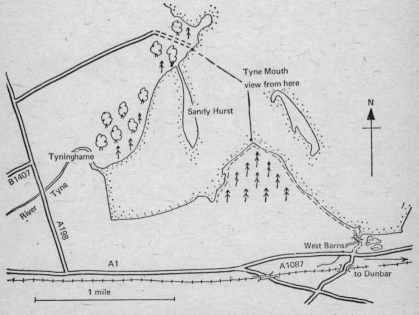

Tyne Mouth: an attractive wooded tidal basin with private land on all sides

offshore are a daytime roost of wildfowl. For the north side, continue on the A1087, turn right on to the A198 and half a mile past Tyninghame village turn right again. Park at car park and continue down track to the sea. The surrounding estate is strictly private.

See Map.

WATCHWATER RESERVOIR (Berwick)   OS 63

The reservoir lies 7 miles west of Duns, is a little over half a mile long and was flooded in 1954. Lying at almost 900 feet, it has a small population of wildfowl that includes the odd whooper swan, but is primarily known as a roost of up to 300 greylag geese from October–December.

WINTER: greylag goose, goldeneye, teal, whooper swan.

Leave Duns westwards on the A6105 and turn right after 1 mile to Longformacus. Turn left before the bridge to the reservoir. No restrictions.

Caithness, Ross, Cromarty & Sutherland

Inverness is over 500 miles north of London, and Caithness and the north coast lie in the same latitude as southern Norway.

The land, which is predominantly deer forest, with its covering of poor grasses and cotton-sedge bogs, is sparsely inhabited and bird-watchers can walk for days without meeting anyone but the odd stalker. Accommodation is difficult and in many places impossible. Enthusiasts looking for the unusual birds that breed will do well to bring their own accommodation plus a large stock of food. It has a bird population distinct from England and much closer to that of Scandinavia. The crows are hooded, the nuthatch unknown, and the common bird around the dwellings is the twite.

The specialities of the area are mainly birds connected with water and include black-throated and red-throated divers, greylag goose, wigeon, merganser, scoter, various waders, Slavonian grebe, skuas and golden eagle. Sporadic breeders include scaup, snow bunting, redwing, brambling, wood and green sandpipers, and Temminck's stint. Much of Sutherland is still poorly known and even holiday notes can be useful.

Undoubtedly one of the best ways of seeing this country is by the tours organised by 'Kyle and Glen'. Their service was started in 1963 specifically for naturalists and they offer alternate weeks in Ross-shire and Sutherland, enabling both counties to be covered in a fortnight's holiday. Their luxury minicoaches seat 8–12 people and there is thus no embarrassment in asking for a stop when something unusual is spotted. Indeed the driver will want to stop too. Accommodation is at hotels, or, if desired, at Youth Hostels with self-catering. The organiser is a bird-watcher.

Transport otherwise is by car or foot. Boats can usually be obtained to visit any island but are expensive unless a group shares the fare.

BEAULY FIRTH (Ross & Cromarty)   OS 28; HT at Inverness

Beauly Firth lies at the head of the Moray Firth system. The western end consists of extensive saltings and mud banks, along the southern shore, and is a favourite haunt of duck. Pinkfeet top 500 in spring and greylag are particularly numerous in autumn. At this time herring shoals enter the firth and an array of predators gather at Kessock. These include up

to 400 each of merganser and goosander with frequently large numbers
of kittiwakes.

WINTER: wigeon, pintail, greylag goose.
SPRING: pink-footed goose, waders.
SUMMER: shelduck, merganser, black-headed gull.
AUTUMN: Canada goose, merganser, goosander, kittiwake, bar-tailed
godwit, greenshank, grey plover.

Leave Beauly eastwards on the A9 and view from convenient lay-bys.
Or leave northwards and turn right at Muir of Ord on to the A832. After
2¼ miles turn right to Redcastle and continue along northern shore to
North Kessock.

BEINN EIGHE (Ross & Cromarty)   OS 19 and 26

Beinn Eighe lies between Loch Torridon and Loch Maree to the south-
east of Gairloch and was Britain's first National Nature Reserve. A
series of Torridon peaks in the neighbourhood reach 3,000 feet, and the
Reserve contains 300 acres of woodland, mainly old Caledonian pine.
The wood at Coille na Glas Leitir, which has much birch, holds the usual
variety of species, plus crossbill and probably siskin. High up on the
tops ptarmigan breed with, possibly, dotterel and snow bunting.

SUMMER: golden eagle, peregrine, ptarmigan, crossbill, siskin, tree pipit,
redstart, goldcrest, woodcock, long-eared owl.

The Reserve lies between the A832 and B858 to the west of Kinlochewe.
A pony track opposite Anancaun Field Station leads into the heart of the
Reserve. Visitors are requested not to enter fenced enclosures and recom-
mended to contact the Warden at Anancaun for further information.
The usual warnings about mountain walking apply.

CLO MOR (Sutherland)   OS 9

Clo Mor lies on the north coast of Sutherland, 4 miles east of Cape Wrath
and form the highest cliffs on the British mainland. They are renowned
for outstanding colonies of sea birds. Ptarmigan breed at an extremely
low level and at Cape Wrath a main attraction is the almost constant
stream of gannets offshore.

SUMMER: guillemot, razorbill, puffin, black guillemot, gannet, fulmar,
peregrine, golden eagle, ptarmigan.

Leave the A838 alongside the Kyle of Durness to Keodale. Take the
ferry across the Kyle and the minibus up to Cape Wrath. Access is
prohibited when the area is used as a naval artillery range which is
sometimes for 2 or 3 weeks in summer, but limited access to Cape Wrath
lighthouse is allowed at certain hours.

Accommodation is very difficult in summer. Kyle and Glen Highland
Safaris include visits to the area in their Sutherland weeks.

CROMARTY FIRTH (Ross & Cromarty)
OS 22 and 28; HT —0:37 Inverness

This is an 18 mile long inlet varying between 1 mile and 5 miles in width with huge bays and areas of sand and mud. The head of the firth around Dingwall has saltings and a huge expanse of foreshore holding very little but a few duck, waders and up to 500 greylags. At Invergordon there are concentrations of gulls, duck and mute swans feeding on the waste outflow from a distillery. Udale Bay on the southern shore holds the best collection of birds on the estuary, including good numbers of passage waders. The Sutors rise to over 450 feet on either side of the entrance and the cliffs on the northern side hold fulmar and cormorant.

WINTER: wigeon, goldeneye, merganser, greylag goose, knot, bar-tailed godwit, turnstone, grey plover.

SPRING: waders.

SUMMER: fulmar, cormorant.

AUTUMN: whimbrel, greenshank, turnstone, knot.

Leave Dingwall northwards and view from the A9 which leads to Invergordon for the distillery. From here there is a foot ferry to the south shore and a good track via Newhallpoint to Udale Bay. The B9163 leads along the north side of Black Isle to the bay. For the North Sutor leave the A9 south-eastwards 2¼ miles north of Kildary and follow lanes through Castlecraig.

DORNOCH FIRTH (Ross & Cromarty)   OS 22; HT +0:43 Inverness

The inner firth beyond Dornoch Point is over 12 miles long and contains a number of the most outstanding bird resorts in Scotland. At the entrance on the southern side there is the expanse of Morrich More with its dune slacks and extensive saltmarsh. Behind the More lies Loch Eye over 1½ miles long and outstanding in its own right. And to the north is Tarbat Ness, an excellent place for a sea watch. The cliffs south of Rockfield on the eastern side of the Tarbat peninsula hold fulmars.

Tarbat Ness is a useful place to go after a day around the estuary. In spring large numbers of long-tailed duck congregate here and in autumn shearwaters, skuas and purple sandpipers can be seen.

From Whiteness Point to Edderton the sandy foreshore is hardly less than 1 mile wide and is the resort of hordes of wildfowl. Geese are most plentiful in spring and autumn and the only flock of white-fronts in east Scotland occurs in March. The roost of these birds is on Morrich More which is used as a military firing range. This is also the roost of the largest flocks of waders in north-east Scotland.

Loch Eye holds most of the wildfowl species found on the estuary, and in autumn fresh waders are excellent. The only other place on the southern

shore is the fresh water pool enclosed by the railway at Fearn. This is a
notable resort of whooper swans in winter and waders on passage.

On the northern shore the sands at Dornoch and Cuthill hold duck
and the usual waders. While to the west, the muddy Skibo Inlet and the
adjacent Loch Evelix provide a resort for duck and whooper swan.

The firth is well worth a visit at any season but is outstanding in autumn.

WINTER: greylag goose, wigeon, pintail, teal, scaup, tufted duck,
pochard, whooper swan, knot, bar-tailed godwit, divers.

SPRING: greylag, pink-footed and white-fronted geese, knot, bar-tailed
godwit, grey plover, turnstone, purple sandpiper.

SUMMER: fulmar, terns, waders.

AUTUMN: greylag and pink-footed geese, wigeon, knot, bar-tailed godwit,
whimbrel, turnstone, sanderling, greenshank, grey plover, purple sandpiper.

Access to all points is directly from the A9 which runs along the north
and south shores:

1. TARBAT NESS: leave the A9 three miles south of Tain on to the B9165.

2. TAIN: bridge over the railway west of the station.

3. EDDERTON SANDS: leave A9 three miles west of Tain northwards to
Ferry Point.

4. FEARN POOL: alongside A9 between Easter and Wester Fearn.

5. SKIBO INLET: leave the A9 southwards at Clashmore and turn right
at T-junction to Ferrytown.

6. CUTHILL-DORNOCH SANDS: at T-junction in 5 miles continue on track
across Cuthill Links. Access to Dornoch Point via golf course and
municipal camping site.

DUNNET HEAD (Caithness)   OS 11

Dunnet Head lies on the north Caithness coast and is the best spot for
sea birds in this area. Near the lighthouse at Easter Head there are large
colonies of auks, and where the head joins the mainland the sandy bay
on the western side holds Arctic tern and ringed plover. St John's Loch
holds wildfowl in winter.

SUMMER: guillemot, razorbill, puffin, kittiwake, fulmar, peregrine,
raven, rock dove, Arctic tern, ringed plover, twite.

WINTER: wigeon, pochard, tufted duck, whooper swan.

Leave Castletown north-eastwards alongside the bay. At Dunnet turn
left on to the B855 to the Head. St John's Loch lies alongside the B855
and A836 north of Dunnet.

FARAID HEAD (Sutherland) OS 9

The head lies on the north coast, to the east of the Kyle of Durness and is offered as an alternative to those who either do not wish, or are unable to go to Cape Wrath and Clo Mor. There are excellent colonies of sea birds on the head and on the offshore stacks of Clach Mhor and Clach Bheag na Fharaid, and ptarmigan breed nearby.

SUMMER: black guillemot, guillemot, razorbill, puffin, kittiwake, fulmar, corncrake, ptarmigan.

Leave the A838 at Durness westwards to Balnakeil. A military track runs from here out to the radar station at the head, but fork off to the right to the north-eastern side of the peninsula.

LOCH FLEET (Sutherland) OS 22; HT —0:30 Inverness

The loch lies on the east coast and is a virtually land-locked basin 3 miles by 1 mile. At low tide it is almost totally dry providing a fine habitat for waders and wildfowl. Attempts to reclaim the upper estuary by building an embankment called The Mound in 1815 were only partially successful. The 2 miles above The Mound are now a dense alder swamp giving shelter to a variety of breeding birds. The fresh water pool is a favourite haunt of many species. Mergansers reach a high peak in autumn and waders are plentiful in winter and are joined by the usual array on passage. Eiders are particularly numerous at the mouth and now breed amongst the dunes in Ferry Links. Both scoter and velvet scoter winter off Embo in rafts of up to 1,000, and long-tailed duck gather in Golspie Bay.

WINTER: wigeon, teal, goldeneye, scoter, velvet scoter, eider, long-tailed duck, knot.

SPRING: shelduck, waders.

SUMMER: eider.

AUTUMN: knot, greenshank, turnstone, merganser, eider.

Leave Dornoch westwards on the B9168 forking right outside the town. Join the A9 and immediately fork right on to the unclassified road to Skelbo. Continue over the railway to the pier. Leave Skelbo westwards along the southern shore, join the A9 and cross The Mound.

HANDA ISLAND (Sutherland) OS 9

The island lies half a mile offshore 3 miles north-west of Scourie on the west coast of Sutherland, and is an RSPB reserve. The island covers 766 acres with 400 foot cliffs, sandy beaches, moorlands and lochs. The cliffs hold fulmar (2,000), shag (3,000), kittiwake (7,000), razorbill (6,000), guillemot (2,500), puffin (400). A wide variety of other species breed or can be seen in summer.

SUMMER: razorbill, guillemot, puffin, kittiwake, fulmar, eider, Arctic tern, rock dove, twite, skuas.

Day visitors do not require permits and landings can be arranged with local boatmen. There is a reconditioned bothy which accommodates members on a hostel basis and bookings for this should be made with the RSPB Scottish Office. Camping is not allowed.

Accommodation is limited, there is a small hotel in Scourie, but Kyle and Glen Minicoaches include Handa in many of their holidays.

INVERNAVER (Sutherland)   OS 10

Invernaver lies at the mouth of the River Naver and is a National Nature Reserve covering 1,363 acres. It was declared in 1960 to protect the fine boreal plant communities but has the advantage of typical Sutherland species within a small area and without the danger of being lost on the open moors.

SUMMER: red-throated diver, common sandpiper, greenshank, ring ouzel, twite.

Leave the A836 on the west side of the bridge over the River Naver northwards to Invernaver. There is a footpath over Druim Chuibhe to Borgie.

INVERPOLLY (Sutherland)   OS 13

This area is a National Nature Reserve covering 26,827 acres of the wildest and remotest country in Britain. It includes high summits, streams, moorland, cliffs and woodland, and, lying on Lewisian Gneiss, is very wet and boggy with innumerable lakes. Though primarily of interest to geologists, bearing some of the oldest rock in the world, the area around Elphin and Knockan, is limestone and is a green and fertile jewel amongst the wild surrounding landscape. The centre of the Reserve is the large Loch Sionascaig. Wild cats and pine martens are the mammal stars but breeding birds are excellent.

SUMMER: black-throated diver, black guillemot, merganser, ptarmigan, raven, golden eagle, buzzard, stonechat, ring ouzel.

Permission is required from The Warden, Strathpolly, Inverpolly, by Ullapool; and from Assynt Estate Office, Lochinver, for parties of more than 6 and for any visit between 15 July and 15 October. Leave the A835 by Old Drumrunie Lodge westwards. After 4 miles a footpath on the right runs to the centre of the Reserve. A track leads off to the right to Inverpolly in a further 5 miles. Approaching from the north, leave Lochinver southwards to Inverkirkaig, pass through the village and park at the bridge. Continue up the southern bank of the River Kirkaig.

Accommodation is limited.

KYLE OF TONGUE AND ROAN ISLAND (Sutherland)
OS 10; HT +1:00 Stornoway

Situated on the north Sutherland coast, the Kyle is a long tidal inlet with extensive mud banks for most of its length. It holds numbers of waders on passage, but is not outstanding for wildfowl though a number of species breed in the neighbourhood. Roan Island, or correctly, Eilean nan Ron, lies at the entrance to the estuary and held a small human population until 1938. It is mainly noted as the winter haunt of up to 200 barnacle geese, often 300 in spring; but is also a good summer spot for breeding birds. Tongue village has a rookery, the most northerly on the British mainland.

WINTER: barnacle goose.

SUMMER: duck, rook, storm petrel, fulmar, peregrine, kittiwake, common and Arctic terns, black guillemot, rock dove.

AUTUMN: waders.

The wintering barnacles can be seen from the adjacent mainland with a telescope. Trips to the island are by private charter at Tongue or Skerray.

Tongue Pier is a good vantage point for the estuary and the A838 runs down the western shore extended northwards by an unclassified road.

Accommodation is limited but there is a Youth Hostel at Tongue.

KYLESKU (Sutherland)
OS 13

Kylesku is between Loch Cairnbawn and Lochs Glendu and Glencoul on the west Sutherland coast. There is a ferry here on the A894 and a small inn on the southern shore. It is a good spot for a stop and walk.

SUMMER: golden eagle, Arctic tern, buzzard, heron, common sandpiper, black guillemot.

On A894 the northern shore has a large fenced cattle ranch that restricts access.

LOCH LAXFORD (Sutherland)
OS 9

The loch is on the western coast of Sutherland, 15 miles south of Cape Wrath. The landscape is bleak, and a glance at the OS map shows the loch-studded scenery. For those who like searching for unusual breeding species this is the area, and time can be taken off to visit nearby Handa Island. But the going is severe.

SUMMER: black and red-throated divers, mergansers, dunlin, greenshank, woodcock, twite.

The A894 crosses the area, the A838 leads south-eastwards, and the unclassified road to Foindle and Tarbet runs north-westerly. Otherwise the area can be explored on foot. The Badcall Islands 3 miles south of

Scourie are excellent for birds but arrangements to visit them must be
made locally.

INNER MORAY FIRTH (Ross & Cromarty)

OS 28; HT at Inverness

Situated at the northern end of the Caledonian Canal between the Moray
and Beauly Firths. It is 8 miles by 3 miles with limited areas of foreshore.
The main haunts of wildfowl and waders are at Castle Stuart Bay and
west to Inverness, and the muddy inlet of Munlochy Bay, which is the
favourite haunt of pink-feet in April and greylags from February. Waders
are quite good and breeding species include fulmar on the low cliffs at
Rosemarkie and heron at Munlochy.

WINTER: wigeon, pintail, shelduck, greylag goose.
SPRING: pink-footed and greylag geese, waders.
SUMMER: fulmar, eider, heron.
AUTUMN: knot, bar-tailed godwit, whimbrel, greenshank.

On the south side the A96 between Inverness and Milton runs along
the shore. Continue and 3½ miles east of Milton turn left on to the B9039
to Castle Stuart. There is a footpath to the shore.

On the north side leave Beauly northwards on the A9 to Muir of Ord
and turn right on to the A832. Past Munlochy a footpath leads to Munlochy Bay and further on the road runs beside the Firth to Rosemarkie.
Chanonry Point and Avoch are good places during migration.

NOSS HEAD (Caithness)   OS 16

The head stands 3 miles north of Wick on the east coast. Its cliffs barely
reach 100 feet but are good for breeding sea birds and for sea watching.

SUMMER: guillemot, razorbill, black guillemot, puffin, kittiwake, fulmar.

Leave Wick northwards on the unclassified road across the airport.
There are sometimes delays here due to aircraft movements but they are
never prolonged. Walk westward from the lighthouse over boggy fields
to Sinclair Castle.

SUMMER ISLES (Ross & Cromarty)   ·   OS 13

The islands lie at the mouth of Loch Broom and are a notable bird haunt.
300 barnacle geese winter on Glas Leac Beag which is the summer haunt
of large gull colonies. It is also the island chosen as the moulting ground
of the Summer Isles greylags in July and August. The major island and
the one most likely to be visited is Tanera More which holds greylag,
red-throated diver, Arctic tern and buzzard, while the smaller Carn non
Sgeir, which is en route to Tanera More, holds black guillemot and eider.
Storm petrels breed on Priest Island.

WINTER: barnacle goose.

SUMMER: greylag goose, storm petrel, red-throated diver, Arctic tern, black guillemot, eider, rock dove, buzzard, heron.

Boats run quite frequently from Ullapool. Time ashore is limited unless the boat is chartered.

Dumfriesshire, Kirkcudbrightshire, Wigtownshire (Solway)

CAERLAVEROCK (Dumfries)   OS 75; HT +1:10 Liverpool

Caerlaverock, on the northern shore of the Solway, is one of the most outstanding bird haunts in Britain. The area treated here stretches from the Nith to the mouth of the Lochar Water. Throughout this length the Merse salt marsh is anything up to a mile wide and inter-tidal mud stretches out into the estuary for another 3 miles. The eastern third of the Merse, covering 13,514 acres, was established as Caerlaverock National Nature Reserve in 1957 and is one of the principal haunts of barnacle geese in Britain. Over 4,000 have been recorded. This number is totally dwarfed, however, by the 10–12,000 pink-feet that arrive in autumn and the 10,000 that winter. Greylag geese number 1,000 in winter with 2,000 in spring, and waders are plentiful. Autumn brings the best collection of waders on the Scottish west coast.

On the farmland behind the Merse the Wildfowl Trust is developing Eastpark Farm as a sanctuary and observation centre for the geese. Embankments shield the geese from disturbance and a series of hides, including towers, give excellent views of the birds at close quarters. A 20-acre enclosure attracts wild birds to close range.

WINTER: barnacle, pink-footed and greylag geese, whooper swan, wigeon, pintail, knot, hen harrier, peregrine, merlin, golden plover.

SPRING: greylag goose, waders.

AUTUMN: pink-footed goose, black-tailed godwit.

Access to Caerlaverock National Nature Reserve is usually only granted on Sundays and then by prior arrangement with the Warden, Mr E. L. Roberts, Tadorna, Hollands Farm Road, Caerlaverock, by Dumfries.

There are, however, several public roads which, with the 7 miles of the B725, make observation of all species straightforward without disturbing the Reserve at all. Indeed the best place for whooper swans is the Nith above Glencaple.

View from any point on the B725 between Kelton and the wood south of Caerlaverock Castle, the track south of this wood continues these views eastwards. Further east there are decent views from the road again at the mouth of the Lochar water near Stanhope.

Caerlaverock Wildfowl Refuge can be visited throughout the winter between 11.00–14.00 hours except Tuesdays and Wednesdays. Apply in advance to the Warden, Eastpark Farm, Caerlaverock, Dumfriesshire. Leave the B724/B725 southwards at Bankend and turn eastwards at T junction after 1 mile. Follow signposts to East Park.

CARSE SANDS (Kirkcudbright)   OS 75; HT +0:30 Liverpool

The sands lie at the mouth of the Nith, immediately west of Caerlaverock and are generally rather better for duck. There is little salting and to the south there is a great deal of rock and a comparatively small area of fore-shore. The Sands themselves hold up to 1,000 each of wigeon and pintail which are found at Caerlaverock at high tide. High water brings scaup to Carsethorn, large numbers of waders are present and greylag geese are always about.

WINTER: wigeon, pintail, scaup, greylag goose, knot, redshank, oyster-catcher, hen harrier.

AUTUMN: black-tailed godwit.

Leave the A710 at Kirkbean to Carsethorn. Further north on the A710 view direct from main road.

CLATTERINGSHAWS (Kirkcudbright)   OS 73

The area lies to north and south of the A712 between New Galloway and Newton Stewart, though the large Clatteringshaws Loch is too high for wildfowl and has little but scenic attraction. The black water of Dee flows through the new plantations of conifers and forms an attractive area for birds in summer.

SUMMER: black and red grouse, golden plover, peregrine.

Take the A712 between New Galloway and Newton Stewart and stop near the Upper Bridge of Dee at the south-west corner of the loch. General access.

DEE VALLEY (Kirkcudbright)   OS 73, 74, 80 and 81

The entire length of the valley between Castle Douglas and New Galloway, a distance something over 12 miles, is worth exploring. Greylag (600), white-fronted (500), pink-footed (200) and bean geese (50) are all present, though the latter are fast declining.

The major area of interest in the valley lies above the hydro-electricity dam near Townhead of Greenlaw. Loch Ken is up to half a mile wide in places and provides one of the most important roosts in the area. The marshes below the dam at Threave, together with Carlingwark Loch outside Castle Douglas are important areas.

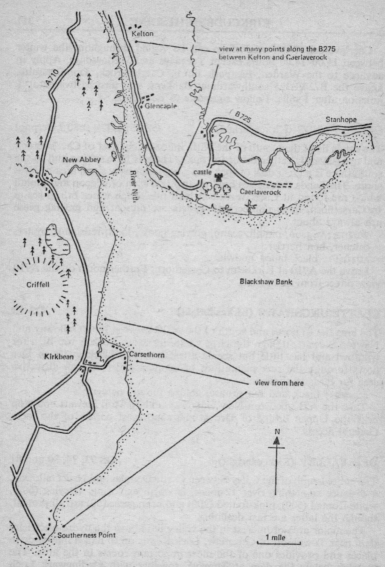

Kelton

view at many points along the B275
between Kelton and Caerlaverock

A710

Glencaple

B725

Stanhope

New Abbey

castle

Caerlaverock

River Nith

Criffell

Blackshaw Bank

Kirkbean

Carsethorn

view from here

N

Southerness Point

1 mile

Dumfries—Kirkcudbright: showing Caerlaverock National Nature Reserve and Southerness Point and the vast wildfowl haunt between the two. Most of the area can be worked from classified roads

The whole area is best treated in three parts:

1. CASTLE DOUGLAS-THREAVE: this is the main area for the bean geese, with greylags numerous and a few white-fronts. It also holds the largest numbers of duck. Carlingwark Loch is a shallow pool of 105 acres and holds large numbers of diving duck. Whooper swans are regular.

2. THE RIVER DEE up to 1 mile north of Crossmichael: greylag and white-fronts frequent this area with quite good numbers of duck on the wider part above Livingston.

3. LOCH KEN: begins properly above the Loch Ken viaduct. There is a larger area of open water in this part which, together with the marsh at the head of the loch, attract numbers of duck and some white-fronts.

WINTER: greylag, white-fronted, pink-footed and bean geese, whooper swan, wigeon, pintail, shoveler, goldeneye, gadwall, smew.
SPRING AND AUTUMN: wildfowl.
The three areas are reached as follows:

1. CARLINGWARK LOCH can be seen from the A75 south of Castle Douglas but the geese move around the area so much that a general exploration to the south-east and north-west of the town is recommended. The Threave marshes can be penetrated from the A75, but the road to Netherhall north from Bridge of Dee repays investigation.

2. Leave the A713 westwards at Townhead of Greenlaw. Cross the dam on the B795 and turn right immediately. This unclassified road gives excellent views for 2 miles to Livingston.

3. LOCH KEN: the A762 runs alongside the Loch for the top 4 miles including the marshy north end, and the A713 gives more intermittent views from the east bank.

All of these areas contain valuable farm land and watchers should not enter fields without permission or disturb stock. Many farmers dislike the geese and carelessness or lack of understanding of other interests by bird-watchers will make things worse for the birds in the end. Generally satisfactory views can be obtained from public roads without disturbing either farmers or geese.

GLENTROOL (Kirkcudbright)   OS 73

Glentrool is 10 miles north of Newton Stewart, east of the A714. The area is Forestry Commission property and consists of young forest, with old oakwood, and open moorland. Loch Trool forms the centrepiece.
SUMMER: black grouse, whinchat, stonechat, ring ouzel, buzzard, grass-

hopper warbler, woodcock, grey wagtail, dipper, common sandpiper, pied flycatcher, tree pipit, redstart, raven.

Leave Newton Stewart northwards on the A714 and turn right at Bargrennan. Turn right again in 2 miles.

LOCHINCH (Wigtown)   OS 79

Lochinch lies 2 miles east of Stranraer north of the A75 and between the prime habitat areas of Loch Ryan and Luce Bay. Lochinch Castle is the home of the Earl of Stair and the grounds include the remains of Castle Kennedy, and the two important White and Black Lochs which are kept as a private reserve. The lochs act as a roost for the greylag geese for miles around and are the breeding headquarters of a flock of feral greylags. Over 5,000 geese sometimes come in to roost.

WINTER: greylag geese and feral greylags, shoveler, tufted duck, golden-eye.

The grounds are open from 2–5 pm on Sunday and Wednesday from Easter to 1st August and at other times by arrangement. As, however, the only true attraction is the greylag roost, visitors should be content with watching the hordes flight in at evening. Perhaps a good place to watch from would be the hills immediately to the north.

LOCHMABEN (Dumfries)   OS 75

This is a small town 10 miles east of Dumfries on the A709. It is a good wildfowl centre with large numbers of duck on the surrounding lochs and along the meandering course of the River Annan where there are numerous floods and oxbow lakes. The most important area is Castle Loch which covers 210 acres and holds up to 1,000 greylag geese. Part of the area, including Castle Loch, is a local nature reserve.

WINTER: greylag goose, wigeon, shoveler, pochard, goosander.

Castle Loch lies alongside the A709 south of Lochmaben. Views can also be obtained from the western side from the B7020. Kirk Loch and Mill Loch can be seen from public roads ref. OS 75.

The Annan meadows and floods are the major feeding ground of the geese and a search is often necessary. The bridge over the river on the A709 is a useful vantage point looking south, and there are several unclassified roads running north and south along both sides of the river.

MERSEHEAD SANDS (Kirkcudbright)
OS 74 and 81; HT +0:30 Liverpool

On the north Solway shore, between Southerness Point and Rough Firth, there is an area of merse at Southwick with an area of pasture and huge expanse of open sandbank. This is a major resort of greylag geese which reach a peak of 1,000 in the late winter. Pink-footed geese are increasing here, but barnacle are irregular. Flocks of waders gather on a rising tide.

WINTER: greylag and pink-footed geese, wigeon, pintail, shoveler, scaup, redshank, oystercatcher.

View from the A710 for almost aerial views near Lot's Wife pinnacle.

MILTON LOCH (Kirkcudbright)   OS 74

The loch is about a mile south of the A75 between Dumfries and Castle Douglas. It is perhaps the best of a number of good places in the neighbourhood for wildfowl, which include Lochrutton Loch and Auchenreoch Loch. Milton Loch, less than a mile long, holds 300 greylag geese and up to 1,000 duck.

WINTER: greylag goose, teal, wigeon.

Take the A75 from either Dumfries or Castle Douglas and turn southwards at Ninemile Bar just west of its junction with the A712. Fork left in threequarters of a mile and view from the road in a further threequarters of a mile.

MULL OF GALLOWAY (Wigtown)   OS 79

This is the southernmost point of Scotland and lies at the end of a long peninsula west of Luce Bay. Its cliffs hold an interesting collection of breeding sea birds.

SUMMER: guillemot, razorbill, black guillemot, kittiwake, shag, cormorant, fulmar.

Leave Drummore at the end of the A716 southwards on the B7041 and continue to the Mull. Permission to enter the lighthouse area can be obtained from the keepers.

PRIESTSIDE BANK (Dumfries)   OS 75; HT +0:30 Liverpool

This spot is the easternmost of the main geese resorts on the Scottish shore of the Solway, and is separated from the huge Blackshaw Bank off Caerlaverock by the channel of the Lochar Water. A narrow strip of merse lies between the flat lowland and the huge banks. Pink-feet are often very numerous and greylags can usually be seen, with, sometimes, a flock of barnacles. Duck are not notable but like the waders are regularly present in numbers.

WINTER: pink-footed, greylag and barnacle geese, wigeon, pintail, waders, peregrine, merlin.

Leave Annan westwards on the A75, cross the river and in 600 yards turn left on to the B724. Turn left after 3½ miles in Cummertrees and after 1 mile a track leads down to the shore.

ROUGH FIRTH (Kirkcudbright)   OS 74 and 81; HT +0:24 Liverpool

The firth is probably the most interesting of the group of inlets lying south of Dalbeattie. It is 3 miles by 1 mile and is almost completely dry at low water. At such times there are flocks of waders, but at high tide there is a flock of up to 600 scaup present.

WINTER: scaup, merganser, shelduck, waders.

Leave the A710 at White Loch to Rockcliffe (do not confuse with the Cumberland 'Rockcliffe'). A road down to Kippford leaves the A710 2 miles nearer Dalbeattie. Both places are 'touristy'.

LOCH RYAN (Wigtown)   OS 79; HT —0:50 Greenock

Loch Ryan is the northern water that cuts off a large part of the Rhinns of Galloway from the rest of Wigtownshire. Luce Bay to the south is still largely inaccessible for military reasons. Loch Ryan, in spite of its large area, has only a fairly small area of muddy foreshore at the head of the bay. It does, however, hold greylag geese as well as numbers of duck and waders.

WINTER: greylag goose, merganser, scaup, goldeneye, eider, wigeon, waders.

The A77 for 2 miles east of Stranraer runs alongside the head of the bay.

SOUTHERNESS POINT (Kirkcudbright)

OS 75; HT +0:30 Liverpool

The point juts out into the Solway to the west of the Nith. Though the flatness of the area is reminiscent of other marshes it is the rocky fore-shore and the sea that provide the main attractions. The sea often holds vast flocks of sea duck and occasionally a few surf scoter.

WINTER: scoter, velvet scoter, scaup, merganser, surf scoter, great crested grebe, red-throated diver, purple sandpiper, turnstone, knot, bar-tailed godwit.

Leave the A710 by any one of three unclassified roads south of Kirk-bean and follow through to Southerness Point. See Map.

WIGTOWN BAY (Kirkcudbright/Wigtown)

OS 80; HT +0:19 Liverpool

A vast area of inter-tidal sands stretching 7 miles from Spital to the mouth at Jultock Point and up to 3 miles across. The upper estuary in particular has large expanses of merse salt marsh, and the 2 square miles of the Moss of Cree lie immediately inland. The area attracts a wintering flock of up to 2,500 greylags which are joined in March by 2,000 pink-feet. The level of duck is high with total reaching several thousand every winter. An unusual occurrence is the flock of up to 2,000 scoter that assemble at the mouth of the bay in late July. The waders are the usual and sometimes very numerous.

WINTER: greylag goose, wigeon, pintail, shoveler, shelduck, whooper swan, waders.

SPRING: pink-footed goose.

SUMMER: scoter.

The main area for wildfowl is the western shore which is particularly difficult of access. On the eastern side, the A75 gives good views over the entire estuary at many points and particularly at Creetown and Spital. An unclassified road running north from Wigtown between the estuary and the Moss of Cree offers the best chance of observation on that side.

Orkney Islands

The Orkneys are separated from Caithness by the Pentland Firth which is at one point no more than 6 miles wide. There are 29 inhabited isles, 38 holmes, and a vast number of skerries. The landscape is generally low and rolling though Hoy rises to over 1,500 feet, and has fine cliffs and stacks. It is basically an agricultural land with a large number of small farmers. There are extensive lochs and a considerable area of damp moorland. Its sea bird cliffs are excellent, especially on Hoy and many divers and waders breed around its inland lochs. The red-necked phalarope still breeds on one island and both skuas are increasing and spreading.

The islands have long been famous as the stronghold of the hen harrier, and due in no small measure to the work of Eddie Balfour, they have increased and spread back to the Scottish mainland.

ORKNEY FIELD CLUB.
The Club holds monthly field meetings and studies most branches of natural history. It extends a welcome to all casual visitors to join its outings. The RSPB has a local representative to contact.

The North of Scotland and Orkney and Shetland Shipping Company Ltd, Matthews Quay, Aberdeen, run a twice weekly service from Aberdeen to Kirkwall. Ships may be joined one day earlier at Leith. There is a daily service from Scrabster, Thurso, Caithness to Stromness (2 hours) during the summer. There are daily flights from London, Edinburgh, Glasgow, Aberdeen, Inverness and Wick to Kirkwall. Enquiries should be made of British Airways.

Within the islands there are frequent boat services and most parts of the mainland are served by bus. Cars can be hired – even on Hoy.

READ: *Orkney Birds: Status and Guide*, E. Balfour.

COPINSAY   OS 6

Together with its associated islands, Copinsay covers 210 acres. It was purchased by a number of conservation bodies co-ordinated by the World Wildlife Fund, as a memorial to the late James Fisher, who died in a car accident in 1970, and is administered by the RSPB. The Old Red Sandstone rises to 200 feet in the south-east and is topped by a lighthouse and its attendant buildings. The three keepers are now the only residents, though a farm was abandoned only twenty years ago. Sheep are still grazed on the island.

Copinsay is best known for the colonies of seabirds along the cliffs. There are 10,000 pairs of kittiwakes and 9,000 pairs of guillemots, but all the other species are well represented.

SUMMER: fulmar, cormorant, shag, great black-backed gull, lesser black-backed gull, kittiwake, Arctic tern, razorbill, guillemot, black guillemot, puffin, rock dove, rock pipit.

Access is by private charter from the Orkney mainland. Contact the RSPB Orkney representative.

COSTA HEAD   OS 6

The head lies at the very northern tip of the mainland north of the Loch of Swannay. The cliffs here rise to over 400 feet and hold extensive colonies of sea birds.

SUMMER: guillemot, razorbill, puffin, kittiwake, fulmar, shag, raven.

Stop on the A966 at the northern end of Loch of Swannay and walk north-eastwards to the head.

LOCH OF HARRAY AND LOCH OF STENNESS   OS 6

These two lochs lie in the south-west of the mainland north of Stromness and are linked in the south-east. Though Stenness joins the sea it can only be called brackish, while Harray is all but fresh. Their summer population includes a wide variety of breeding wildfowl and other species. In winter both lochs are excellent for wildfowl, with the sea duck on Stenness and the others on Harray.

WINTER: scaup, long-tailed duck, goldeneye, pochard, tufted duck, whooper and mute swans.

SUMMER: dunlin, common gull, eider, merganser, tufted duck, common tern.

The A965 from Stromness leads to the B9055 which runs between the lochs giving access to both. Boats for hire are available at different places, and Harray is noted for trout.

HOY   OS 7

Hoy is the most westerly island of the Orkney group, the second largest, being 14 miles by 6 miles, and scenically the most varied, rising to over 1,500 feet and exposing an extensive line of cliffs on the western coast. These culminate in the Old Man of Hoy, a noted tourist spot, and hold numerous colonies of sea birds. Manx shearwaters breed in the north. The hills hold Arctic and great skuas.

SUMMER: guillemot, razorbill, puffin, kittiwake, fulmar, raven, Arctic and great skuas, Manx shearwater, red-throated diver.

Hoy is reached by the motor vessels of the Bremner Shipping Co, which sail from Stromness to Longhope 3 days per week throughout the year; and almost daily in the summer. A hostel has been created from the old school at Rackwick on the west coast. Enquiries and booking to the Orkney County Youth Leader, Education Office, Kirkwall. Bremner also call at Graemsay, Fara and Flotta by arrangement.

MARWICK HEAD   OS 6

The promontory on the north-west coast, 2 miles south of Brough Head is generally acknowledged as one of the best sea bird cliffs in Orkney. Many thousands of birds can be seen and peregrines are regularly noted.

SUMMER: guillemot, razorbill, puffin, kittiwake, fulmar, shag, raven, peregrine.

Leave the A967 westwards, quarter of a mile north of its junction with A986. At B9056 turn right and first left to Mar Wick Bay. Walk along the cliffs northwards.

ROUSAY   OS 6

Rousay is one of the northern isles and is separated from the mainland by Eynhallow Sound. Its 6 miles by 4 miles is sufficient for a holiday and its cliffs and moorlands hold an interesting variety of species among which Arctic skua and hen harrier are outstanding.

SUMMER: guillemot, razorbill, puffin, kittiwake, fulmar, Arctic skua, hen harrier.

Rousay is reached by boats of the Orkney Islands Shipping Co from Kirkwall. There are regular sailings and stops are made at Egilsay as well. Accommodation limited.

WESTRAY   OS 5

This is one of the largest of the northern isles and fortunately well populated by man and birds. Its cliffs hold sea birds and the hills Arctic and great skuas. No place in its 10 miles by 5 miles is further than a mile from the sea and it would take a good holiday to fully explore. There are large sandy beaches, fresh water lochs and it forms a convenient stepping off point for Papa Westray.

SUMMER: guillemot, razorbill, puffin, kittiwake, fulmar, raven, Arctic and great skuas.

The Orkney Islands Shipping Co run a regular service almost every day in summer from Kirkwall.

Outer Hebrides

These islands lie at the north-western corner of Britain and stretch 130 miles from north to south. The coastline holds numbers of long sea lochs that stretch inland for several miles and the islands are divided by only shallow sandy straits. The geology of the Hebrides is of paramount importance to bird and human distribution. The western side of the group faces the open Atlantic and has received large deposits of shell sand. A glance at any map of the Uists shows the smooth and sand strewn western coast and the rocky indented and sheltered eastern coast.

The western dunes have created a soil rich in lime giving rise to the characteristic sweet grass machair, and both weather and man have carried seaweed on to the land and enriched it. This fertile area is in sharp contrast to the central and eastern peat ridden sections of the islands. The western side has farms with cattle and arable farming, the eastern has a mass of acid lochs and is mainly barren.

There are some interesting areas of woodland. The most famous being at Stornoway Castle, but there are others at Little Loch Roag; Glen Valtos in Uig, Lewis; Borve, Lewis; Newton Hotel, North Uist; and Alt Volagir, South Uist.

Birds are nowhere more plentiful than on the western cliffs, and the southern isles of Berneray and Mingulay are outstanding. The eastern sea lochs hold numbers of feeding divers and the sea is a favourite feeding ground of gannets. Golden eagle, buzzard, hen harrier, short-eared owl, raven and heron all breed amongst the peat of the interior where the outstanding species are skuas and greylag geese. The latter breed on Loch Druidibeg but move west on to the lochs of the machair with their young. These lochs shelter dunlin, duck, and very rarely, red-necked phalarope, while the beaches hold oystercatchers, terns and ringed plovers.

In spite of their isolated geographical position the islands are easy to reach. BEA have regular flights to Stornoway and the internal air service connects Barra, Benbecula and Stornoway. MacBraynes run regular steamer services from Mallaig and Kyle of Lochalsh to Stornoway, and from Oban to Castlebay in Barra, and Lochboisdale in South Uist. This company also runs a car ferry service between Uig in Skye and Tarbert in Harris and Lochmaddy in North Uist. There are bus services about the islands and boats are not prohibitive to charter.

For information contact Western Isles Tourist Association, 21 South Beach Street, Stornoway, who publish an official *Guide* and *Where to Stay in the Western Isles.*

BERNERAY AND MINGULAY   OS 32

These are situated at the southern end of the Hebridean chain and have much the same sort of romance as Muckle Flugga and St Kilda. There

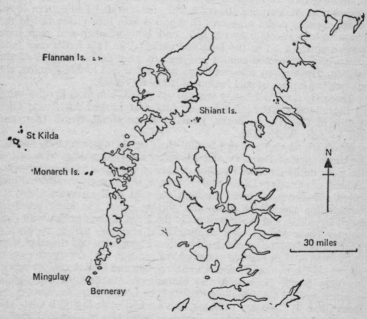

The Ultimate Challenge: these isolated islands are not all covered in this guide, but all are outstanding for birds. They hold the most elusive of all sea-birds, Leach's petrel, as well as gannets, storm petrels, and thousands (millions?) of auks. For the expedition minded they present the ultimate challenge of British ornithology

is a lighthouse on the southernmost tip at Barra Head but they are otherwise uninhabited. The outstanding sea bird colonies are on the western side of Mingulay on the 800 foot cliffs at Bagh nah-Aoineig and the stacks of Lianamull and Arnamull. The bird population of these islands is still comparatively unknown.

SUMMER: guillemot, razorbill, black guillemot, puffin, kittiwake, fulmar, corncrake.

Access is by expedition or by Sunday pleasure trips from Castlebay, Barra. Contact the Western Isles Tourist Association, Post Office, Castlebay.

THE FLANNAN ISLES   OS 12

The Flannans lie 17 miles north-west of Gallan Head on the west side of Lewis, and consist of 7 islands and many skerries. The largest island, Eilean Mor, covers 39 acres, rises to 288 feet, and has a lighthouse. All of the isles are cliff bound. Leach's petrels breed abundantly, this being one of their five British breeding stations.

SUMMER: Leach's petrel, puffin, guillemot, razorbill, shag, kittiwake, fulmar, black guillemot, eider.

The end of June is the best time for a visit which will be a matter of arrangement and negotiation with previous visitors and the lighthouse authorities. The Scottish Ornithologists' Club is a good source of information.

LOCH DRUIDIBEG   OS 23

The loch is in the northern half of South Uist near Howmore. It was declared a National Nature Reserve in 1958 and the Reserve now covers 4,145 acres of peat loch together with innumerable islands, machair, farmland and open sandy shore. It thus covers the full needs of the native greylag geese that are its principle attraction. Some 40-50 pairs breed annually and form the most important remaining colony in Britain. After the breeding season up to 300 geese congregate on the machair between Howmore and Eochar. The huge Loch Bee to the north is an important haunt of wildfowl in winter.

SUMMER: greylag goose, ringed plover, dunlin.

A permit is required to visit the Reserve in summer, and there is a small hostel attached to the Reserve at Grogany Lodge Annex. Enquiries for both should be addressed to The Warden, Stilligarry, Lochboisdale, South Uist.

NORTH UIST   OS 17

Connected to Benbecula and South Uist by bridge, North Uist is generally

accepted as the complete gem of the Outer Hebrides, at least ornithologically speaking. Like the other islands it is sweet and green in the west
with huge shell beaches sweeping the gentle coves, and brown and acid
in the east and centre. Some 110 plus species have summered in recent
years and the RSPB has established a reserve of 1,500 acres in the extreme
west at Balranald. This little area is exceptionally rich in plant and bird
life and is noted as the stronghold of the red-necked phalarope in the
Outer Isles. Over 50 other species have bred including wigeon, red-breasted
merganser, corncrake, snipe, dunlin, Arctic tern, sedge warbler and tree
sparrow.

Though seldom visited except in summer there are many attractions
in winter and during passage seasons. Of note are great northern diver,
whooper swan, merlin and hen harrier. Other parts of the island should
not be ignored. Griminish Point is good for passage plus breeding Arctic
terns and black guillemots. Golden eagle, hen harrier, buzzard and
merlin breed, as do golden plover, greenshank, Arctic skua and raven.

SUMMER: black-throated diver, red-throated diver, little grebe, teal,
gadwall, wigeon, shoveler, tufted duck, pochard, eider, merganser,
shelduck, water rail, corncrake, oystercatcher, ringed plover, red-
necked phalarope, snipe, redshank, dunlin, Arctic skua, Arctic tern,
common tern, buzzard, golden eagle, merlin, golden plover, greenshank.

Access is by ship or by air via Glasgow to Benbecula. Accommodation
is plentiful. No permits are required for Balranald but report to the
warden.

ST KILDA   OS 17

St Kilda stands 45 miles west of Griminish Point, North Uist, Outer
Hebrides. There are seven islands and stacks in the group of which Hirta
is the largest covering 1,575 acres and rising to a height of nearly 1,400
feet. The Ard Uachdarachd buttress of Conachair is the highest sea cliff
in Britain, and the western face of Boreray rising to 1,250 feet is amongst
the best cliffs for sea birds in the country. St Kilda was inhabited until
1930 and has since 1957 been used as a radar station by the Army. It
was made a National Nature Reserve when it was repopulated.

St Kilda holds the largest gannetry in the world, a recent estimate
showing 44,000 pairs. It also has large colonies of fulmar (20,000 on
Hirta, perhaps 40,000 in the group), Leach's and storm petrels, and
Manx shearwater all four of which breed on Carn More. The puffin,
once the commonest bird has declined drastically but is still abundant.
The other auks are quite numerous. The St Kilda wren is unique and
about 100 pairs breed on Hirta.

SUMMER: gannet, fulmar, Leach's and storm petrels, Manx shearwater, puffin, guillemot, razorbill, kittiwake, black guillemot, gulls, eider, St Kilda wren.

Access is unrestricted but difficult. The National Trust for Scotland owns the group and organises expeditions periodically. The 'Island's Cruise' of that body calls at Hirta. All enquiries to the Nature Conservancy Scottish Office, 12 Hope Terrace, Edinburgh 7, or the Scottish National Trust, 5 Charlotte Square, Edinburgh 2.

READ: *St Kilda Summer*, K. Williamson and J. Morton Boyd.

SOUND OF HARRIS OS 17

The sound lies between Harris and North Uist and is included here as an important winter area which will be inaccessible to all but the really determined. Barnacle geese are plentiful and can be regularly found on the islands of Shillay, Coppay, Ensay, Pabbay and Berneray from December onwards. Greylags are also present as are large numbers of sea-duck. Long-tailed duck are plentiful and the usual divers and gulls are present.

WINTER: barnacle and greylag geese, eider, shelduck, long-tailed duck, scoter, merganser.

SUMMER: storm petrel.

Access is by boat from Leverburgh in Harris, or Lochmaddy in North Uist. There is usually something of interest off Port nan Long at the end of the B893, North Uist.

READ: *A Mosaic of Islands*, K. Williamson and J. Morton Boyd.

SOUTH UIST OS 23 and 32

The island is connected by causeways northwards to Benbecula (1939) and further north to North Uist (1960). The visitor can thus easily explore all three islands though it is likely that he will make this island his headquarters. Apart from Loch Druidibeg, which is treated separately, the lochs of the machair, moor and sea hold a rich variety of species including Arctic skua. The sands hold the usual summer species and a good selection of migrant and wintering waders. The promontory of Rudha Andvule and its lochan is an excellent spot at all seasons.

WINTER: white-fronted and barnacle geese, bar-tailed godwit, sanderling.

SPRING: whimbrel, turnstone, purple sandpiper.

SUMMER: Arctic skua, black-throated diver, eider, merganser, Arctic tern, dunlin, ringed plover.

AUTUMN: waders, gannet.

Accommodation is available in Lochboisdale and in private homes in other parts of the island, see *Where to stay in the Western Isles*.

STORNOWAY HARBOUR AND LOCH BRANAHUIE OS 8

The Stornoway area is not only convenient of access but also has a wide
variety of habitat. The woods are dealt with separately and we are here
concerned with the water and muddy, rocky edges of the harbour and
with the small Loch Branahuie lying on the isthmus that connects the
Eye Peninsula to the mainland. The Iceland gull is a regular winter visitor
to the harbour and is commoner than the glaucous which also occurs.
In spring the scoter and velvet scoter that winter in the bay to the north
are joined by up to 500 long-tailed duck.

WINTER: merganser, long-tailed duck, scoter, velvet scoter, Iceland and
glaucous gulls, turnstone, purple sandpiper.

The harbour is the town centre. Loch Branahuie lies 3 miles east on
the A866.

STORNOWAY WOODS OS 8

The woods form part of the castle grounds, now belonging to the people
of Stornoway. Though not the only trees in the Outer Hebrides the
nearest comparable woodland is 40 miles to the east. The bird population
is one of the most outstanding in the Outer Hebrides.

SUMMER: wood pigeon, rook, blue tit, treecreeper, robin, whitethroat,
chiffchaff, goldcrest, tree sparrow, buzzard, corncrake, raven, hooded
crow, dipper, grey wagtail.

Access direct from Stornoway.

Shetland Isles

The Shetlands lie in latitude 60° north, which is the same as Cape Farewell in Greenland and 6° south of the Arctic circle. They extend for 70 miles from north to south, and 37 from east to west. The mainland occupies about two-thirds of the total area but the coast is so indented that no place is more than 3 miles from the sea. Only nineteen of the hundred odd islands are now inhabited and the mainland has over half of the population of 17,000. Every one of these islands is good for birds and choice is limited by ease of access, and time available. If, amongst so many wonderful places, some can be said to be outstanding, they are Noss, Fetlar and Hermaness, and the intending visitor should try to include at least one of these in his travels.

Shetland is a rugged land which fact is belied by the modest maximum height of 1,475 feet. It is essentially igneous in geology and its mantle is rough grass underlain by a thick layer of peat. Only Fetlar and the southern half of Unst have a semblance of green fields and pasture.

For information and accommodation contact the Shetland Tourist Association, Information Centre, Alexandra Wharf, Lerwick.

READ: *Birds and Mammals of Shetland*, L. S. V. and U. M. Venables; *Bird Haunts in Northern Britain*, G. K. Yeates; *A Guide to Shetland Birds*, Bobby Tulloch and Fred Hunter.

The RSPB has a local representative who may be contacted.

FAIR ISLE   OS 4

Fair Isle is 24 miles south-west of Sumburgh Head between the Orkneys and the Shetlands and is completely isolated. Its 'drawing power' is thus very high though its geographical position is off the main migration routes. It is not a mere speck in the ocean, being 3 miles by 1 mile, and has some of the finest cliff scenery in Britain; it supports a crofting population of over forty. Eagle Clarke's pioneer studies put Fair Isle on the ornithological map in 1912 and it has retained its pre-eminence ever since. After the last war the island was purchased by George Waterston and the Bird Observatory was opened with Kenneth Williamson as

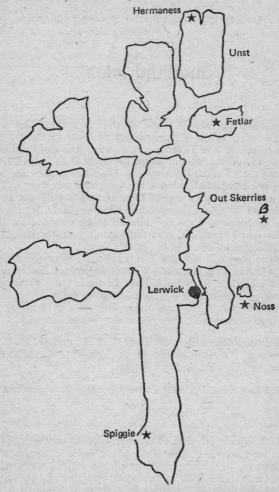

Hermaness ★

Unst

★ Fetlar

Out Skerries
ℬ
★

Lerwick

★ Noss

Spiggie ★

The Shetland Isles showing the position of the main islands: a piece of the Arctic in Britain, lying a few degrees south of the Arctic circle.

the first Warden. The National Trust for Scotland purchased the Isle in 1954. Though Fair Isle is a migration study post it does have an interesting variety of breeding species.

Vagrants occur every week of the autumn season and many birds have been added to the British list from their occurrence on this tiny island. Several species are almost 'regular' at Fair Isle but virtually unknown elsewhere in the country, yellow-breasted and little buntings, citrine wagtail, and scarlet grosbeak fall into this category. Barred warblers, bluethroats and Lapland buntings are commonplace. Anything can turn up.

SPRING: migrants, shrikes, rarities.

SUMMER: great and Arctic skuas, guillemot, razorbill, puffin, storm petrel, kittiwake, fulmar, wren (Fair Isle subspecies), twite.

AUTUMN: migrants, rarities, short-toed lark, barred warbler, bluethroat, vagrants.

The *Good Shepherd* runs between Grutness, Sumburgh, Shetland and Fair Isle three times a week through the summer and once a week during autumn and winter. It is thus convenient for Sumburgh Airport and the south. Accommodation is available at the new Fair Isle Bird Observatory opened in 1969. It offers a variety of accommodation and a cafeteria food service. In comparison with most observatories it is sheer luxury. Full details from The Warden, Fair Isle Bird Observatory, by Lerwick, Shetland.

FETLAR

This is the smallest of the main islands and often called the green island because of its fields and cultivation. Fetlar has been well known as the haunt of red-necked phalarope and whimbrel for many years, though there has always been a feeling that such facts should be kept quiet. In 1967 the full light of ornithological fame descended on Fetlar when a pair of snowy owls bred in Britain for the first time. With commendable speed the RSPB promptly established a reserve covering 1,600 acres of the northern part of the island and set up a continuous guard system and facilities for visitors to see the birds. They have bred ever since.

Some 40 other species breed within the reserve as well as grey and common seals, but the island, which has a population of a hundred souls, is almost one large reserve. The East Neap in the north is a formidable 400 feet high cliff with offshore stacks that boast one of the largest shaggeries in Britain and all the usual cliff-nesting seabirds. These include Manx shearwater and storm petrel.

The promontory of Urie, once the site of a fishing village, now provides living space for Arctic and common terns and the elusive red-necked phalarope.

SUMMER: great and Arctic skuas, Manx shearwater, storm petrel, whimbrel, red-recked phalarope, guillemot, razorbill, puffin, black guillemot, shag, merlin, golden plover, snowy owl.

There are regular boat and air services from Lerwick, and cottage accommodation offers genuine island hospitality. The RSPB reserve with snowy owls may be visited from May to August. Contact the wardens at Bealance Bothy.

MAINLAND OS 1, 2, 3 and 4

The Mainland of Shetland is 33 miles long and an outstanding bird haunt in its own right. The visitor arriving for a trip to Hermaness and seeing gannets diving in Lerwick Harbour would be foolish not to explore further. Had he arrived in winter the same site would provide glaucous gull! A short exploration to Ronas Voe would produce surf scoter or some other rarity and perhaps Unst would have to wait.

There are innumerable cliffs with breeding auks and kittiwakes. Arctic skuas breed in several places and great skuas are spreading from their northern strongholds. In winter interesting species include a variety of sea duck, glaucous gull, great northern diver and wild swans. During migration periods almost anything may turn up almost anywhere.

WINTER: divers, scoter, velvet scoter, long-tailed duck, eider, merganser, glaucous gull.

SUMMER: guillemot, razorbill, black guillemot, kittiwake, fulmar, raven, hooded crow, twite, wren, eider, merganser, scoter, gannet, divers, curlew, dunlin, common sandpiper, skuas, common and Arctic terns, red-necked phalarope.

AUTUMN: waders, sea birds, passerines, rarities.

Amongst many sites worth a visit are:

1. SUMBURGH HEAD: extreme south with seabird cliffs and possible passage migrants.

2. LOCH OF SPIGGIE: excellent lowland loch in south of Mainland with whoopers and grebes. Also look over Loch Brow.

3. POOL OF VISKIE: first-class autumn migrants especially little stint, purple sandpiper, godwits, etc. Iceland and glaucous gulls in winter.

For details of accommodation write to Shetland Tourist Association, Alexandra Wharf, Lerwick. The North of Scotland and Orkney and Shetland Shipping Co Ltd, Matthews' Quay, Aberdeen, run a twice weekly service from Aberdeen to Lerwick via Kirkwall, Orkney. Ships may be joined one day earlier at Leith. A direct overnight service from Aberdeen to Lerwick leaves on Monday and Thursday pm. BEA run daily air services to Sumburgh from Kirkwall, Aberdeen and Wick, with connections to other parts of Britain.

NOSS OS 3

Noss lies 3 miles east of Lerwick and its sandstone cliffs drop almost 600 feet to the sea. It is an outstanding sea bird colony made all the more attractive by its convenient situation and the fact that it is best seen from a boat. Over 3,000 pairs of gannets were counted in 1949, and the colony has probably grown since. A large assembly of eiders congregate below the Noup of Noss in late summer and both skuas breed.

SUMMER: gannet, guillemot, razorbill, puffin, black guillemot, kittiwake, razorbill, eider, great and Arctic skuas.

Frequent tourist trips by boat from Lerwick around the island. The RSPB administered reserve can be visited from June to August every weekday (not Tuesdays) from Lerwick via Brissay. Ferry details are posted in Lerwick Harbour.

RONAS HILL NATIONAL NATURE RESERVE OS 2

The Reserve lies on the north-western side of Mainland and extends along 12 miles of coast including cliffs towering to over 750 feet. Apart from the usual sea birds, the Reserve is one of the strongholds of great and Arctic skuas on mainland.

SUMMER: great and Arctic skuas, guillemot, razorbill, black guillemot, red-throated diver, merganser, raven.

Leave Lerwick northwards on the A970. All enquiries to the Nature Conservancy Scottish Office.

UNST OS 1

Unst is 12 miles by 5 miles and is the most northerly island of Britain. The southern half is well cultivated and the village of Baltasound is quite sizeable by local standards. The cliff scenery has been described as amongst the finest in the country, culminating in the cliffs of Hermaness. Only a few stacks stretch further northwards to Muckle Flugga with its lighthouse and Out Stack the most northern rock of Britain.

At Hermaness the cliff tops are honeycombed with the burrows of puffins while on the cliffs themselves is a truly magnificent gathering of sea birds. These species breed right round the headland and on to the cliffs along Burra Firth. Both Arctic and great skuas breed on the moorland and have increased under protection to such an extent that the bonxie has been able to spread from what was once almost its last stand. Gannets have bred since 1917 on the offshore stacks and skerries and are now firmly established and easily seen. All of these marine species regularly flight to the freshwater of the Loch of Cliff which is separated from Burra Firth by only a narrow strip of land. During migration periods virtually the whole island is of interest though the extreme north-west has proved a good spot.

WINTER: whooper swan, eider, long-tailed duck, divers.

SUMMER: guillemot, razorbill, puffin, black guillemot, kittiwake, fulmar, Arctic and great skuas, gannet, whimbrel.

Baltasound is in regular steamer contact with Lerwick. The ferries between the Mainland and Yell, and Yell and Unst, provide an overland route. There is also an air service from Sumburgh. The Hermaness Reserve established in 1955 covers 2,383 acres but there are no restrictions on access.

YELL   OS 1

Yell is the second largest of the Shetlands, 17 miles by 6 miles, and is the least visited by outsiders. It is a land of moor, rough grass and peat and though it has some magnificent cliffs, especially on the western coast, its main attractions lie inland. Whale Firth on the west and Mid-Yell Voe in the east almost cut the island in half and the village of Mid Yell forms an admirable centre.

Of many places to go the following areas contain most of the typical species: the ridge of Alin Knowes and, to the north-west, the deserted crofting area of Lumbister which has been described as the loveliest place in Yell. Both species of skua breed on the rising ground to the north of Loch of Lumbister and on the Whale Firth Peninsula.

SUMMER: great and Arctic skuas, kittiwake, guillemot, razorbill.

There are two main routes to Yell by sea from Lerwick to Mid Yell or 'overland'. The overland route leaves Lerwick by road to Mossbank where passengers are ferried across Yell sound to Ulsta. The route continues by road to Mid Yell.

Appendix

BIRD OBSERVATORIES

The British Bird Observatories consist of amateur organisations established by the enthusiasm and dedication of small groups of bird-watchers sharing a passion for bird migration. They are in no way official, and though representatives meet to discuss general scientific policy, each observatory is completely separate from the others. For these reasons British observatories are liable to change. Amateur officials move or retire, and just occasionally observatories close down for good – as did the superbly sited St Agnes station in the Isles of Scilly.

Most observatories offer accommodation of varying standard but usually on a hostel basis. Their main occupations are recording the numbers of migrants and ringing individual birds. Visitors are expected to participate in these endeavours.

Though this list is accurate at the time of going to press some changes will be bound to occur. In case of difficulty contact the British Trust for Ornithology, Beech Grove, Tring, Herts., and be sure to enclose a stamped addressed envelope. Better still enclose a subscription.

Many observatories are more fully described within this guide.

Fair Isle: a classic site and one of the most exciting migration watch-points in the world. Excellent new hostel with full catering service. Book well in advance for busy autumn period. The Warden, Fair Isle Bird Observatory, Shetland.

Isle of May: small island in Firth of Forth. Hostel for 6 visitors but no resident warden. Ringing activities dependent on presence of qualified personnel. Bookings: A. Macdonald, Threeways, 5 Larkfield Road, Eskbank, Dalkeith, Midlothian.

Spurn: southern end of lengthy shingle spit at mouth of Humber. Hostel caters for 17 visitors. The Warden, Spurn Bird Observatory, Kilnsea, via Patrington, Hull, Yorkshire.

★ Fair Isle

★ Isle of May

Calf of Man ★
Walney ★

Spurn ★
Gibraltar Point ★
★ Holme

Bardsey ★

Skokholm ★

Lundy ★

★ Sandwich Bay

Dungeness ★

Portland ★

Gibraltar Point: at mouth of The Wash. Venue of several ringing and field study courses. Accommodation for 29 visitors. The Administrative Officer, The Lincolnshire Trust for Nature Conservation, The Manor House, Alford, Lincolnshire.

Holme: proved rarity site at mouth of The Wash. Details of local accommodation from The Warden, Holme Bird Observatory, Holme-next-Sea, Hunstanton, Norfolk.

Sandwich Bay: ringing station with nearby estuary facing continental migration routes. Hostel: No. 1, Old Downs Farm, Sandwich Bay Estate, Sandwich, Kent.

Dungeness: tip of large shingle peninsula, particularly good in spring. Hostel 10 visitors: write H. A. R. Cawkwell, 3 Lovers Walk, Brighton, Sussex.

Portland: attractive converted lighthouse offering first-class hostel accommodation for 16 visitors. Excellent sea-watching in season. The Warden, Old Lower Light, Portland, Dorset.

Lundy: romantic island in Bristol Channel ideally suited to receive American vagrants. Hostel for 12-15 visitors. Write to The Agent, Lundy, Bristol Channel, via Ilfracombe, Devon.

Skokholm: good research migration station with bonus of good breeding seabirds. Hostel accommodates 12 visitors. Resident warden through season. Bookings to D. Miles, 4 Victoria Place, Haverfordwest, Pembrokeshire.

Bardsey: island off North Wales temporarily closed.

Walney: low lying island connected to the mainland north of Morecambe Bay. Hides for waders, huge gullery, hostel accommodation. J. Mitchell, 82 Plymouth Street, Walney Island, Barrow-in-Furness, Lancashire.

Calf of Man: small island off Isle of Man with resident choughs and seabirds in season. Resident Warden and hostel for 12: write to The Secretary, Manx Museum and National Trust, Douglas, Isle of Man.

Please send information on any locality worthy of inclusion in this book or any error or change in any area already included to:

John Gooders, c/o Pan Books Ltd, Cavaye Place, London SW10 9PG.

It would be helpful if information could be set out under the following headings:

1. Name of area;

2. Exact locations and brief description, Ordnance Survey one inch sheet number. (i.e. nearest large town etc., if reservoir, concrete or natural banks);

3. Access details: i.e. path to follow, etc. (illustrate if necessary or give OS reference);

4. Limitations on access to part or whole; and/or permit details (i.e. from whom available, etc.);

5. Most interesting regular species (or group of species), and best times of year for visits;

6. Any other information about the area you think might be helpful to intending visitor;

7. Name and Address.

Index

Other Pan books that may interest you
are listed on the following pages

Alan Young
Sea Angling for Beginners 50p

Sea angling remains basically the problem of getting the fish to take a baited hook — by following the author's expert advice the new fisherman will avoid much disappointment. The book deals in a practical way with all the many aspects of fishing — what fish you may catch, what are the best baits to use, and there is a full coverage of tackle and techniques.

Kenneth Seaman
Canal Fishing 60p

Traditional methods and tackles are critically examined, and there is advice on bait selection and preparation. There are chapters on angling — for well-known species as well as the more unusual ones — match fishing techniques and the problems of canal maintenance.

Trevor Housby
Shore Fishing 50p

Comprehensive and straightforward, this book covers in detail the tackle and techniques of both rock and beach fishing. Essential reading for the holiday-maker and the veteran angler alike.

Shark Fishing in British Waters 40p

Many varieties of shark may be found and fished within easy distance of Britain's coastline. Trevor Housby draws on a fund of shark-fishing expertise and experience to show how the use of light-tackle techniques and a sound knowledge of each individual species can place shark fishing at the top of the big-game fishing league, with its demands upon courage, endurance and skill.

Tony Soper
The New Bird Table Book 60p

'If you are among those thousands of bird lovers who put out food for your
feathered visitors in winter, erect bird boxes in summer and try to maintain
a bird table all the year round — and then find that somehow the birds don't
come; here is the book for you . . .' THE DALESMAN
'Most comprehensive, containing everything that anyone could possibly
want to know on the subject' CAGE AND AVIARY BIRDS
'One of the best introductions to ornithology in a long time'
TEACHER'S WORLD

Edited by Michael Wright
(Hardback edition £6.00)
The Complete Indoor Gardener £3.95

The complete answer for everyone who loves growing plants but has no
garden. Whether you are a beginner or possess 'green fingers', whether you
live in a penthouse or a single room, these clear, easy-to-follow instructions
show how simple it is to grow all kinds of plants both indoors and on patios
and terraces, window ledges and balconies, roof gardens and back yards.
With 110 sections written by fourteen specialist contributors, and over 600
illustrations, the majority in colour, this is the ideal companion for the
gardener without a garden.
The book includes advice on: houseplants and indoor gardening; outdoor
gardening without a garden; dual-purpose plants; exciting special features;
and techniques and technicalities.

Selected bestsellers

☐ **The Eagle Has Landed** Jack Higgins 80p
☐ **The Moneychangers** Arthur Hailey 95p
☐ **Marathon Man** William Goldman 70p
☐ **Nightwork** Irwin Shaw 75p
☐ **Tropic of Ruislip** Leslie Thomas 75p
☐ **One Flew Over The Cuckoo's Nest** Ken Kesey 75p
☐ **Collision** Spencer Dunmore 70p
☐ **Perdita's Prince** Jean Plaidy 70p
☐ **The Eye of the Tiger** Wilbur Smith 80p
☐ **The Shootist** Glendon Swarthout 60p
☐ **Of Human Bondage** Somerset Maugham 95p
☐ **Rebecca** Daphne du Maurier 80p
☐ **Slay Ride** Dick Francis 60p
☐ **Jaws** Peter Benchley 70p
☐ **Let Sleeping Vets Lie** James Herriot 60p
☐ **If Only They Could Talk** James Herriot 60p
☐ **It Shouldn't Happen to a Vet** James Herriot 60p
☐ **Vet In Harness** James Herriot 60p
☐ **Tinker Tailor Soldier Spy** John le Carré 75p
☐ **Gone with the Wind** Margaret Mitchell £1.75
☐ **Cashelmara** Susan Howatch £1.25
☐ **The Nonesuch** Georgette Heyer 60p
☐ **The Grapes of Wrath** John Steinbeck 95p
☐ **Drum** Kyle Onstott 60p

All these books are available at your bookshop or newsagent;
or can be obtained direct from the publisher
Pan Books, Cavaye Place, London SW10 9PG
Just tick the titles you want and fill in the form below
Prices quoted are applicable in UK
Send purchase price plus 15p for the first book and 5p for each
additional book, to allow for postage and packing

Name _____
(block letters please)
Address _____

_____

While every effort is made to keep prices low, it is sometimes
necessary to increase prices at short notice. Pan Books reserve the
right to show on covers new retail prices which may differ from
those advertised in the text or elsewhere